Church and Synagogue Affiliation

**Recent Titles in
Contributions to the Study of Religion**

Choosing the Dream: The Future of Religion in American Public Life
Frederick Mark Gedicks and Roger Hendrix

Death and Afterlife: Perspectives of World Religions
Hiroshi Obayashi, editor

Buddhist Ethics and Modern Society: An International Symposium
Charles Wei-hsun Fu and Sandra A. Wawrytko, editors

Religion and Political Conflict in South Asia
Douglas Allen, editor

Popular Religion in America: The Evangelical Voice
Erling Jorstad

Politics and Religious Authority: American Catholics Since the Second Vatican Council
Richard J. Gelm

Drums of Redemption: An Introduction to African Christianity
Harvey J. Sindima

Being Religious, American Style: A History of Popular Religiosity in the United States
Charles H. Lippy

The Veneration of Divine Justice: The Dead Sea Scrolls and Christianity
Roy A. Rosenberg

Toward Universal Religion: Voices of American and Indian Spirituality
Daniel Ross Chandler

Nineteenth-Century English Religious Traditions: Retrospect and Prospect
D. G. Paz, editor

Church and Synagogue Affiliation

Theory, Research, and Practice

Edited by
Amy L. Sales *and* Gary A. Tobin

Foreword by Rabbi Renni S. Altman
Afterword by James P. Wind

Contributions to the Study of Religion, Number 42

GREENWOOD PRESS
Westport, Connecticut • London

Acknowledgment

This volume is an outgrowth of the Think Tank on Congregational Affiliation, a conference held at Brandeis University in October 1992. The conference and this publication were made possible by a grant from the Lilly Endowment, Inc., an Indianapolis private family foundation with a long-standing interest in American religion.

Library of Congress Cataloging-in-Publication Data

Church and synagogue affiliation : theory, research, and practice /
   edited by Amy L. Sales and Gary A. Tobin ; foreword by Renni S.
   Altman; afterword by James P. Wind.
      p. cm.—(Contributions to the study of religion, ISSN
0196–7053 ; no. 42)
   Includes bibliographical references and index.
   ISBN 0–313–29681–2
   1. Church membership—Study and teaching. 2. Synagogues—
Membership—Study and teaching. I. Sales, Amy L. II. Tobin, Gary
A. III. Series.
BV820.C48 1995
262'.15—dc20   95–6671

British Library Cataloguing in Publication Data is available.

Copyright © 1995 by Amy L. Sales and Gary A. Tobin

All rights reserved. No portion of this book may be
reproduced, by any process or technique, without the
express written consent of the publisher.

Library of Congress Catalog Card Number: 95–6671
ISBN: 0–313–29681–2
ISSN: 0196–7053

First published in 1995

Greenwood Press, 88 Post Road West, Westport, CT 06881
An imprint of Greenwood Publishing Group, Inc.

Printed in the United States of America

The paper used in this book complies with the
Permanent Paper Standard issued by the National
Information Standards Organization (Z39.48–1984).

10 9 8 7 6 5 4 3 2 1

Contents

Figures and Table   vii

Foreword
Rabbi Renni S. Altman   ix

Introduction
Amy L. Sales and Gary A. Tobin   1

Part One: Defining the Issues   15

1. A Framework for Understanding Congregational Affiliation: Suggestions from Research within the Christian Tradition
David A. Roozen   17

2. Definitions of Congregational Growth
Rev. Loren B. Mead   27

3. Interdenominational Dialogue: Seeking a Common Language for Affiliation Research and Practice
Gary A. Tobin   41

Part Two: The Unaffiliated   55

4. Congregational Involvement of Young Adults Who Grew Up in Protestant Churches
Dean R. Hoge, Benton Johnson, and Donald A. Luidens   59

5.	Four Styles of Religious Marginality *Penny Long Marler and C. Kirk Hadaway*	77
6.	Profiles of the Disaffiliated: Four Case Studies *Amy L. Sales*	95

Part Three: Programs and Practices — 109

7.	Reaching Out to the Unaffiliated *Rabbi Steven E. Foster*	113
8.	Luther Place Memorial Church: A Church as Refuge/Sanctuary *Rev. John F. Steinbruck*	127
9.	Bethany Baptist Church: Growth through Planning and Social Action *Dr. James A. Scott*	135
10.	Congregation B'nai Jeshurun: The Power of a Relevant Message *Rabbi Marshall T. Meyer*	143

Part Four: The Institutional Context of Affiliation — 153

11.	Leadership, Ministry, and Integrity Amid Changing Roles for Clergy and Laity *James R. Wood*	155
12.	The Role of National Religious Institutions in Congregational Affiliation and Growth *William McKinney*	167

Afterword
  James P. Wind — 177

For Further Reading — 183

Index — 185

About the Editors and Contributors — 191

Figures and Table

FIGURES

Figure 1.1	Factors Affecting Congregational Affiliation—Affiliation is, most immediately, a relationship between individuals and congregations	18
Figure 4.1	Baby Boomer Sample by Religious Type	62
Figure 4.2	Core Belief Index—% Believing in Central Christian Teachings	68
Figure 4.3	Christ Only Index—% Believing in Central Christian Teachings	69
Figure 12.1	Conservative Protestants—% Entering and Leaving	170
Figure 12.2	Oldline Protestants—% Entering and Leaving	171
Figure 12.3	Jews—% Entering and Leaving	172

TABLE

Table 7.1	Synagogue Affiliation by Region	114

Foreword

Rabbi Renni S. Altman

Congregational affiliation is a matter of interest to both the academic and religious communities. Yet the two hold fundamentally different perspectives on the matter, and they rarely articulate their views in mutually intelligible ways. Religious leaders may (or may not) use the findings of academic studies to guide their decisions about which populations to target in an outreach effort or which programs to create. Likewise, academics might (or might not) turn to local religious institutions or congregations as models for their research or as testing grounds for their theories. Collaborative inquiry involving clergy, lay leaders, and scholars is rare.

The Maurice and Marilyn Cohen Center for Modern Jewish Studies at Brandeis University and the Union of American Hebrew Congregations (UAHC), with a grant from the Lilly Endowment, recently embarked on a joint project—an unusual effort of an academic and a religious institution collaborating on a topic of shared concern. The project was initially conceived of as a study of methodological issues in affiliation research. Our plan was to begin with an in-depth survey of congregational membership studies (using Reform synagogues in North America as our sample) and then hold a conference at which researchers would present scholarly papers on their most recent work in the study of congregational affiliation. Underlying these activities was the goal of building a working relationship between the university and the religious movement and establishing modes of communication to bridge the academic and religious worlds.

SURVEY OF CONGREGATIONAL MEMBERSHIP STUDIES

The initial stage of the project confirmed our sense that there was an unbridged gap between academic and congregational approaches to affiliation. For one, we found a notable *underutilization of research* in congregations. Although a number of synagogues in our sample had undertaken membership studies, few had produced a report of the results or disseminated the findings in any way. Information was much more likely to be utilized if the congregation received assistance and consultation from an outsider skilled in research, organization development, or related areas of expertise. Our findings indicated that synergy between the research world and the congregational world significantly improves the chances of a membership study being used successfully.

Moreover, there is at times a *misuse of data* at the congregational level. For example, we discovered that in certain congregations the ostensible purpose for conducting a survey is to solicit input from the membership, but the true purpose is to gather ammunition for dismissing the rabbi. In such instances, the research fails the test of objectivity and the social scientist experiences the research process as quite foreign, unusable, and even reprehensible.

Almost 90% of the membership surveys undertaken by the synagogues in our study focused exclusively on current members, a population of convenience. Yet we know that much of what we need to learn about affiliation can come only from past or prospective members. The congregations engaged in these membership studies feel they are doing methodologically sound research and analyzing their populations well, but for the most part their efforts are limited. We thus agreed that maximizing the objectivity, validity, and utility of affiliation studies (which are *already* being carried out in local congregations) requires dialogue between the congregations' leaders and the researchers who are engaged in studies of the same phenomena.

CONFERENCE ON AFFILIATION

As we moved to the next phase of our work, planning an academic conference on congregational affiliation, it became clear that our goals of mutual dialogue, open exchange, and collaboration between the academic and the religious institution were more readily espoused than achieved. An advisory committee comprised of academics and UAHC professionals was assembled to guide the planning of the conference. At the advisory committee's initial meeting, all concurred that, given the joint sponsorship of Brandeis and the UAHC, the conference should not be limited to social scientists and university researchers, but should involve, as well, members of the religious community. Following the meeting, a detailed outline of topics for the conference was circulated along with a request for suggestions of speakers.

It was at this stage that the conference planners (Gary Tobin, Lawrence Sternberg, Gabriel Berger, and Amy Sales of Brandeis and Rabbi Renni

Foreword xi

Altman, Dru Greenwood, and Audrey Wilson of the UAHC) realized that, despite the intent to create a forum for dialogue, the emerging conference was being cast in an academic mold. Reviewing a draft plan for the conference, UAHC professionals saw no real dialogue and little of interest or value to the religious community. Indeed, much of the language in the draft seemed foreign to them, and some of the proposed sessions without meaning. If the planners themselves were talking past one another, speaking in completely different languages, what expectation could we have that those attending the conference would be able to bridge perspectives and what hope could we have for facilitating dialogue between members of the academic and religious worlds? We returned to the drawing board to redesign the conference, this time with an uncompromised focus on creating opportunities for true dialogue.

The resulting conference brought together fifty eminent scholars, clergy, and other professionals from the major denominations across the United States for a creative conversation on the current state and future direction of research, theory, and practice related to congregational affiliation. Most critically, the conference attempted to chart a course through the multiplicity of languages, perspectives, and expectations of this diverse group, literally building a network across denominations and across the boundaries of those who study congregational life and those who serve on the "front lines."

Scholars and clergy alike left the meeting encouraged by positive exchanges with individuals from other faiths who wrestle with similar challenges of affiliation. They were touched by the words of the unaffiliated who came to speak about their broken relationships with the church or synagogue, and they were inspired by the stories of congregations that, driven by a sense of mission, have turned from dying institutions into thriving religious centers. They left the conference motivated to better understand how to build religious communities that will attract the participation of those distanced from religious life.

CHURCH AND SYNAGOGUE AFFILIATION: THEORY, RESEARCH, AND PRACTICE

Our survey of synagogue membership studies revealed the lack of communication between academic researchers and congregational leaders. Our creation of a conference that would benefit both scholars and clergy taught us a great deal about the challenges inherent in such a dialogue. The present volume is comprised of the papers that emerged from this project. In the aggregate, they present research and practical areas of concern in congregational affiliation, and they suggest future steps for researchers, clergy, and church/synagogue professionals. By melding the scholarly with the practical, this volume can perhaps help each enjoy the contributions of the other.

The work is far from complete. The chapters in this volume are at once informative and provocative; they answer some questions, but raise others. The pluralism of approaches—the obstacle to true exchange between clergy and scholars and across the lines of religions, denominations, and academic disciplines—remains a great strength and challenge. It is hoped that the work presented here will encourage readers to think about congregational affiliation and growth in new ways and so inspire their work, both in academe and in religious congregations.

Introduction

Amy L. Sales and Gary A. Tobin

Recently, in casual conversation, we asked a Jewish coworker if she belonged to a synagogue. She admitted that she did not. But she blushed and clearly looked uncomfortable, as if she had the feeling that she *ought* to belong to one. "It's all right," we found ourselves reassuring her. "You're not that different from most American Jews."

This book is about church and synagogue affiliation in the United States today. The reports of research and practice presented in these pages explore the dynamics of congregational affiliation: the motivations that impel people to join a congregation, drop out, or remain unaffiliated; the practices within churches and synagogues that attract or repel membership; and the ways in which contextual religious, social, and cultural factors influence patterns of congregational affiliation. The book is principally concerned with churches and synagogues in the more liberal denominations of Christianity and Judaism, those where the greatest membership losses have been occurring.

THE NEED TO UNDERSTAND CONGREGATIONAL AFFILIATION

Understanding congregational affiliation seems a particularly urgent task in contemporary America. Congregations play a significant role in our society; at the same time, membership in many denominations is on the decline, and churches and synagogues are facing ominous challenges.

The Congregation's Contribution to Personal and Communal Life

Membership in churches and synagogues carries significant implications for individuals and families, and for society at large. Congregations have a special set of purposes and functions, which range from everyday concerns to the loftiest of human expression. We might cast some of these in the following way:

- On the one hand, the congregation offers the weekly ritual and regularity of Sabbath worship. On the other hand, it is the institution that serves major life-cycle events such as birth, marriage, passage into adulthood, and death.
- The congregation is the institution that supports everyday life by offering a wide array of human services such as preschool care or a gathering place for the elderly. At the same time, it is the institution that links individuals to their spiritual selves; it helps them transcend everyday life and experience their connection to God.
- The nature of the congregation focuses its energy inward, helping to form a cohesive community of individuals who work and pray together. In this sense, the congregation exists to serve the needs of its members. But the congregation is also the institution that connects individuals to neighborhood and the wider community. Indeed, it is the congregation that helps build internal strength by reaching out to the external world through charity, philanthropy, or other forms of community involvement.
- Congregations represent stability and tradition. They embody the most ancient of thoughts and behaviors and attempt to provide continuity of ideologies and ritual practice that links the generations one to another. Congregations have likewise been institutions that encourage and facilitate growth and change. Congregations have been at the center of major political, social, and cultural innovations and continue to be a major source of change.

We might also think of the purpose of the congregation as the creation of linkages among individuals, families, and communities. To begin, the congregation can help individuals connect to themselves. Worship, community involvement, and other congregational activities produce deeper understanding and greater self-knowledge—the church or synagogue's contribution to the individual's learning and growth. Congregations likewise facilitate connections to family as they bring family members together in worship, community service, and social and other activities that promote family well-being and development. Congregations connect the individual to those in need. They provide a setting in which people are able to serve the hungry, the homeless, and those in economic, physical, or emotional distress. And they provide connections to the wider religious community of Catholics, or Lutherans, or Jews. They thus provide linkages to communities that are greater than neighborhood, municipality, or even nation.

Congregations further connect the individual to the past. Churches and synagogues are places where tradition and history are learned and where ritual, study and communal worship link people to their ancestry. Congregations also provide linkages to the future as they serve to transmit the same knowledge and values to children, grandchildren, and generations beyond. Most importantly, congregations connect individuals, families, and communities to God. Their central purpose is communal worship, and they are uniquely concerned with the spiritual, with providing a core of meaning, direction, and value to human life.

No other institution serves the individual, the community, and God in the ways that the congregation does. The congregation is something of a central switching terminal that provides a complex array of connections not available elsewhere. The individual's decision about affiliation is thus a quintessentially human act, and overall affiliation rates are inextricably attached to the quality of personal, social, and communal life. Ultimately those of us who care about the quality of life need to be concerned with the health of the congregation (Chapter 2).

Declines in Affiliation

Membership has a dynamic quality; it ebbs and flows, changing over time. The 1990s have been marked by declines in "mainline" churches in the United States. After the mid-1960s, for example, the Episcopal Church, the Presbyterian Church, and the United Church of Christ each lost over 20% of their membership (Hoge & Roozen, 1979). In 1990, Lutheran congregations reported having 500,000 fewer baptized members than they had in 1970 (Aid Association for Lutherans, 1992). Rates of synagogue affiliation have also declined. Four decades ago, 60% of all Jews were religiously affiliated (Sloan, 1955); today that number is just under 40% (Goldstein, 1993), and in the western United States it is below 30% (Tobin & Berger, 1993).

The work of some authors in this volume suggests that congregational participation may continue to decline. A host of demographic and cultural changes have been working to erode the traditional roles of the congregation. In the marketplace of social and communal organizations, the congregation is facing unprecedented competition. The normative pressure to belong to a congregation has given way to a vast array of acceptable individual choices. These include not belonging at all, joining and resigning as need or mood dictates, switching congregations within denominations, or switching to a congregation in a different denomination, joining ethnic, cultural or religious groups that substitute for congregations, and even taking part in religion through the media (radio or television). Many people do not feel they "need" a congregation in order to be religious or even to live a life of faith.

Congregational affiliation and the causes of membership decline have riveted the attention of religious scholars, church leaders, and social commentators who seek explanations for shifting demographic and social trends in this country and insights into how to sustain and grow our religious institutions. The topic has been tackled from a variety of perspectives and a host of academic disciplines. Indeed, represented in the current volume are the views of Christian and Jewish clergy, as well as scholars from sociology, psychology, history, demography, and religion. Their methods of research include quantitative surveys, qualitative interviews, and case studies. The membership programs and practices they describe range from the deeply spiritual (a true reconnection to God and to faith) to the unabashedly political (a serious recommitment to the Biblical commandments to care for others).

THE NATURE OF AFFILIATION

As David A. Roozen notes in Chapter 1, affiliation is a relational concept; it is most immediately a relationship between the individual and the local congregation. When the individual and the congregation are well suited to each other, affiliation is likely to result. When the match is less felicitous, the outcome is likely to be unaffiliation or disaffiliation (dropping out). This simple relationship, however, is laden with intricacies because both sides, the individual and the congregation, are highly complex, ever-changing entities.

The individual is part of a social group which often has great influence on the decision to affiliate. The views of friends and family, for example, can affect the value that an individual places on congregational affiliation. Familial and friendship needs (e.g., the need to educate one's children or the need for social support) may be influential determinants, as well (Chapter 3). The individual's affiliation behavior is also affected by a host of background and personal characteristics: childhood experiences; early socialization into a religious community; later life experiences; motivations, needs and interests; and values or ideology. Any or all of these may be important to consider in understanding the individual's side of the relationship.

The congregation is equally complex. People join a congregation because they have been attracted to one or more aspects of what the congregation is and/or what it has to offer. Elements that define a congregation include, for example, the social nature of the institution (its congregants, leaders, educators, and so on), clergy, structures and processes, politics, practices, and ideology. Churches and synagogues may also be identified with the specific programs they undertake to reach out to the unaffiliated, to draw in new members, or to retain and involve those already in the fold. These programs, too, form part of the texture of a congregation.

Not only are both sides of the relationship complex, but the relationship itself changes over time. At the individual level, affiliation is linked to stages of life, so that we see people move in and out of religious institutions over the life span. We repeatedly hear, for example, that the most difficult to reach are eighteen- to twenty-year olds (Chapter 4). A developmental perspective, however, reminds us that this is the age at which people enter the wide world, look beyond the institutions of their youth, and experiment with new structures. These young adults are likely to reaffiliate at another point in life when they have a felt *need* for the church or synagogue—when they want a religious wedding ceremony, Bible education for their children, or consolation at the death of a loved one (Chapter 7). We would suggest that there are ages of affiliation and ages of disaffiliation, a reality which needs to be reflected in our work.

At the macro level, there is an historical ebb and flow in the growth and strength of America's churches and synagogues. In certain decades, there is clearly an upsurge in religious affiliation, in others a decline. Moreover, the relationship shifts with geography. Research consistently shows differential trends in religious affiliation depending on the region of the country and on geographical population shifts which occur over time (Chapter 2).

Finally, these complex and changing relationships occur in larger contexts which themselves are multifaceted and in flux. For one, local congregations belong to national denominations, which may encourage and support the growth of local congregations (Chapter 12) and which may be an important source of religious identification for individuals (Chapter 3). What takes place at the level of the local congregation may thus be affected by the rise or decline of the national denomination.

Moreover, our religious behavior occurs within the context of the broader American culture in which we live. Congregational affiliation takes place amidst the pervasive secularism of the twentieth century, amidst materialism, relativism, and other social forces that shape the tone and tenor of society and ultimately the role of religious institutions in America. Today's cultural context also includes, many would argue, an environment of beleaguered social institutions. People are questioning what has happened to public education, the family, volunteerism, and the family doctor, and they are holding on to nostalgic views of old neighborhoods, ethnic ties, safe streets, and American holidays once celebrated without controversy. As we work to understand religious affiliation, we need to consider the special opportunities congregations face in such an environment.

OVERVIEW OF THE BOOK

This book is divided into four parts, each of which explores a different dimension of the affiliation relationship. Part One defines the issues related to congregational affiliation: the multiple aspects of the affiliation relationship (Chapter 1), the various ways in which religious institutions and their membership can grow (Chapter 2), and the plurality of languages we use for describing these various affiliation dynamics (Chapter 3).

Part Two focuses on the individual side of the relationship: the motivations and beliefs of active congregants in contrast to those of the religious and nonreligious "unchurched" (Chapter 4); the values and beliefs of marginal members—inactive Protestant Americans who claim church membership but who attend worship services infrequently (Chapter 5); and the experiences of church and synagogue dropouts (Chapter 6).

Part Three looks at the congregational side of the relationship and describes what synagogues and churches are doing to reach out to new members and to nourish and sustain those who are currently in the fold. This section presents programs and practices that have had significant and positive impact on affiliation and congregational growth in a Reform synagogue in Denver, Colorado (Chapter 7), a Lutheran church in Washington, D.C. (Chapter 8), a black Baptist church in Newark, New Jersey (Chapter 9), and a Conservative synagogue in New York City (Chapter 10). Each of these congregations has defied the trend of weak recruitment and retention of members common in liberal congregations. The case studies presented here suggest some of the ways that liberal churches and synagogues can achieve high commitment from their members while remaining true to their ideology and mission.

The final section, Part Four, is dedicated to the institutional context in which the affiliation relationship takes place. It examines the role of religious leadership (Chapter 11) and national religious institutions and denominations (Chapter 12).

THE UNIQUE PROPERTIES OF AFFILIATION

Affiliation is a uniquely human behavior particularized by its essential religious and communal nature. This section explores three premises: (1) religious institutions are special organizations; (2) affiliation is an emotional issue; and (3) affiliation must be disentangled from related concepts.

Religious Institutions as Special Organizations

Churches and synagogues share a great deal in common with other organizations, and indeed, discussions about congregational growth are infused with the language of organization development. When Mead (Chapter 2), for example, talks about *organic growth,* he is referring to the capacity of a congregation to develop as a community—as an effective organization able to work, make decisions, and take action. Concepts from private-sector corporations are borrowed freely. One rabbi framed declines in synagogue membership in the following way: "People purchase services with money. The consumerism perspective is part of real life and the unaffiliated and disaffiliated aren't buying our product. So how do we get them to buy?" Words like *market niche, dues, tickets, board of trustees, bottom line,* and *research and development* all suggest a corporate model of understanding and intervening to affect congregational affiliation and growth.

Ironically, corporate consultants would undoubtedly advise congregations to clarify and commit to their unique mission and to communicate this to laity (see Chapter 8, Chapter 9, Chapter 10). Marketing specialists would emphasize the uniqueness of the congregation as the institution in society established to bring people together in prayer, to replenish the soul, and to help people deal with the existential issues of life and death. They would tell congregations to make certain that the language of economics and business not corrupt the language of the congregation and to ensure that concepts like *love, beauty, faith, hope, justice, peace* and *solace* remain at the forefront of the congregational lexicon.

Affiliation as an Emotional Issue

The topic of congregational affiliation is an emotional one for clergy, lay leaders, congregants, researchers, and scholars alike. In this regard, it differs from other arenas of inquiry in which the behavioral scientist might feel neutral about the outcome of the research or be satisfied to merely let the data "speak for themselves."

The chapters on marginal members (Chapter 5) and the disaffiliated (Chapter 6) demonstrate clearly that decisions about affiliation or dropping out are highly charged emotionally. Unlike decisions about which automobile to purchase or what color to paint one's house, decisions about church or synagogue membership touch on an individual's identity, ideology and beliefs, faith and spirituality, and on how all these will play out in the context of the family. These issues involve deep feeling. Moreover, it is not uncommon for individuals to leave a congregation out of anger, frustration, or disappointment at expectations unmet (Chapter 7). In such cases, the motivation to disaffiliate is mediated through strong negative emotions that are used to justify the rejection of the church or synagogue.

Congregations, too, experience questions of affiliation with great emotion. In our work with synagogues, in which we meet with boards, talk with the laity, and work with rabbis in addressing issues of affiliation, we find a tendency to blame those who are not a part of the congregation. "They're not carrying their own weight." "They have walked away from their religious obligation." "They're cheap. They won't pay their dues." Complaints about what is wrong with those outside the fold swirl around these meetings expressing of despair, or even anger, that the unaffiliated are not committed enough or conscious enough to share in what the congregation has to offer.

Distinguishing Affiliation from Related Concepts

Finally, we cite the need to distinguish affiliation from a variety of related concepts. Failure to recognize the unique behavior represented by affiliation leads us to false conclusions about the affiliated and the unaffiliated and hence to incorrect decisions about our research and the interventions that might help congregations grow and develop.

Most important, as several authors in this book emphasize, affiliation is not tantamount to religiosity. An individual may be intensely religious, hold deep spiritual beliefs, and be well educated in a religious tradition but not be a member of a congregation. Conversely, it is equally possible to find individuals who are not religious and have little faith but do belong to a congregation. Such congregants may be motivated by communal concerns, a desire to provide Bible education to their children, social needs, family history, or some sense of tradition. We therefore err when we equate religiosity with affiliation and make judgments based on a faulty merging of the two concepts.

Congregational affiliation is also not the same as religious identity. Affiliation is a behavior that results from the decision to become a member of a congregation. Identity is a psychological construct that defines who the person is—it is an internal judgment which may or may not be commensurate with overt behavior. Thus a person may be strongly identified as a Jew or a Baptist, but not formally belong to a synagogue or church. And conversely, it is possible to be on the formal rolls of a congregation but not to embrace that membership as a central element in defining one's identity.

CONGREGATIONAL RESPONSE TO THE CHALLENGES OF AFFILIATION

Given that churches and synagogues are unique institutions and affiliation an emotional issue with complex motivations, how might congregations respond to challenges of affiliation and growth? The issues presented by such a question are discussed throughout this book. They include congregation mission, passion, and relevance; the societal value placed on pluralism, relativism, and individualism; and finally programmatic inreach and outreach.

Mission, Passion, and Relevance

Market analysis, which often dominates discussion of congregational affiliation, cannot sufficiently show congregations how to respond to declines in membership or to their own desires for growth. The corporate answer is to offer the public what it wants. Marketing specialists determine that Americans want more comfortable casual clothing or breakfast cereal with less sugar, and the next season these appear in stores. Should public opinion and prevailing fashion change in the future, the marketing consultant is there to help business respond. We see such an approach in the movie *Sister Act*. In this film, rock and roll music replaces the chants and hymns of the traditional mass, and the gates to the church are literally torn down as the public flocks into church for what is now perceived to be a relevant and exciting church service.

But the issues for congregations in real life are not quite so simple. For one, there may be a danger in giving people what they think they want, of diluting the church's message so that it will be noncontroversial, undemanding, and palpable to all. Clergy obviously have a critical role to play in maintaining the special value and mission of the church or synagogue (Chapter 11). Healthy congregations are not taking the approach of seeking to appeal to the "lowest common denominator" of the laity. The success of the conservative religious groups—whether fundamentalist, evangelical, or orthodox—suggests that churches which ask much of their members grow while those which ease the burdens of belonging are more likely to decline (Finke & Stark, 1992). Marler and Hadaway's study (Chapter 5), for example, describes one group of Protestants who became marginal to the church because they had heard that church attendance was optional and they found little was expected of them as church members.

Some in the religious community argue that churches and synagogues are neglecting difficult issues and are therefore failing to address the realities of the community. Clergy are reluctant to offer sermons on sexuality, environmentalism, poverty, civil rights, and other topics which they fear might offend or divide members of the congregation, and they thus represent a religion with limited relevance to people's lives.

Others define the problem as a loss of spirituality in our religious institutions. The liberal denominations are particularly open to this charge. Many people in search of a spiritual path reject the institutional machinery of the church or synagogue, and/or they determine that these institutions are the last place one should look to find God (Chapter 6). Indeed, we have heard clergy talk about the church's embarrassment with spiritual feeling, the avoidance of spiritual language in the synagogue, and the resistance of both clergy and lay people to "the fires of faith and passion." A rabbi who has dared to offer spirituality workshops reports being accused by Jewish colleagues of "Christianizing Judaism," as if Judaism had nothing to say about spirituality.

In responding to the challenges of congregational growth, it is clear that the church and synagogue must not pander to the wishes and desires of lay people, but rather offer something strong enough to change people's lives.

Congregations often use programs to attack the problem of membership decline. They might establish an outreach program, an educational program, or a social action program—program upon program in an attempt to attract and maintain membership. Programs alone, however, are insufficient when what may be needed is greater passion. What is the vision of the church or synagogue? What does it stand for? Programs are concrete, manipulable, and measurable, but they provide poor spiritual nutrition. People hungry for spirituality are attracted not to programs but to those centers that offer vision and passionate belief.

The church and synagogue thus need a reawakening, one which fulfills the initial intents and purposes of the institution, dares to ask much of its congregants, and sends forth a powerful message into the world. As we see in the profiles of congregational growth presented in this volume (Chapter 7, Chapter 8, Chapter 9, Chapter 10), churches and synagogues grow when their mission is an imperative. It is this mission—whether it be connecting people to God, studying Torah and Biblical texts, being a moral force in the community, or helping the congregation to take action in the world in *imitateo dei*—that will draw in people and make the institution worth saving.

Pluralism, Relativism, and Individualism

A second recurring set of issues concerns the value placed on relativism and pluralism in contemporary society. We appear to be experiencing an explosion of options for those seeking a path to a more meaningful and useful life. Established religious institutions consequently need to move faster and farther in providing sufficient options to potential congregants in order to be "competitive" in the marketplace. In this view, there is not one Lutheran church, one Presbyterian church, or one Conservative synagogue that can appeal to those who would affiliate within these denominations. Rather than homogenize the message and the structures and forms that are conduits for that message, congregations may need to diversify and offer the "consumer" products closer to what they seek. In such a pluralistic world, the future vitality of a congregation depends upon its ability to redesign a unique position amongst the multitude of available organizational and institutional options and to reestablish its legitimacy and authority. The uniqueness of a congregation resides in the combination of elements that define it rather than in any singular characteristic. After all, worship, charity, moral guidance, and a range of human services to serve the family can be obtained in one way or another outside the congregation.

Relativism is a position that accepts multiple paths to faith. This perspective, prevalent today, maintains that regardless of what religion we may choose for ourselves, we believe that all religions are valid and that we need to be tolerant of differences in doctrine and moral teachings. There are, in this view, no absolute truths, no single path. Relativism, however, is somewhat paradoxical: it entails a commitment to one's own religion along with an openness to other religions. This is a difficult stance to maintain and one which may be inadequately robust to sustain a religious community. At the very least, relativism provides a plausibility structure (see Chapter 4) that makes unaffiliation possible, and it thus potentially threatens the health of congregations.

Individualism is another threat to established religions and their congregations. Individualism maintains that we can fashion our own religion either by combining elements of various religions (as in movements of the 1960s which melded Eastern and Western religious traditions to form a new path toward spirituality) or by selecting from the belief system of existing religions to create a version of Catholicism, Protestantism, or Judaism that fits our individual needs and beliefs. Such liberalism has certain values, but it also has high costs. For example, individualistic approaches to Judaism have been linked to high levels of assimilation and declines in commitment to the synagogue. Catholics in the 1990s are debating who is and who is not an "authentic" Catholic. In their consideration of which tenets and universally held teachings are truly central, some American Catholics see themselves "in faithful dissent," while the Papacy considers such a position oxymoronic. Can we have a cafeteria style religion, in which each of us chooses the elements we will believe in and abide by, yet still retain the religion and its institutions? This is a question that challenges liberal approaches to religion.

Inreach and Outreach

Affiliation is not just about bringing in new members. It is also centrally concerned with maintaining current members and helping them to grow in their faith and in their capacity to live religiously (Chapter 2). Membership without involvement and other forms of growth is nominal at best, shallow, and devoid of meaning. A church or synagogue can neither thrive nor even survive with mere nominal membership. We conclude, therefore, with a reminder that the purpose of understanding affiliation is not merely to increase membership numbers but to increase involvement and active participation in congregations as well. Congregations require ideological, structural, and programmatic responses to the challenge of enhancing participation in all of its many forms—financial contribution; volunteerism for the congregation, or through the congregation for the community; study; outreach to non-members; ritual practice; and last, but not least, worship.

All of these forms of participation are relevant to congregational growth. Thus the practical side of affiliation will necessarily be not just outreach to the unaffiliated, but inreach to those already in the fold who need to have their souls nourished and their religious lives sustained. We must be careful in studying the unaffiliated, in reaching out to them, and in dedicating volumes to them that we not forget the affiliated, what they bring to the religious congregation, and what they need to receive from it.

CONCLUSION

Despite the complexity of the topic and the multiform routes to its exploration and implementation, affiliation is a valued act, and the congregations to which people attach themselves are unique and remarkably enduring institutions. It is often said that religious community is central to a life of faith. Indeed, Judaism requires the minimum of a *minyan*, ten Jews above the age of thirteen, for congregational worship, public Torah reading, and the recitation of *Kedusah* (prayers praising the holiness of God). The tradition thus mandates prayer as a communal act, undertaken by the community on behalf of the community. Without a *minyan*, there can be no wedding, no prayers for the deceased, no confession of sins. The congregation is vital for carrying out the tasks of the religion.

The responsibility for meeting the challenges posed by membership declines and high rates of unaffiliation rests with the religious institutions. A society that craves communal and personal intimacy, moral and ethical guidance, and spiritual fulfillment cannot afford to have any less than the most innovative and creative congregations. Mead's words on the importance of congregations and our need to understand congregational affiliation (Chapter 2) set the tone for this volume as a whole.

The congregation is one of the few places in society in which we as individuals can come together, restore our wholeness, recover our sense of direction, receive the power to do what we must do, and be assured of the community with God and with one another that makes life worth living. The congregation is the arena for the restoration of life and mission. That arena itself needs repair and restoration very critically at this moment in history. Those who care about the quality of life in our society need to care about the health of religious congregations and their ability to grow—not just in numbers, but also in faith, ministry, and mission.

No other institution has shown the ability to affect so positively not only the lives of individuals but our society and culture as well. But religious congregations must grow in many ways if they are to meet their greatest potential in the next century and be the place where people can fulfill their deepest needs.

REFERENCES

Aid Association for Lutherans. (1992). *Findings Report at Completion of Phase I for the Church Membership Initiative*. Appleton, WI: Author.

Finke, R., & Stark, R. (1992). *The Churching of America, 1776–1990*. New Brunswick, NJ: Rutgers University Press.

Goldstein, S. (1993). Profile of American Jewry: Insights from the 1990 National Jewish Population Survey. In D. Singer (Ed.), *American Jewish Year Book* (pp. 77–173). NY: American Jewish Committee and the Jewish Publication Society.

Hoge, D. R., & Roozen, D. A. (Eds.). (1979). *Understanding Church Growth and Decline: 1950–1978*. NY: Pilgrim Press.

Sloan, J. (1955). Religion. In *American Jewish Yearbook: Vol. 56*. NY: Ktav Publishing, Inc.

Tobin, G. T., & Berger, G. (1993). *Synagogue Affiliation: Implications for the 1990s (Research Report 9)*. Waltham, MA: Brandeis University, Cohen Center for Modern Jewish Studies.

PART ONE

Defining the Issues

The chapters in Part One focus on the conceptual and definitional issues that underlie any discussion of congregational affiliation. Each of the constructs related to affiliation theory, research, and practice is complex and multiform. Our language for discussing them is equally rich and diverse. We need, therefore, to clarify common terms so that affiliation can be discussed across denominations and academic disciplines with mutual understanding and precision. Part One addresses the need for a clarification of affiliation-related constructs.

David A. Roozen first presents a framework for defining *congregational affiliation*. The framework is grounded in the assertion that "*individuals* affiliate with *congregations* which are affiliated with *denominations*; and that all three shape and are shaped by their *social context*." Roozen arrays these various levels of interacting factors in a matrix, graphically demonstrating the complexity of affiliation. He shows the need for more elaborated models for generating research questions and designing strategies for congregational growth.

Roozen suggests that the most critical questions—and those least emphasized in past research—involve the interaction between these various factors. Thus, for example, affiliation can be seen as a bridge between individual motivations, predispositions, and loyalties and the abilities of a congregation to satisfy or build upon these. Rather than devise research and strategy from the point of view of the individual or from the perspective of the congregation, key questions rest on the interrelationship between the two. Affiliation does not result from what the congregation does or what it is, but from how its actions and identity relate to the needs, values, and beliefs of the individual.

In the second chapter, Loren B. Mead offers a complex definition of *congregational growth* that encourages us to think about this concept in ways that transcend mere numbers on the membership rolls. Mead recognizes the importance of increases in the number of active members or the number of attendees at worship services, but he argues that other types of growth are necessary, as well.

In addition to numerical growth, Mead presents the concept of "maturational growth," an increase in the church's capacity to nurture its congregants within the tradition. This type of growth entails enhanced religious knowledge, greater ability to deal with life issues, and most critically, deeper capacity for worship. "Organic growth," another type of growth defined by Mead, refers to the church's development as an organism that can make decisions and take action. Such growth centers on leadership, involvement of congregants, effective organization, and an institutional culture that supports such activity. Defining roles, examining and making explicit congregational norms and values, and developing systems for effective decision making are key to healthy growth of the religious organization. A final model of growth is what Mead calls "incarnational," growth in the congregation's ability to make an impact on the world with its faith and values. Mead acknowledges that not all congregations can grow in all ways at the same time. But he sets forth a framework that enables us to think of growth in the most extensive terms possible.

In Chapter 3, Gary A. Tobin explores the inherent challenge in discussing affiliation and models of growth across denominations. At the most fundamental level, Tobin explains, we find vast differences in the way language is used to talk about concepts related to affiliation and growth. "Membership," for example, is variously considered to reside in baptism and/or attendance at religious services and/or expression of faith and/or participation in the religious community, or (particularly in Jewish congregations) full payment of annual membership dues. "Outreach" for Christian groups refers to reaching out to the unconverted, the disenfranchised, and the suffering—undertaking evangelism or acts of compassion in the surrounding community in God's name. Jewish outreach, in contrast, targets interfaith families (where one partner is Jewish) and is seen primarily as a response by the liberal movement to the current high rate of intermarriage in the Jewish community.

Based on a survey of fifty clergy and scholars, Tobin finds that definitions of membership, outreach, denominational affiliation, the unaffiliated, and growth all vary substantially from one religious group to the next. The multitude of definitions demonstrates the rich pluralism of perspectives necessitated by diverse churches and synagogues. But it also signals the need for care in transporting research and practice from one faith community to another.

The three chapters in Part One lay the groundwork for the discussion of affiliation, congregational growth, and related concepts that take place in the remainder of this volume. Together they indicate the complexity of the constructs that form the building blocks of our understanding of congregational affiliation.

CHAPTER 1

A Framework for Understanding Congregational Affiliation: Suggestions from Research within the Christian Tradition

David A. Roozen

The longer I look at an issue, the greater my appreciation for its complexity; and the more complexity I see, the less I hold any illusion of adequately encapsulating that complexity within any single theoretical or theological formulation. While we have not as yet arrived at a grand theory of congregational affiliation, we do have frameworks which are helpful for organizing our thinking about the multiple factors and relationships that any comprehensive understanding of congregational affiliation needs to consider. That is to say, I think we have a reasonable idea of the general areas to be visited in understanding congregational affiliation, even if we do not yet have adequate recognition of their specifics and interrelationships.

The framework laid out in this chapter integrates my earlier experiences with empirical research on church growth and congregational studies (Hoge & Roozen, 1979; Roozen & Hadaway, 1993; Stokes & Roozen, 1991). It is important to state at the outset that this framework is based on my work in the Christian tradition. Obviously the reader will have to judge whether the concepts presented here are translatable to the situation of Jewish synagogues and congregations of other faiths.

A FRAMEWORK FOR UNDERSTANDING CONGREGATIONAL AFFILIATION

The framework I want to suggest is grounded in the assertion that:

Individuals affiliate with congregations which are affiliated with denominations; and that all three shape and are shaped by their social context.

Figure 1.1
Factors Affecting Congregational Affiliation—Affiliation is, most immediately, a relationship between individuals and congregations

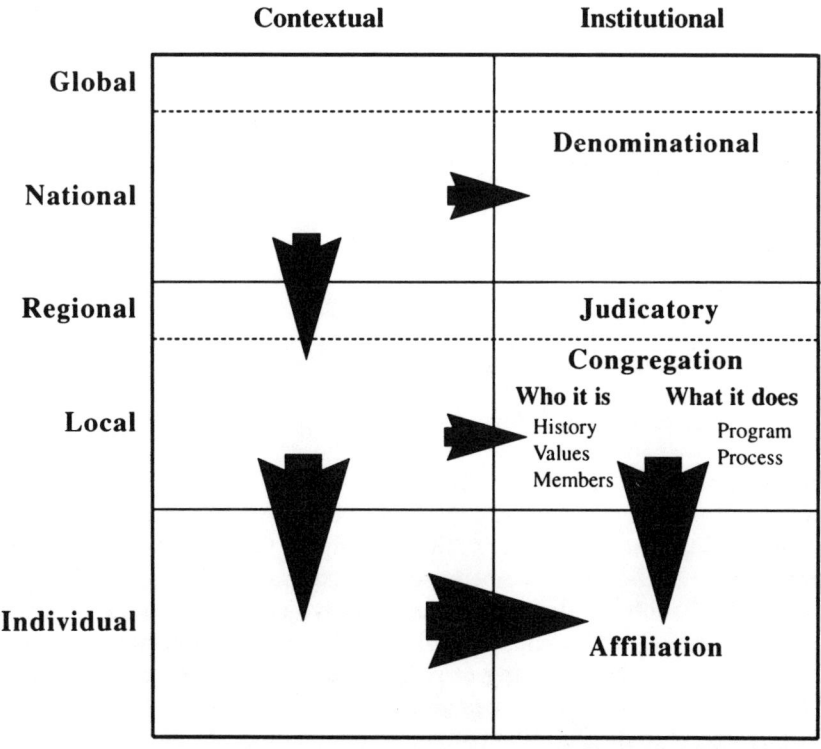

The different sizes of the arrows indicate the magnitude of importance.

One way of schematizing this assertion is to crosscut a contextual/institutional axis with a national-to-local-to-individual axis. This provides the six cells shown in Figure 1.1, essentially an extension of Hoge and Roozen's (1979) original four cell typology. The individual to national dimension is, obviously, intended to parallel my grounding assertion. The institutional/contextual distinction is important for at least two reasons. First, it has strategic implications. Religious leaders have some control over the nature of the institutions they lead, but they have relatively little control over the social context. For example:

- At the national level. Immigration is a social contextual factor over which a denomination or a congregation has relatively little control. But a denomination or congregation does have control over the language used in worship and other programming. Language, in turn, has considerable impact on how closely a congregation will be tied to immigration.

A Framework for Understanding Congregational Affiliation   19

- At the local level. During the 1960s, racial transition was a dominant contextual reality for many urban congregations over which they had little direct control. But a congregation did have control over whether or not it would relocate its building.
- At the individual level. It is often noted that baby boomer's have a preference for programmatically diverse congregations. A congregation has little control over that preference. But it does have some control over its program diversity.

Second, the contextual/institutional distinction points to an important difference in the social location of religious leaders and "lay" affiliates (see Chapter 11). As seminary professor and church consultant Doug Walrath (personal communication) puts it:

The cognitive home of church leaders is religious; they tend to view the world through the church. But laity view the church through the "world." It is even part of our everyday language to say, "people come to the church." Where do they come from? Their cognitive home is the "world."

The difference between taking the church or the world (the church's social context) as one's primary reference point has significant implications for how the two groups communicate or miscommunicate with each other.

For persons interested in tracking membership change, the contextual/institutional distinction also has implications for the measure of change that one uses. Market share measures (e.g., membership as a percentage of the population) direct our attention outward to social contextual opportunities. In contrast, growth rate measures (e.g., change as a percentage of starting membership) direct our attention inward toward the capacity of institutionally available resources (e.g., to the resource of the "starting" membership).

Individual and Congregation

Let me begin my elaboration of the framework with the individual/congregation nexus. Religious professionals and academics with strong religious commitments tend to express their interest in the individual/congregation nexus from the institutional perspective. That is, they tend to ask:

What can a congregation do or be to attract affiliates and sustain the affiliation of existing members?

Phrasing the question in this way points to several important insights. First, putting the question this way recognizes that what motivates someone to affiliate initially is often different from what will sustain that person's motivation. Although we may recognize these as separate dynamics and we may be equally concerned with understanding new members and dropouts, the vast majority of correlational national survey research on affiliation does not distinguish between the two sets of motivations.

Second, the "do or be" in the question calls attention to the fact—increasingly recognized in the emerging field of congregational studies—that a congregation itself is a complex system with many analytically distinct, but closely interrelated components. There are any number of conceptual models available for thinking about the interrelated dimensions of congregational life. One of the more popular is that contained in the *Handbook for Congregational Studies* (Carroll, Dudley, & McKinney, 1986). It suggests four primary components to a congregation: (1) a congregation's *identity or corporate culture*—including its historical and immediate theological affirmations; (2) a congregation's *organizational structure and processes*—including leadership and decision making; (3) a congregation's *program*—worship, education, mission, and so on; and, (4) a congregation's *social context*.

For present purposes, it is not necessary to advocate any given congregational model, only to call attention to the fact that any and all dimensions of congregational life can be a bridge or a barrier to affiliation. Building somewhat on the framework suggested in the *Handbook for Congregational Studies*, however, recent research on church growth has found it helpful to differentiate between at least two aspects of congregational life: (1) *who a congregation is*—that is, its identity and the characteristics of current affiliates; and, (2) *what a congregation does*—its programs and organizational processes. The major implication of this distinction is, again, strategic. It is easier for a congregation to change what it does than who it is.

Third, and most important, implicit in putting the question this way is the recognition that *affiliation is a relational concept*. It is most immediately a relationship between individuals and congregations. That is, it is a relationship between individual motivations, predispositions, and loyalties and the ability of a congregation to satisfy or build upon those motivations, predispositions, and loyalties.

We all know experientially that individual motivations and predispositions for religious affiliation are multiple and diverse, even within the same individual, much less across individuals. And we know from the research literature that the list of possible *individual* motivations and predispositions includes at least the following:

- the content and saliency of an individual's religious belief and practice
- an individual's embeddedness in ethnic subcultures and communal or friendship networks, and, somewhat related to the latter, his or her geographic mobility
- a host of family-related factors, including the presence of young children and the religious affiliation of one's spouse

- social economic status, generation, and an individual's broader meaning system and/or lifestyle
- an individual's perception of whether a church or synagogue is to his or her liking—a factor which is becoming increasingly important as the prevalence of expressive individualism increases within American society

We also know that congregations come in different sizes and shapes. From research on church growth, we know, for example, that it does make a difference:

- that some congregations' leadership and/or expressed theology is more relational than dogmatic/hierarchical
- that some congregations have diverse programs, while others have little formal programming
- that some congregations see themselves as primarily oriented to the comfort of their members, while other congregations are primarily oriented to engaging the world
- that some congregations are dominated by long tenured members, while others have very young members
- that some congregations proclaim their denominational affiliation, while others hide it
- perhaps most importantly for present purposes, that some congregations are very intentional about member recruitment and assimilation, while others are not

Either list could be extended; but the broader and more important point is that extending either list independently does not take us very far. Rather, the relational nature of affiliation really demands that we ask: *What kinds of people affiliate with what kinds of congregations?* What kinds of people like relational theology? hierarchical theology? What kinds of congregations do blue collar families find supportive? Upper-middle-class singles?

Unfortunately, most research in the past has addressed the individual/congregation nexus either from the point of view of the individual (i.e., what are the characteristics of affiliates?) or from the perspective of the congregation (i.e., what are the characteristics of a vital congregation?). What I am suggesting is that the key question of affiliation is really the interrelationship between the two. *Affiliation is, most immediately, a relationship between individuals and congregations.* Unfortunately, despite a long history of research on Christian membership in congregations, we are just beginning to develop an empirical literature that directly focuses on this interrelationship.

Local Contextual Factors

The individual/congregation nexus is at the core of the affiliation question. But there are, obviously, several other cells in my framework. I comment on them only briefly, starting with the *local contextual*. The main influence on affiliation of the vast majority of local contextual factors identified in past research is mediated through their influence on individuals. Indeed, much of what have been called local contextual factors in the past are nothing more than aggregates of individual characteristics. In the Christian context, we are apt to say, for example, this is Bible Belt country, this is a commuter suburb, this is a family-oriented community, this is a transitional neighborhood, and so on. In each case, the designations are little more than shorthand for saying you are going to find a lot of certain kinds of individuals here.

There are other kinds of local contextual factors that exert an influence on affiliation through their effect on the congregation rather than through the individual. Unfortunately, I am aware of little comparative, empirical research on the subject. To the extent there is a literature or conversation about such factors, it is primarily focused on very specific and isolated cases. We know of situations, for example, where public building or zoning codes put constraints on what a congregation could do with the size, shape, or location of its physical facilities. For established congregations, adding extra parking or a new educational wing are especially sensitive to the availability of property.

We also know that different cities, towns, or states can have different interpretations of the boundary between public funding and religious use. We also know that congregations located near a denominational office, seminary, university, or ecumenical agency have greater access to their programmatic resources than more distant congregations. But again, there is no systematic research on the relationship between such phenomena and affiliation.

However, there has been a flurry of conflicting empirical studies in the last few years on the effect of the number of congregations in a given area on membership growth. The studies that find a positive relationship between the two tend to offer two explanations. The first is that the presence of many congregations creates an enhanced ethos of religiosity and thereby raises the affiliation rate of the entire area—an effect which is, of course, mediated through individuals. The second reason given, however, is an institutional effect—namely that the increased competition fostered by many congregations in an area pushes all congregations to increase the quality of their programs.

National Institutional Factors

At the national level, the most visible religious institutional influences on congregation affiliation tend to emanate from the denomination (see Chapter 12). Let me just note a few possibilities by way of example:

- Although it is a factor of diminishing importance in American Protestantism, there remain many people who affiliate with a congregation because of the congregation's denominational affiliation. They are what Donald Luidens (1987) has called, in his research on the Reformed Church in America, "denominational loyalists." They are as self-consciously Lutheran or Baptist as they are members of Grace Church or Center Church.
- Most denominations "require" a certain kind of local congregational polity.
- Most major denominations produce programmatic resources for congregations, in some cases even requiring the use of certain denominational resources (e.g., the Episcopal Prayer Book or the Methodist Book of Discipline).
- Many denominations control or at least influence the seminary training of parish clergy.
- Most denominations control or at least influence the intellectual conservation and development of the denomination's theological and liturgical traditions.
- All denominations can advocate for congregational priorities.
- Denominations can provide funding to congregations.
- Most denominations have some responsibility for what in the Christian tradition we typically call evangelism and new church development.

That should be enough examples to provide a feel for the range of possibilities. The extent to which such possibilities actually can and do influence congregational affiliation is a question which needs to be explored in our research and in our work with local congregations.

National Contextual Factors

That leaves us with *national contextual* factors. If the issue before us was denominational membership growth, we would have to spend a lot of time examining such factors as the national birth rate, immigration patterns, the relative strength of various religious and ethnic subcultures, and the increasing prevalence of expressive individualism and religious volunteerism in American culture. But since the issue is congregational affiliation, the direct influence of national contextual factors is difficult to specify. It is difficult to specify because most, if not all, of it is mediated and filtered down through the local contextual cell and ultimately through the individual. The recent surge in the Hispanic population in the United States, for example, is relatively irrelevant to the affiliation patterns of Protestant congregations in Dubuque, Iowa—a city with virtually no Hispanic population; but it is increasingly significant for congregations in Hartford, Connecticut—where, according to the 1990 census, nearly one-third of the population is Hispanic.

As we saw to be the case for the local contextual cell, institutional to institutional influences at the national level, such as federal policies or new breakthroughs in religious scholarship, are conceivable, but I am hard pressed to think of any recent, concrete examples. One possible exception was President Bush's proposed voucher system for increasing educational choice, a move which could increase the appeal of congregations with parochial schools. Another might be recent work in contextual theology, which could provide new approaches for relating the particularity of local situations to the universality of historical faith traditions.

Added Complexity

Before leaving my framework let me add one important footnote. The outer boundaries of any system's framework are always somewhat arbitrary and heuristic because most systems are really a subsystem of some more extensive system. Similarly, the identification of subsystems within any social system is typically heuristic. Both statements are certainly true for the framework I have just suggested. I hope it is obvious, for example, that each cell in my framework is really a complex system in its own right, such as I have indicated for the congregation. One could, therefore, elaborate any system's framework almost endlessly. Let me note only two possibly important, additional layers of complexity for my framework.

First, many Christian denominations have one or more layers of regional bureaucracy in their overall organizational structure. We often refer to these generically as judicatories, although different denominations have different names for them—synods, dioceses, conferences, presbyteries, associations, and so on. They are the least studied and understood layer of denominational structure. But they are important in a consideration of congregational affiliation because: (1) judicatories are often a mediator of or gatekeeper for denominational influences; and (2) judicatories can have direct responsibility for many of the functions I listed earlier in regard to denominations. Many Catholic dioceses, for example, have their own seminaries; and most regional judicatories in the Christian tradition have more direct responsibility for clergy placement and/or resourcing congregations than do their respective national structures.

Second, there is obviously a global or international layer "above" my national layer. I would venture to say that this is of almost negligible influence on congregational membership for most American Protestant congregations—except for congregations heavily invested in global justice issues or foreign missions, or those whose local context is heavily impacted upon by either immigration and/or global economics. The Catholic situation, however, is very different. Any comprehensive examination of Catholic parish life, even in the United States, must consider Rome. Given the significance of Israel on the one hand and the marginalization—if not outright oppression—of Jews in many countries on the other hand, I would suggest that the "global" is as important a sphere of influence for American Jewish affiliation as it is for American Roman Catholic affiliation.

Text and Context

I have not said anything about God or the transcendent, and little about theology. As a sociologist, I am probably not the most appropriate person to address this subject. But I do think my framework has several implications for theological reflection.

What can possibly be unique about congregations as organizations if it is not that congregations are self-conscious carriers of faith? What can possibly be unique about congregational leadership, program, and affiliation, if not that they are self-conscious efforts to embody commitment? I agree with Loren B. Mead's important insight that congregations need to be shaping laity in ministry and equipping lay religious leaders with working theologies (Chapter 2). My hope, however, is that academic theologians could be more directly engaged with congregations in this task. My experience is that they seldom are, and that when they are, they are not very helpful for at least three reasons.

First, Protestant theologians have raised "criticism" to an art form. But they are often short on the empathetic understanding necessary to move from deconstruction to construction. If they want to be truly helpful to congregations, they need to balance their preoccupation with what should be, with some realistic concern with what can be.

Second, theologians tend to thrive on the "simplicity" of abstraction or specialization. In contrast, the reality of congregations is complex and messy. Single issue theology, even with all the positive nuances of scholarly rigor, is of limited value to congregations. To do theology that takes the reality of the congregation seriously, one has to be willing to wallow in ambiguity and imperfection, without becoming paralyzed by analysis or hopelessness.

Third, the theology of congregations is necessarily contextual. The natural home of most academic theologians is the "text" (i.e., sacred scripture and tradition). However, the day in and day out challenge of lived theology is the relationship between "text" and context. *Affiliation is most critically, therefore, a relationship between individual, congregation and "text."*

REFERENCES

Carroll, J. W., Dudley, C. S., & McKinney, W. (1986). *Handbook for Congregational Studies*. Nashville: Abingdon.

Hoge, D. R., & Roozen, D. A. (Eds.). (1979). *Understanding Church Growth and Decline: 1950–1978*. New York: Pilgrim Press.

Luidens, D. A., & Nemeth, R. J. (1987). 'Public' and 'Private' Protestantism Reconsidered: Introducing the 'Loyalists.' *Journal for the Scientific Study of Religion*, 26(4), 450–464.

Roozen, D. A., & Hadaway, C. K. (Eds.). (1993). *Church and Denominational Growth*. Nashville: Abingdon.

Stokes, A., & Roozen, D. A. (1991). The Unfolding Story of Congregational Studies. In J. Wind, J. W. Carroll, & C. S. Dudley (Eds.), *Carriers of Faith: Lessons from Congregational Studies* (pp. 183–192). Louisville: Westminster/John Knox.

CHAPTER 2
Definitions of Congregational Growth

Rev. Loren B. Mead

Church statisticians and clergy are aware of the historical trends in church membership—increases in the 1930s and 1940s, a high peak in the late 1950s and 1960s, and then a drop-off. Although the general pattern may vary somewhat by denomination, the essential fact of religious life in the 1990s remains clear: most mainline churches are not growing numerically.

I personally have come to look on "number of members" as an important but problematic statistic. It does tell something, and our religious institutions get into trouble if they fail to attend to it; but its simplicity hides a great deal. I want to enlarge the context in which we think about the growth of congregations by laying out a framework which encompasses several varieties of growth, instead of a unique focus on numbers.

The framework was first suggested by Ted Buckle, former archdeacon and now assistant bishop of the Anglican Church of New Zealand (Buckle, 1978). In his attempts to start up new churches, Buckle struggled to understand why some of his congregations grew in numbers and others did not. He came to the realization that numerical growth is not the only possibility for congregations. There are, he proposed, four different kinds of church growth. This chapter describes each of these in detail:

Numerical growth. This is growth in the ways we ordinarily describe it: growth in numbers of active members, attendance at worship services, size of budget, numbers of activities, and so on.

Maturational growth. This is growth in stature and maturity of members, in their ability to grow in their faith and deepen their spiritual roots.

Organic growth. This is growth of the congregation as a functioning community, as an organism that is able to work, decide, move, and take action.

Incarnational growth. This is growth in the ability of the congregation to have an impact on the world, with the meanings and values of the faith-story. It is growth in the ability to manifest in the community the principles and faith of the religion.

Congregations, over time, need to pursue and achieve more than one kind of growth; numerical growth is necessary but not sufficient for congregational health.

NUMERICAL GROWTH

Numerical growth has been our conventional way of measuring church growth. Numbers, however, are not easy to derive. At the denominational level, for example, we may see a greater decline in church membership if we calculate the relative percentage of the population that is affiliated rather than the absolute number of church members. At the congregational level, there are other problems. When I ask a church leader about the number of members in the congregation, I am usually greeted by a pained look. "Do you mean 'active' or 'on the mailing list' members?" I am asked, or, "Do you mean 'on the rolls,' or 'pledges'?" The definition seems to change from year to year and from place to place (Chapter 3).

Church events affect numbers as well. We know that lists of congregational members generally get sharply pared whenever a per capita assessment system is installed. We also know that many new pastors take out the shears to "clean up the membership list" as one of the first acts of taking over leadership of a congregation. It is also true that a long-term pastor tends to leave on the rolls people she or he remembers and does not want to drop, even though the last time that person was within the church walls was a decade ago. All of these inclinations undermine valid and reliable counting of church members.

The numbers we count, moreover, need to be understood as a product of both gains and losses in membership. I first became aware of the issue of church growth in the late 1950s when I was a young pastor in the Episcopal Church. The church at that time was concerned with "evangelism," by which it meant the number of church faithful. To research this number, it established a commission under the direction of Charles Kane, then a rector in Washington, D.C. Kane went out, studied all the statistics, and returned with his report. "The Episcopal Church," he said, "is a fantastic organization. It just brings people in from everywhere. It's like a vacuum cleaner—it sucks people up all over the place. There is just one problem. There's no bag on the other end, so, out they go as soon as they are done."

As Kane's report illustrates, numerical growth depends on bringing in new members—through new births in the congregation, conversion, and missionary work, or outreach to those currently unaffiliated. It depends equally on retaining current members, and minimizing the number of

Definitions of Congregational Growth 29

dropouts or those leaving through the "back door." Simply put, religious institutions that do not replace their losses will die.

Environmental Factors

Three environmental factors are related to numerical growth: regional culture, geographical population shifts, and birth and death rates.

Regional Culture. Differences in regional culture exist and exert noticeable impact on church membership. For example, in California perhaps 15% of the people in a community go to church, while in a similar community in Alabama some 80% are likely to attend (Bradley, Green, Jones, Lynn, & McNeil, 1992). If we were to move a church to California, it probably would not enjoy much growth. Alternatively, if we could move the California environment to other parts of the country, churches there would experience low growth.

Geographical Population Shifts. There are also sections of the country where membership is likely to decrease for a completely different reason: the population itself is in decline. Throughout the Great Plains states, population has been slowly shrinking for generations. Some towns and cities are victims of local causes of population decline (e.g., in the rust belt, Appalachian mining areas, towns where a major employer goes bust, or areas where environmental catastrophe occurs). It is probable that congregational membership in those areas will match the declines in the general population, no matter what church leaders do.

Birth and Death Rates. The balance between births and deaths leads to increases of membership during baby booms and decreases during times of widespread illness and mortality. Other factors can be influential: a religious group's position on birth control, a discovery of how to preserve life or conquer a terrible illness, or the outbreak of a virulent epidemic (like AIDS). Birthrates, moreover, are related to socioeconomic status. Churches, such as the Southern Baptist churches, that experience a shift from blue collar to white collar, discover that the birthrate of their membership declines. Across our society, it has been demonstrated that as denominations move up the socioeconomic ladder they tend to have lower birthrates and, consequently, lower congregational growth rates.

The environmental factors (regional culture, geographical population shifts, birth and death rates) are factors over which congregations have almost no control. A wise congregation, however, will analyze these in its own life in order to plan and make informed choices.[1]

Individual Decisions

Numbers are also affected by individuals' decisions whether or not to become or remain a part of a congregation. These decisions account for transfers in, transfers out, converts, and dropouts (Roof & McKinney, 1987). Transfers are individuals who move from one church or denomination to another. Already numbered among the faithful, they affect the membership count of a given church but not the total census of the affiliated. Converts and dropouts, in contrast, are those who have moved between participation in a particular church and detachment from any religious institution at all. As they move in (convert) or out (dropout), they affect the congregational membership numbers, as well as overall statistics on religious affiliation.

Transfers In and Out. Many transfers are attributable to environmental factors (e.g., the presence of a high-turnover industry in the community or the location of a congregation in a university setting). Some transfers-in may result from specific qualities of the church, such as the appointment of a charismatic minister or priest; conversely some transfers-out may be motivated by an individual's disappointments with the church or by his or her failure to establish connections to the congregation.

There may be little the church can do to bring transfers-in to its doors. There is, however, much it can do to assure that those who arrive as newcomers are received and cared for, formally and visibly welcomed into membership, and connected to groups and people in the congregation. Likewise, the congregation may be unable to prevent some transfers-out. But it can make certain that those who experience disappointments have an opportunity to reevaluate the meaning of membership, confess feelings of resentment, and begin to build more realistic expectations for the future.

Converts and Dropouts. Converts are often people who were virtual strangers to religion. To bring them into the church, congregations must be able to present the case for faith to those who are illiterate in the faith-story and have no firsthand experience of commitment. The congregation has to learn to receive and nurture people converted from radical lack of faith to faith.

Equal skill is needed to respond to the contemporary phenomenon of dropouts, the fastest growing religious group in this country (Roof & McKinney, 1987). Dropouts are a complex group which comprises a spectrum from those who still attend church to those who have "given up" on religion entirely (Chapter 4). It is important to note that while some drop out because of factors internal to the church, many do so in response to external forces. These dropouts are not angry or disillusioned; they simply find life outside the church attractive and relatively fulfilling (see Chapter 6). For them, the need for church is not convincing, and they see few forces in society encouraging or supporting church membership.

Dropouts are very hard to reclaim, so congregational energy is better spent in prevention than in pursuing those who have left. The most effective course of action is to build strong, challenging communities of faith, communities that will stretch and empower congregational members. Where such communities exist, the need to drop out is diminished.

MATURATIONAL GROWTH

Maturational growth concerns the ability of a congregation to mature in its faith, to deepen its spiritual roots, and to broaden its religious imagination. Such growth does not depend on numbers. I know of congregations where there is no numerical growth—indeed there is loss of membership—but where there is significant maturational growth.

The first congregation I ever served was in a little place called Hell Hole Swamp, South Carolina. During the course of three years, we gained three members, and we lost three: two were shot, and one was put in jail for shooting one of the other two. But the congregation was an extraordinary group of people in terms of their ability to learn and to minister to one another, a remarkable community of people who were trying to grow in faith. When people grapple together with personal dimensions of faith, search the Scriptures in depth, try to make connections between their faith and the life of their community, they are working toward profound maturational growth.

Maturation of Faith through Ministry of Education

Maturational growth means the congregation is taking seriously its ministry of education and is bringing its people along in understanding the faith in new ways. To meet the religious challenges of the next century, I would argue that congregations have to be reinvented as new kinds of seminaries—they must become congregations that shape *laity in ministry* as effectively as seminaries of the past century shaped the professional clergy. Ministry in the twenty-first century is going to demand persons equipped with the Biblical story, with working theologies that translate into everyday realities, and with an operational grasp of ethics. Such understanding and knowledge do not come with a sermon or two a year, but rather require serious, long-term engagement with the content and meaning of the faith.

Maturational growth also implies the application of theology to everyday life situations—at work or in the community, in homemaking or retirement, or in the experience of unemployment or being sick in a hospital. These are the situations in which ministry is carried out, and the congregation needs to have a system that helps lay persons reflect on their encounters with God's concerns in daily life. In this model, the clearest path to theological discovery rises not from grounding in traditions of scholarship, but from engagement with the life of the world, through the ministry of ordinary people. Our future challenge, as I see it, is building slowly and steadily toward a comprehensive, lifelong program which helps each congregational member gain the knowledge, skills, and perspective necessary for a frontline ministry.

Maturation of Faith through Life-Crisis Ministries

Maturational growth means doing a good job of helping people grow and be nurtured through life transitions and crises. The church provides a framework for the dramatic changes of life, the turning points that almost by definition destroy the homeostasis of life: birth, acceptance into maturity, marriage, birth of one's own children, illness, and death. These developmental earthquakes have shaped lives for thousands of years and still do. They are the framework for a process of spiritual development, the moments when people have to face anew the ultimate questions: who am I? what am I called to be? what do I believe? what must I do? The religious task has been to facilitate in those moments a conversation with God, bringing to bear all the wisdom of Scripture and the power of liturgy. We call this work *pastoral care*. Its purpose is to facilitate the dialogue between the self and God, as the self faces new challenges in life transitions.

Unfortunately, the life-crisis ministries we have developed for maturational growth largely reflect the crises of life as conceived in medieval Europe, and they completely overlook some of the major crises faced in the modern world. For example, what the medieval church did as ministry at the time of birth was challenging enough, but today pastoral care requires the competence to minister in moral quandaries about reproduction and abortion, prenatal care, premature birth, and birth defects. Similarly, the congregation or pastor who helped a bride and groom prepare for spiritual and physical union did not ordinarily deal with issues of divorce and remarriage, much less birth control and genetic testing. We even have life transitions and life stages that did not exist in the medieval world or were not included in its pastoral care syllabus. Adolescence is a relatively new concept. And never before has the category of "senior citizen" existed in the way it does in this country and century.

We need to update our pastoral care. There is a "growth industry" awaiting our religious institutions if they would only look carefully at the crises of life described by contemporary social scientists (e.g., Erikson, 1968; Gilligan, 1982; Levinson, 1978) and develop models for congregational ministry based on the challenges of modern life. Such models would be valuable tools for maturational growth.

Maturation of Faith through Worship

The other side of maturational growth is worship—the common, ordinary, week-by-week worship that is at the heart of congregational life. Spiritual maturity or growth is one of the most elusive subjects one finds around church people. Everybody has a stake in it, but few have much sense of what it actually means. Laity, by and large, leave it (like "theology") to the professionals, the clergy and the professors. Let me say, however, that any congregation that wants to produce a ministry for the future needs to have a clear picture of what it wants to accomplish in the area of spiritual growth and a program for doing it.

The religious congregation has the task of providing guides and resources for the spiritual development of its members. People spend most of their time in "homeostasis," spiritually stuck. When homeostasis is threatened, as it often is for most of us, we learn to rebuild our walls and shore up our defenses against spirituality as fast as we can—just to keep going with our daily routine. So it is that we come to our worship each week with scantily patched defenses, looking for, but also afraid to find, the dialogue between who or what we are and God's purposes for us. That dialogue, which alone can strengthen us for the next steps of life, is the essence of spiritual development. The role of worship each week is to help us let down our defenses and enter once more into the religious dialogue that feeds our spirit.

The primary task of the congregation in helping spiritual growth is thus very simple: it is maintaining the steady rhythm of exposure to Scripture and worship week in and week out, year after year. A congregation that allows its worship to become sloppy or routine is compromising its central opportunity to provide for spiritual growth of its members. A pastor who gets caught up in anything else—from pastoral counseling to social action to theological study—and neglects the task of preaching and leadership for worship is in the wrong business.

ORGANIC GROWTH

A third kind of growth is organic growth, developing as a community, as an organism that is able to work, make decisions, and take action. Many people find the formal structures of their congregation an obstacle to its ministry, draining rather than generating energy. Organic growth helps the organizational structures of the congregation become a launching pad for ministry, rather than an institutional albatross around the collective neck of the members. All congregations have potential for organic growth; those that neglect it will undercut their ability to sustain any of the other kinds of growth.

Organic growth raises questions such as these: what form of community best supports ministry and mission? how are decisions to be made—by majority vote or by inspired leadership? who owns this congregation and where does legitimate power reside? how do you handle the fights that come up over allocation of space or budget? how do you handle changes in size and deal with losses or with the assimilation of new members? Organic growth assures that growth in numbers or maturation or mission takes place within a strong and effective organization, one that is able to make decisions and carry them out over time. A congregation cannot accomplish much without paying some attention to its underpinnings as an organism.

The systems analysis for organic growth is quite elaborate. I will simply point to a few of the key elements and processes here, ones we can most readily affect.

Organizational Culture

Organizational culture is a term borrowed from anthropological conceptions of society that explain how people live and organize themselves. Culture has a superficial and a deep structure. The surface realm includes roles, role relationships, and norms that describe and prescribe how one is to act in the culture. The deep structure is comprised of the values and beliefs that give significance to behavior and legitimacy to organization.

Roles. People in local congregations fulfill different roles—the pastor, the treasurer, the head of the board, the head of the education program, the teachers, the ushers. Some of the roles are long-term ones, some relatively short. Some are more central and visible, others are less so. The congregation that is growing organically will clarify roles and role relationships and make certain adequate training and support is available for people in various roles.

Confusion over roles, insufficient authority for those in a given role, burnout from a role poorly circumscribed, or behavior inappropriate to a given role (e.g., abdicating the power of one's role or co-opting the power of someone else's role) all hinder the smooth functioning and growth of the congregation as an organization. The clearer the roles are and the better the training for them, the more likely the system will work well.

Norms. Congregations also have norms, unwritten rules which set limits of behavior. Norms may have consequences which are not in the best interest of the congregation. For example, a norm that no one ever criticizes anybody or anything makes it difficult for a congregation to deal with conflict, or even with differences of opinion. A congregational norm of "we are like a family around here" may make it extremely hard for a newcomer to break in.

Often norms are so ingrained in the culture of a congregation that they operate outside the realm of awareness and it is possible to see them only in their violation. In order to understand the influence of norms on congregational functioning, they need to be made explicit, brought into conscious awareness. Healthy norms can undergird healthy interactions for years; unhealthy norms can inhibit the organic growth of a congregation.

Values. Every social system has at its heart a set of values and beliefs that are its center of gravity. When individual or congregational behavior becomes separated from deeply held beliefs and values, problems are inevitable. We often say, "We must practice what we preach" or "you've got to walk the talk." Keeping beliefs and values yoked with behavior is important. It is easy to construct a congregation in which people are used rather than loved, in which a stranger is ignored, in which people are unforgiving and rigid, or in which they hide what they find unacceptable rather than bringing it out in the open for healing. A congregation that seeks to grow as a ministering community will work hard to match its behavior to its values and beliefs.

Organizational Processes

Organic growth also entails attention to how the congregation makes decisions and takes action. For many years, management studies have been providing us with tools for enhancing leadership and organization effectiveness (e.g., Carroll, Dudley, & McKinney, 1986; Friedman, 1985; Mead, 1993). Properly implemented, these tools can help congregations develop as religious organizations, by improving decision making, socialization of new members, and other congregational processes.

Decision Making. Decision making is a key process in any social system, including congregations. Exactly what decisions get made is sometimes not as important as how they get made. A congregation needs to be certain there is a dependable, accountable system for making decisions. It needs to build confidence that decisions are made in the service of values and beliefs, and it needs to provide appropriate opportunity for input into decisions.

There are many ways to make decisions (e.g., majority rule, consensus, or the dictates of an authority). If the organization has different decision-making patterns for different kinds of decisions, it needs to be clear about what pattern operates where. Confusion about how decisions are made produces anger, poor motivation, and a sense of victimization. Congregations that want to grow as effective human systems need to have as much clarity as possible about who makes what decisions and how one can have input or register protest.

Socialization of New Members. Another important process in congregational life is the socialization of new members of the congregation. Where it is done well, the new member rapidly becomes an effective, contributing member. Where it is not done well, the new member is frustrated and unproductive, and frequently disappears from the group before long.

Congregations tend to pay little attention to socialization. We are told that half the new members who join a congregation leave within two years. From a strict systems point of view, such a rate of loss is extremely costly. The gifts those people brought and wanted to contribute are now cut off, while their complaints about the congregation are likely to be spread to their friends. The congregation has also violated its own beliefs and values. It has failed to receive and give hospitality to one of God's children who was seeking to make a home in the community.

Other Congregational Processes. Other processes congregations need to work on include the following:

communication (upward, downward, and across groups in the system)

boundary maintenance (e.g., the distinguishing characteristics or behaviors that constitute membership, the meaning of membership, different categories of membership, entry points and training for membership, ways of dealing with those who do not live up to membership standards or those who leave)

leadership development (the distribution of power and authority in the system, training for various roles, the dialogue between clergy and lay leadership, and so on)

conflict management (helping people and congregations deal more effectively with their differences and the divisiveness that occurs in religious families)

Understanding the congregation as a human system and thinking strategically about points of intervention opens possibilities for organic growth.

INCARNATIONAL GROWTH

In the final variety of growth, incarnational growth, the principles and faith of the congregation are made manifest in the structures of the community. Congregations undergoing incarnational growth are developing the ability to affect the social environment with their religious values and beliefs. Those that care about incarnational growth want their faith to make a difference in the world.

Relationship to the Community

There are a multitude of ways by which congregations get involved in social ministries within their communities (Dudley, 1991). There are, for example, the activists in church life who try to incarnate their values by demonstrating in the community for social change. There is *outreach*, an organized effort by the church to go into the community to alleviate suffering—poverty, homelessness, disease, or other social ills. And there is what used to be called the *apostolate of the laity*, that is, lay people incarnating the values of the faith, taking individual action out in the community on behalf of the faith.

Roozen, McKinney, and Carroll (1984) suggest a four-part typology of how a congregation might orient itself toward the wider community: civic, activist, sanctuary, and evangelistic.

Civic Orientation. Civic orientation describes congregations in which there is concern for the life of the community and a sense of responsibility for public life. Civic congregations tend to be supportive of the orderly processes of government and systems of law. At times members of civic congregations will become involved in political campaigns, working, as private individuals, for or against particular candidates or issues. Pastors and other leaders in such civic congregations will encourage members and young people to participate in the political process. Civic congregations seek to produce members who, as responsible participants in society, are active in shaping a community that cares for human needs.

Activist Orientation. The activist orientation describes congregations that sometimes operate as countercultures, seeking redress of wrongs, protesting public policies their members consider unjust, joining public demonstrations to voice their concerns. Whereas the civic congregation tends to support the structures of society, the activist congregation is more often suspicious and confrontational toward those structures.[2] Activist congregations seek to create a community with a higher consciousness of justice issues. They are interested in changing laws and practices in the community and in producing members skilled at and committed to action for social justice.

Sanctuary Orientation. The focus in sanctuary congregations is on developing a relationship with God in this world that will carry over into a triumphant life after death, where the trials and tribulations of this present time will be overcome. The outside community is not the focus of change efforts. Instead, the secular community is seen as a dangerous but necessary testing place from which to return to the congregation for restoration and renewal. The congregation with a sanctuary orientation is not interested in influencing society directly; it is interested in producing people of faith who can stand against the powers of the world and finally attain everlasting glory.

Evangelistic Orientation. The evangelistic orientation, like the sanctuary orientation, is primarily concerned about the world beyond this one. It differs, however, in its understanding of a powerful calling to relate to those outside the congregation in order to win them over to faith. These congregations may share with sanctuary congregations a real suspicion of society, seeing it as a dangerous place of personal testing. But their members also see a calling to witness their faith and to thereby win outsiders to faith. Like the sanctuary congregation, the ultimate focus of the evangelistic congregation is on producing saints for glory. However, the evangelistic congregation is also characterized by an aggressive output of energy into the environment in order to recruit members. Its secondary output, therefore, is a highly visible effort to increase the size of the community of the faithful and to enhance its character as a sustainer of the faithful for religious struggle in the secular world.

These four orientations describe something of the diversity of how congregations see their relationship to the world, but we should also remember that these descriptions are artificial constructs. No one congregation fully fits any of the descriptions, and every congregation probably has people or groups who share a quite different orientation from that which predominates in the congregation.

Caveats

For congregations that seek incarnational growth, let me offer two caveats: avoid temptation, and remember, at all times, the primary mission of the church (Mead, 1993).

The temptation I speak of is the temptation to reconstruct "Christendom," to reconstitute a marriage of church and state. This is sometimes seen in attempts to build a coalition of "the right people," religious and political leaders who will establish a consensus in which the church sets the moral agenda for society at large. Such temptation creates a twofold problem. It assumes that religious people have a corner on knowing what justice looks like and that the power to enforce such a society can be administered and organized coherently and fairly.

To take one example of the problem, what is "justice" on abortion? Most of the people I know are clear about the answer to the question. The problem is their answers do not agree. More than that, the most passionate on whatever side have what I can only call contempt or outrage for those on the other side. And many of the people on both sides who are most articulate have deep religious convictions they call upon as support for their position. Religious people who care about the state of society have a hard time not projecting their passion onto God, seeking to build a society that enforces their own convictions about what is true and good. When they do, they often become the antithesis of their faith—hard, unforgiving, rigid, monomaniacal, intolerant.

The temptation to rebuild a religious-secular coalition leads congregations to make outreach to the social world, and not relationship to God, their primary task. Congregations, however, must be clear that they are in business to help people find God and be found by God. They must build themselves up as religious communities, as bases from which ministry is done, as places where God's word is studied and reflected upon, as communities in which people are nurtured, healed, and fed. In society, there is no "second team." No other institution has this primary task or will become this religious community if congregations do not.

The more congregations can resist the temptation to universalize their approach and avoid any temptation toward Christendom, the more they will learn about incarnational growth. The better the congregation gets at building up its base as a religious community and sending its people to engage the world, the more it will generate incarnational growth.

CONCLUSION

I have presented in this chapter four varieties of congregational growth—numerical, maturational, organic, and incarnational. Underlying this framework is the message that congregations need to grow and they can grow. I am arguing here for as wide a definition of growth as possible and an appreciation of the importance of many kinds of growth. Each congregation is asked very simply to become more of what God calls it to be; each one will have its own path. I do not believe that all congregations can grow simultaneously in all four ways. A congregation that makes a disaster of one kind of growth may experience another kind, and it may even come back several years later and succeed where before it had failed.

The congregation is one of the few places in society in which we as individuals can come together, restore our wholeness, recover our sense of direction, receive the power to do what we must do, and be assured of the community with God and with one another that makes life worth living. The congregation is the arena for the restoration of life and mission. That arena itself needs repair and restoration very critically at this moment in history. Those who care about the quality of life in our society need to care about the health of religious congregations and their ability to grow—not just in numbers, but also in faith, ministry, and mission.

NOTES

1. This chapter presents an overview of categories of church growth and the dynamics entailed in each. For a guide to specific activities and programs for diagnosing a congregation's potential for growth and for planning action steps to effect each type of growth, the reader is referred to L. B. Mead (1993), *More Than Numbers*.

2. Although the experiences of the 1960s and 1970s called attention to congregations with an activist orientation, the United States has a long tradition of such congregations. Activist congregations date from the time of abolition and temperance, and reach into the more recent concerns of civil rights and poverty, the rights of women, and pro- or anti-choice issues.

REFERENCES

Bradley, M. B., Green N. M., Jr., Jones, D. E., Lynn, M., & McNeil, L. (1992). *Churches and Church Membership in the United States 1990*. Atlanta: Glenmary Research Center.

Buckle, T. (1978). *The House Alongside*. Auckland, New Zealand: Anglican Diocese.

Carroll, J. W., Dudley, C. S., & McKinney, W. (1986). *Handbook for Congregational Studies*. Nashville: Abingdon.

Dudley, C. (1991). *Basic Steps Toward Community Ministry*. Washington, D.C.: The Alban Institute.

Erikson, E. H. (1968). *Identity, Youth, and Crisis*. New York: Norton.

Friedman, E. (1985). *Generation to Generation: Family Process in Church and Synagogue*. New York: Guilford Press.
Gilligan, C. F. (1982). *In a Different Voice*. Cambridge: Harvard University Press.
Levinson, D. J. (1978). *The Seasons of a Man's Life*. New York: Knopf.
Mead, L. B. (1991). *The Once and Future Church*. Washington, D.C.: The Alban Institute.
Mead, L. B. (1993). *More than Numbers*. Washington, D.C.: The Alban Institute.
Roof, C. W., & McKinney, W. (1987). *American Mainline Religion*. New Brunswick, NJ: Rutgers University Press.
Roozen, D., McKinney, W., & Carroll, J. W. (1984). *Varieties of Religious Presence*. New York: Pilgrim Press.

CHAPTER 3

Interdenominational Dialogue: Seeking a Common Language for Affiliation Research and Practice

Gary A. Tobin

The literature on church membership has grown dramatically in the last twenty years. Scholars have undertaken serious examination of various facets of this issue: changes in the populations of the major religions in the United States, growth and decline in the membership of particular denominations, and individual attitudes and behaviors associated with involvement in religious institutions. They have examined in detail the contextual and institutional factors influencing growth and decline: demographic shifts, changes in the cultural milieu, congregational characteristics, the role of religious leadership, and even the economic benefits of belonging to churches.

This vast literature exhibits little commonality in the language and definitions used in discussing church affiliation. *Churched* and *unchurched, affiliation, nonaffiliation* and *disaffiliation, membership* and *non-membership, growth* and *decline, outreach* and a variety of other terms are used to discuss the phenomena related to church and synagogue participation, but their connotations and denotations shift from one faith tradition to another, from scholar to clergy, and from one academic discipline to another.

This chapter explores the definitional issues surrounding the study and discussion of congregational affiliation and growth. The first sections examine the range of definitions used by clergy and scholars. The final section suggests using the concepts of ideology, participation, and identity as a basis for sorting out the confusion and complexity in affiliation-related terminology.

RESEARCH DEFINITIONS OF THE *CHURCHED* AND THE *UNCHURCHED*

The attempt to define who is inside the church or synagogue and who is outside takes many forms. Gordon Turner (1984), for example, proposes nine concentric rings starting at the "hard core" members who are most involved in the life of the church, moving outward to "soft-core church dropouts," and ending with "hostile reactors." Location within these concentric circles—being a member, an affiliate, or a nonmember—is seen as a fluid experience rather than a permanent state of being.

Others seek more categorical, objective definitions based on Gallup's guidelines (Gallup Poll Organization, 1978) although the specific terms employed vary from study to study. Dean R. Hoge, Benton Johnson and Donald A. Luidens (Chapter 4), for example, use the terms *churched* and *unchurched*; Penny Long Marler and C. Kirk Hadaway (Chapter 5) choose to refer to these persons as *active* or *inactive*. Both studies use frequency of church attendance as a measure to sort people into these two groups; Hoge, Johnson, and Luidens further require church membership for an individual to be considered "churched." *Church member* in their study means that the person has self-consciously joined a local congregation and now has his or her name on the rolls.

It is recognized that the term *unchurched* encompasses a broad array of individual relationships to the church and ought to be subdivided into more meaningful and conceptually useful categories. Hoge, Johnson, and Luidens (Chapter 4) divide the unchurched into four types based on membership and attendance: (1) people who are attenders but not members; (2) people who are members but not attenders; (3) people who are neither but see themselves as religious; and (4) people who are inactive and also see themselves as non-religious. Marler and Hadaway (Chapter 5) add religious identity as a basis for classification. In their schema, the inactive population includes: (1) "nones," those with no religious identity or preference; (2) "mental affiliates," persons who claim a religious preference, say they attend religious services several times a year or less, and do not claim to be members of a church or synagogue; and (3) "marginal members," persons who claim a religious preference, say they attend religious services several times a year or less, and claim to be church or synagogue members. C. Kirk Hadaway and Wade Clark Roof (1988) further distinguish those who have never had a religious identity ("none stayers") from those who have newly rejected one ("apostates"). They include, as well, the "invisible affiliates"—those who identify with some religion, but who rarely if ever attend religious services.

Disaffiliation is an active term describing a process by which a person moves from being inside to being outside the religious institution. Other terms employed for this concept are *disengagement, defection,* or simply *dropping out*. David Roozen (1980), for example, defines *disengagement* as not attending religious services for a period of two years or more. In distinguishing among these terms, Howard Bahr and Stan Albrecht (1989) suggest that, unlike other processes of withdrawal, disaffiliation entails a change in personal identity. They also offer a typology of disaffiliation based on justifications for the change in religious engagement (e.g., maturation, unmet personal or spiritual needs, or conflict with the church).

DEFINITIONS IN USE

We recently asked a group of fifty clergy and scholars representing diverse professional and religious perspectives for their definitions of (1) congregational membership, (2) denominational affiliation, (3) the unaffiliated, (4) outreach, and (5) congregational growth. A summary of the range of definitions in use for each of these concepts is presented in the following pages. The denomination of respondents is noted in parentheses for the reader's information. It is not intended to suggest that any individual's comments represent all views in this denomination or its affiliate churches or synagogues. Indeed, in a number of instances there was significant variation in responses from members of the same denomination.

Congregational Membership

The definitions given for congregational membership were both theoretical and functional.

Theoretical Definitions. Theoretical definitions view membership as based on the ideology and social identity of those who choose to be part of a religious group. These definitions are often ritually based, and in this way they are concerned with membership as a familial identification. In some groups (Lutheran, Presbyterian, Mennonite, Mormon, and others), for example, baptism is a prerequisite for being considered a member of the group.

In addition to ritual initiation, some churches include in their definition of membership a profession of faith. Membership, in these cases, requires a certain ideology or set of religious beliefs apart from the more measurable behavior of baptism or attendance at worship services.

Members are those who have publicly (before the Elders and the congregation) affirmed Christian faith and made a commitment to be responsible for the ongoing life and ministry of the congregation. Members also include the baptized children of such persons. (Presbyterian)

Membership is defined initially as profession of faith, then attendance and/or donations at least once a year. (United Methodist)

Functional Definitions. Functional definitions are concerned with membership as a personal matter. They are based on individual behaviors: how often a person attends worship services, whether he or she pays dues to a congregation, whether he or she volunteers for the congregation, and so on.

A number of respondents (Catholic, Episcopalian, Presbyterian, Jewish, and others) noted that membership entails, at the very minimum, undergoing a formal registration or application which assures that the family's name is placed on the rolls of the congregation. A Reform rabbi said that membership means "a family unit has declared the desire to affiliate, filed an application, come to meet with a membership person, and an annual dues or contribution has been determined." Generally some level of participation is added to this definition of membership.

In most Episcopal churches, membership implies (1) name on the rolls, (2) communion at least twice a year, and (3) at least six months duration since joining. There are different classes of members, though: confirmed, communicant, baptized, and—to beg the whole question—"active" and "inactive" members. (Episcopalian)

Congregational membership is a term that refers to an individual, couple, or family unit who has formally associated themselves to the house of worship and who fulfill all of the financial as well as religious requirements of that given institution. (Conservative Jewish)

In addition to a financial commitment, the most commonly noted form of participation requisite for "membership" is attendance at religious services.

Membership means an active participation in at least the liturgical life of the community. (Roman Catholic)

Congregational membership is with the worshipping community—in its ritual, ceremonial, sacramental, witnessing service and advocacy life together. (Lutheran)

In a few instances, functional definitions are rooted in geography. Catholic respondents, for example, mentioned the demarcation of the local parish, and a Mormon respondent explained how one's home address determines congregational affiliation in the Church of Latter Day Saints.

Complexity in Defining Membership. Defining membership is a complex undertaking because of the subtleties within the concept of membership (especially the distinction between active and inactive members), the multitude of factors that comprise a single definition, and the relativeness of the term.

First, respondents are clear on the attributes and behaviors which distinguish active members, or members in good standing, from other congregants. Attendance at worship services is generally indicative of an active member, although definitions vary from the general "regular attendance," or "regular as defined by local custom," to more highly specified frequency at services: "weekly attendance," "one or more times a month," "at least half of the Sundays," "when in town," or "twice in the past year." Financial support is the other mark of an active member. This too varies across respondents: "financial support as they are able," "a contribution of several hundred dollars or more," or "fulfillment of one's dues obligation." One respondent noted that the best informal definition of an active member or a member in good standing was "anyone whom two or three other persons in the congregation (not otherwise related to him/her) know by name."

Some respondents added other conditions for active membership. These included, among others, willingness to accept assignments and participate in the life and work of the congregation (Mormon), participation in some level of study (Reform Jewish), an attempt to live a life in accordance with the tenets of the congregation (Roman Catholic), and personal involvement and commitment to the goals of the congregation (Roman Catholic).

Moreover, as seen in the preceding definitions, despite our attempt to analyze the various definitions of membership, most are comprised of several conditions—both functional and theoretical—all of which are considered necessary for membership.

Finally, several respondents said that membership is not a fixed concept amenable to such specification. Rather, the criteria for determining the boundary between member and nonmember are relative standards which rest with the individual congregation. "In my research with diverse congregations," wrote one participant, "I accept each congregation's own criteria for membership" (Jewish). Another wrote that a person is a member "when a congregation considers him or her to be a member" (Lutheran). Even active membership was described by several respondents as "whatever the bylaws, customs, and behavior of a congregation prescribe" (Unitarian-Universalist, Jewish, Lutheran, and others).

Denominational Affiliation

Some respondents see denominational affiliation rooted in the individual's self-identity and/or expression of faith. Others regard it as essentially an institutional identity derived from a congregational connection.

Self-Proclaimed Identity. Jewish respondents were most likely to define denominational affiliation as a self-proclaimed identity. "Denomination is operationally defined by the individual's self-reported denomination," wrote one. A person is affiliated with a denomination, explained another, when she or he "is a member of a congregation of that denomination, and/or attends services or functions there, and identifies as a member of that denomination."

For the Church of Latter Day Saints (LDS), denominational affiliation is the same as membership in the Church. A child born to LDS parents becomes a member of record. A child of record or convert (age 8 and over) becomes a baptized member when he or she is baptized into the LDS Church. Catholics, too, defined denominational affiliation as "baptism and acceptance of the basic tenets of the denomination."

Institutional Connection. For others, individuals become affiliated with a denomination when they become members of a church or synagogue which is institutionally affiliated with the national denomination (see Chapter 1). These respondents maintain that the individual's denomination is defined exclusively by his or her connection to the congregation.

For the individual, denomination affiliation goes with congregational membership. For the congregation, this entails compliance with the provisions of the United Methodist Discipline. (United Methodist)

Individuals are affiliated with the Lutheran Church-Missouri Synod (LCMS) through member congregations. Only congregations and ordained/commissioned ministers of the Word (clergy or teachers) are technical "members" of the LCMS. (Lutheran)

The Unaffiliated

Definitions of the unaffiliated are almost as diverse as definitions of members. The term *unaffiliated* is often used as the converse of member. It refers to those who do not formally belong to a congregation or do not participate in the ways described above (are not baptized, do not pay dues, fail to attend worship services, and so on). They are the people who either have no regular contact with a particular church or synagogue, or hold no membership in one. As one rabbi wrote: "Unaffiliated means to me not belonging to a *religious* institution (a church or synagogue). No other Jewish or Christian institution serves the purpose of affiliation (for example a Jewish community center or a Y)." Being unaffiliated is also linked with identity. The unaffiliated, said one respondent, are those "who do not report themselves as 'belonging' to the group or groups in question" (Episcopalian).

Different types may be considered unaffiliated: "those who have never formally become a member of a congregation or those who are 'tasting the wares' with the idea of deciding whether or not they wish to formally become members" (Conservative Jewish); or "those who have either resigned from the congregation membership or have never on their own chosen to become members of the synagogue" (Reform Jewish). Included in this category are persons "who may indicate on a survey a religious preference, but who are not actively involved, and those who have made a faith commitment to a religious story, but who find no sense of place or belonging in any formal congregation" (Presbyterian) (see Chapter 5).

Ceasing to be a Member. Clergy and researchers were also asked about "disaffiliation," that is, how an individual ceases to be a member. Formal declaration of disassociation, the individual or family explicitly requesting

Interdenominational Dialogue 47

to be removed from the rolls, was most often mentioned as the way one ceases to be a member.

The person may either request that his or her name be taken off the list, or by doing nothing his or her name will come off sooner or later. Periodically all churches 'clean' their rolls. In the Presbyterian denomination, the procedure is to contact the person under question to see whether or not he or she wants to remain on the roll, and if so, whether the person expects to attend or contribute. Then a decision is made. (Presbyterian)

Others responded that lack of financial support for some period of time results in removal from the membership list; six months, a year, three years—the amount of time varies before nonpayment cancels membership.

One may simply cease responding to annual statements regarding contributions. In the case of nonresponse to annual dues commitments, our congregation makes written, then telephone contact, and no one is removed from the rolls for at least two years following his/her last contribution. (Reform rabbi)

Still others emphasized that membership ceases through inactivity. At some point, the church "writes you off": the decision is made that someone is not worth pursuing any longer or that the congregation simply does not have the resources to follow up lapsed members. In some cases, names are removed from the rolls because the church or synagogue is unable to contact the member, the person has died or has transferred to another congregation. Finally, in some congregations or denominations egregious acts warrant removal from membership by excommunication.

A person ceases to be a member by session removal after two years of inactivity, after diligent effort has been made by the session to restore such a person to active membership. (Presbyterian)

Members may be removed from the rolls for cause (excommunicated) or because they have not attended worship for extended periods and/or cannot be contacted. (Lutheran)

Outreach

Although they differ in intent and focus, the definitions given for *outreach* agree that the term refers to an effort to extend the church or synagogue to those outside the door. As one respondent explained: "Outreach, by definition, is set in contrast to all activities which revolve around what one might call inreach. Inreach activities have as their focus the lives of those who are currently active participants in the life of the congregation. Therefore, to reach out means to extend the sphere of activity beyond the current active congregation's needs." Basically, outreach is used to refer to one of two endeavors: evangelism, and social/community service (see Chapter 2).

Evangelism. Evangelism, a calling to witness faith, is a "spiritual outreach" intended to win outsiders to faith.

Outreach can be a synonym for evangelism, i.e., witnessing to the Gospel of Jesus Christ among neighbors and friends, seeking their acceptance of Jesus Christ as Savior and Lord and their church membership. (Presbyterian)

Outreach means extending an understanding of faith to those who are unchurched or on the margins. (Roman Catholic)

The term is also used to refer to efforts to bring new members into the congregation—not necessarily to bring them into the denomination or faith, or even into worship, but merely, as a first step, to bring them in as identified members of the congregation. "Outreach is any activity designed to communicate to, serve, or attract those in the community not already affiliated with or active in a Christian congregation," wrote one respondent from the Lutheran Church. Several rabbis referred to outreach as "programs for bringing the unaffiliated into congregational affiliation and membership," "formal and informal methods of bringing previously unaffiliated or inactive members to become involved with congregational activities," "a process to tap the environment for new members," "recruitment," and "enlistment."

Jewish outreach, it should be noted, is directed either toward inactive Jews (those who are born of a Jewish mother but are either unaffiliated or nonobservant) or toward interfaith couples (in which one of the partners is born Jewish). This latter form of outreach is a recent invention, most closely associated with the Reform movement (see Chapter 7) but increasingly engaged in by Conservative synagogues as well. In either case, Jewish outreach, with its focus on Jews and interfaith couples, connotes a very different activity from the Christian concept of outreach as missionary activity.

Even within a single church, "outreach" may have multiple referents. A respondent from the Mormon Church, for example, defined outreach as active proselytizing to those outside the faith and ongoing work with those inside the church.

Outreach consists of two distinct activities. The first is outreach to people who are not members of the church. This proselytizing or missionary activity is carried out primarily by 19–20 year old volunteers who spend two years working full-time as missionaries in various areas of the world. The second outreach activity is directed at members of the church. This consists of a monthly visit to all families in a congregation by members assigned to be "home teachers." The purpose of the visit is to teach doctrinal principles, encourage Christian living, and provide support and assistance as needed. (Mormon)

A Mennonite respondent explained that outreach can refer both to individuals and to congregations:

Congregational outreach is defined in two ways: (1) invitation of nonmembers to become members of the congregation; and (2) the establishment of an "outpost," a new congregation sponsored and perhaps initially staffed by persons from the home congregation. (Mennonite)

Social/Community Service. Social/community service efforts are acts of self-giving on behalf of others as a demonstration of faith at work in congregants' lives.

Outreach can be a synonym for Christian service, i.e., meeting human needs in acts of compassion done in Christ's name. (Presbyterian)

Activities of service and ministry to those outside the church. (Episcopalian)

Outreach means a congregation extends its influence into its neighborhood and/or the wider area for which it assumes responsibility. (American Baptist)

Some express their definitions of outreach in the language of social action:

Outreach is pro-active solidarity with the poor and disadvantaged. (Roman Catholic)

Serving *directly* to meet the needs of the suffering and oppressed (feeding the hungry, healing the sick, sheltering the homeless, etc.) and advocating for justice (working for appropriate legislation, etc.). (Lutheran)

Growth

Definitions of congregational growth generally focus on what Mead (Chapter 2) refers to as numerical and maturational growth.

Numerical Growth. Increase in membership numbers is the most common definition offered for congregational growth. Some definitions are concerned primarily with absolute numbers, others with the rate at which individuals are joining. Thus a number of respondents simply defined growth as "net increase in numbers and/or human resources of a congregation" (Episcopalian), "the percentage net gain/loss in members over the preceding year" (Jewish), "growth in the membership list" (Presbyterian), or "the net growth of persons and baptized children who have affiliated with the congregation plus children born within the congregation" (Protestant). Other definitions include, as well, the attendant increase in financial resources for the religious institution and the increase in participation in church or synagogue functions (including worship).

Maturational Growth. Many of the definitions offered combine numerical growth with spiritual growth—the capacity of congregants to deepen their faith and their spiritual roots. As one Presbyterian scholar explained: "We discuss congregational growth along two tracks: numerical growth and spiritual growth. Numerical growth means simply the increase in the total number of persons who participate in the life of a local congregation. Spiritual growth means the faith maturation of individual members of the congregation."

RESOLVING DEFINITIONAL COMPLEXITY

We clearly face substantial complexity in our attempts to define affiliation-related terms. Most researchers and clergy use membership and/or some level of church attendance as their criteria for affiliation. These, however, fail to eliminate confusion since they are variously understood in different congregations and variously defined in different studies. Is someone churched or unchurched if he or she volunteers for church or synagogue outreach efforts but never attends worship services? What if someone attends worship services regularly but never makes a financial contribution to the congregation? What if someone uses a church social service on a regular basis but does not attend worship services? Is a couple churched if they choose to have their wedding in a synagogue or if they hold a funeral service for a relative in a church?

Moreover, the labels "churched," "unchurched," "affiliated," "unaffiliated," "member," and "nonmember" are not based on religiosity or spirituality. We might encounter individuals, officially unchurched but with strong religious sentiments, who are living deeply religious lives (Chapter 6; Taylor, 1988). Disengagement from organized congregational life is hardly tantamount to nonreligiosity. These issues blur distinctions between member and nonmember, churched and unchurched, and leave us with an obvious need to define our terms and clarify the concepts of being within or without the church or synagogue.

Some order comes to the confusion if we consider that definitions are essentially attempts to describe the extensiveness and intensity of three aspects of association with churches and synagogues: ideology, identification, and participation.

Ideology

Ideology signifies adherence to a set of values and beliefs. One may arrive at an ideology through formal or informal learning, personal exploration, or life experiences. Or the ideology may simply be inherited if membership in the group is mandated or conferred upon the individual regardless of his or her personal choice. For example, according to Jewish theology, a child born of a Jewish mother is considered Jewish regardless of place of birth, the father's religion, or other factors. A child is additionally required to undergo rituals such as circumcision in order to enter the Covenant, but these rituals derive from the ideology inherited at birth.

Identification

Identification refers to a psychological association with a group that shares the values and beliefs of the religion. The identification may be personal (the individual chooses to associate) or it may be familial (one's parents or grandparents identified with or belonged to a particular religious community). People may identify at varying levels within the religion. The more specific their identification, the more likely they are to participate at the congregational level. One may identify with a particular religion (e.g., Jewish, Protestant, Catholic), with a denomination, either local or national (e.g., Conservative Jew, Presbyterian, Jesuit), with a specific subgroup of a denomination (e.g., Southern Baptist or Lutheran Church-Missouri Synod), and/or with a given congregation.

Some may label themselves Southern Baptist or Conservative Jew, not because they have an allegiance to or an identification with the national denomination, but merely because they are members of a congregation which is affiliated with the denomination. Conversely, people may have a denominational identification (e.g., call themselves Episcopalians or Catholics) and have no formal congregational affiliation. Such individuals describe themselves as part of a religion because of birth, family factors, or personal beliefs, but they do not actively participate in church or synagogue life. Finally, individuals may have a denominational identity at variance with their congregational membership. A demographic study in San Francisco, for example, found that almost 20% of synagogue members who identify themselves as Conservative Jews in fact belong to Reform temples (Tobin, Milder, Sternberg, & Seltzer, 1989).

Sources of Congregational Identification. Congregations have histories and cultures which form institutional and communal identities. Individuals who identify at the congregational level may root their identification in the reputation of the congregation or in the activities and programs for which it is noted. They may choose to associate with a congregation because its philosophy or way of conducting its business is attractive to them and fits their own personal beliefs and values.

Identification with a particular congregation may stem from family or personal history. Some "grow up" in a congregation; go through life transitions in that setting; and then, as adults, remain in the congregation which has become a place where they feel at home and where they have a strong sense of belonging.

Identification may also develop through association with clergy or laity. Individuals or families may develop loyalty to a congregation because of a connection they feel to a specific minister, priest, or rabbi. For these people, it is only the charisma or leadership of the cleric that brings them into the church or synagogue. Such people may easily switch congregations since their allegiance is to a particular person rather than to the institution as a whole. If the religious leader leaves the congregation, moves or retires, then the individuals whose religious identity comes through this cleric may also sever their ties to the institution.

Religious identity may come through peer groups. Individuals often join a particular congregation when recruited by friends who have already affiliated. Over time, members may develop a support group within the congregation or meaningful ties to other congregants. For such individuals, identity is less with the clergy, the institution, or even the ideology, but with a group of individuals who are associated with that church or synagogue. Indeed, these social ties can be very strong. Church workers often note, for instance, that peer groups which form early in the life of a congregation can feel like "insider" groups, close and tied to the institution. Others may be prohibited from feeling welcome in a congregation in which peer groups already seem to be formed and exclusive.

Some of the social impetus to identify with a particular congregation converges with geographic area. Newcomers to an area may join a church or congregation seeking to find people with whom they can feel compatible. Parish or other boundaries often define the church that residents in a given district ought to join. Ideology or religious practices may also direct individuals to affiliate with a congregation in a particular locale. For example, an Orthodox Jew who will not ride on the Sabbath generally chooses a synagogue within walking distance of his or her home.

Participation

Most often as we examine questions of affiliation, we focus on congregational or denominational participation rather than on ideology or identification. In part we focus here because levels of participation are more easily examined, measured over time, and compared among groups than are ideology and identification, the somewhat more abstract aspects of membership.

As noted above, participation is most commonly defined as financial contribution and attendance at worship services. Financial participation is considered by many to be the *sine qua non* of membership: if a person does not pay, he or she is not a member. Frequency of attendance at services is an indicator of involvement in the spiritual life of the congregation and in its worship and ritual practices. Congregants may also participate through study—learning about the history, teachings, traditions, and practices of the religion. They may participate by volunteering or engaging in outreach in the institution or in the wider community. These various forms of participation correspond with Mead's (Chapter 2) varieties of congregational growth. Congregations can strive for numerical growth (increase in the number of dues-paying members), maturational growth (enhanced faith and spirituality, greater participation in worship services, in ritual practices, and in learning about the religion), organic growth (volunteering within the congregation), and incarnational growth (volunteering for the community, engaging in outreach).

If affiliation is understood as a complex of ideology, identification, and participation, then the diverse definitions used by congregations and researchers can be gauged along these three dimensions. Analyzing affiliation-related terms in this way can reveal the correspondence among definitions and the points where further specification is needed.

CONCLUSION

Religious scholars and clergy offer a multitude of definitions for similar terms. In some instances, there is agreement about general meanings (e.g., an "active member" is one who participates in worship services and other activities of the church or synagogue) although there is little common understanding of the specifics (e.g., whether active members attend services on a weekly basis or simply a few times a year). In other instances, the same term is used to express vastly different meanings across denominations or religions (e.g., outreach often means activities for interfaith families in the Jewish tradition but more often refers to social missionary activities in various Protestant denominations). Finally, there are terms which are ascribed purely idiosyncratic meanings (e.g., a member is whoever the congregation decides is a member; participation is whatever the local culture defines as the norm).

On the one hand, this multitude of definitions demonstrates the rich pluralism of perspectives necessitated by the diversity among individual churches and synagogues. Some definitions emerge from the particular structure of a church (the division of the Catholic Church into parishes, the maintenance of membership records by the Mormon Church of Latter Day Saints, the use of letters of transfer in the Lutheran Church, the reliance of the Jewish synagogue on annual membership dues, and so on). Others emerge from the ideology or religious practices of particular religions (e.g., baptism as a prerequisite for membership, or public affirmation of Christian faith). Still others come from the historical experience of the religious group (e.g., the Jewish concept of outreach is tightly linked to concerns of Jewish identity and absolute survival of the Jewish people).

On the other hand, the multitude of definitions presents a challenge to research and practice. If concepts are defined and measured in different ways in various research efforts, results cannot be compared across studies, and perhaps not even over time. There is, as well, little common language within and among denominations for addressing policy and planning issues related to increasing congregational affiliation.

Exchange among all the actors—clergy, researchers, national organizations, congregations, denominations, and institutions, including seminaries and universities—is essential. Ultimately, there is agreement that increased participation in religious community is beneficial. Research on factors associated with membership, local recruitment efforts and programs to increase involvement, and national efforts to address major contextual influences on religious life all play key roles in our understanding of participation, growth, and decline. The study of affiliation, membership, and participation must be integrated into the everyday lives of denominations and congregations. Otherwise, isolated individuals, institutions, and movements talking only among themselves (and sometimes not even among themselves) limit the ability of religious groups to increase church and synagogue participation. The first step for a full and productive exchange is to develop a glossary of commonly accepted definitions or, at the very least, to clarify the plurality of meanings underlying the terms being used in our dialogues on congregational affiliation.

REFERENCES

Bahr, H. M., & Albrecht, S. (1989). Strangers Once More: Patterns of Disaffiliation from Mormonism. *Journal for the Scientific Study of Religion, 28*(2), 180–200.

Gallup Poll Organization (American Institute of Public Opinion). (1978). *The Unchurched American*. Princeton: Author.

Hadaway, C. K., & Roof, W. C. (1988). Apostasy in American Churches: Evidence from National Survey Data. In D. G. Bromley (Ed.), *Falling from the Faith: Causes and Consequences of Religious Apostasy* (pp. 29–46). Newbury Park, CA: Sage Publications.

Roozen, D. A. (1978). *The Churched and the Unchurched: A Comparative Profile*. Washington, D.C.: Glenmary Research Center.

Roozen, D. A. (1980). Church Dropouts: Changing Patterns of Disengagement and Reentry. *Review of Religious Research, 21*, 427–450.

Taylor, R. J. (1988). Structural Determinants of Religious Participation among Black Americans. *Review of Religious Research, 30*, 114–125.

Tobin, G. A., Milder, L.K.E., Sternberg, L., & Seltzer, S. (1989). *Synagogue Affiliation among Reform Jews*. Brookline, MA: Union of American Hebrew Congregations, Committee on the Jewish Family.

Turner, G. B. (1984). On the Outside Looking In: The Story of the Church Dropout and What the Church Can Do about It. In G. E. Morris (Ed.), *Rethinking Congregational Development* (pp. 65–80). Lake Junaluska, NC: The World Methodist Council.

PART TWO
The Unaffiliated

In-depth understanding of congregational affiliation requires a clear picture of the *unaffiliated*—those who are currently not active members of a congregation. Included among the unaffiliated are people who were once members and subsequently dropped out, and those who retain some formal membership in a congregation but are inactive and rarely if ever attend a worship service. Part Two elucidates the motivations behind the low levels of involvement of these church/synagogue dropouts and marginal members.

In Chapter 4, Dean R. Hoge, Benton Johnson, and Donald A. Luidens discuss the religious involvement of members of the baby boom generation (those born between the mid-1940s and the early 1960s). Their study of a sample of Presbyterian baby boomers provides valuable insights on the dropout phenomenon.

All of the individuals in the Hoge, Johnson, and Luidens sample were confirmed in the Presbyterian Church. As adults, however, only 29% are active members of the church. Others maintain a formal membership in the church but rarely attend; or they participate in services frequently but they have allowed their membership to lapse. Still others have switched religions or denominations and, although religiously active, are no longer considered a part of the Presbyterian Church. Fewer than 10% of the baby boomers studied are true dropouts—individuals who unequivocally left the church, do not belong, do not attend, and have little if any affinity for religious belief systems or organized religion.

Most importantly, the authors show that the unchurched are not nonbelievers. The majority hold respect for Christianity's inspiration, moral teachings, and power to form vital community life. At the same time, the unchurched are characterized by what Hoge, Johnson, and Luidens call "lay liberalism," a relativistic orientation which tolerates doctrinal differences and the right of individuals to choose what religion they will practice and how they will practice it. As a result, most feel little obligation to participate in the church and will undoubtedly return only if they find that the church has something of value to offer them. Given this analysis of the prevalent beliefs and values among baby boomers, Hoge, Johnson, and Luidens conclude that the potential for congregational growth resides in the church's ability to respond to the needs of this new generation.

Penny Long Marler and C. Kirk Hadaway's research, presented in Chapter 5, is concerned with marginal members—those who have a religious identity and may even consider themselves church members but who are inactive and rarely attend church services.

Marginal members are a diverse group. Marler and Hadaway's analysis of survey data from a Protestant sample yields a description of four types of marginal members. The first type are the traditionalists, religious persons who are removed from the congregation by circumstance (illness, work schedules, or other obligations). Liberals, similar to the "lay liberals" described by Hoge, Johnson, and Luidens, are individuals who choose to be inactive because they feel no obligation to participate in regular worship services. Critics, the third type, are marginal to the institution because they are critical of the church, its form of worship, and its actions, and they feel alienated from the religious experience. The last type, lifelong marginals, includes people who grew up on the periphery of the church. This group holds no negative feelings toward the church, but has no sufficiently positive motivation to participate actively.

Marler and Hadaway point out that most marginals are not antagonistic toward the church and, indeed, already have some positive association with the church. Marginals are thus a likely target for cultivating greater involvement. Protestant demography corroborates the potential benefit of reaching out to the marginals. This group now constitutes 17% of the population, and it is likely to grow in numbers. Like other authors in this volume, Marler and Hadaway call for more pro-active steps by the church to reinvolve these individuals in the religious community. They suggest that making the church more accessible—physically, socially, and spiritually—could reconnect marginal members to the congregation.

In Chapter 6, Amy L. Sales presents case studies of four individuals who have formally dropped their congregational membership. Each of these individuals came from different religious background: Jewish, Presbyterian, Methodist, and Catholic. They all dropped out of the church or synagogue at some point in their adult life and subsequently arrived at some kind of *modus vivendi* with their religious institution and with organized religion. Importantly, Sales finds that these disaffiliated individuals all continue to engage in some religious practices and to dwell on theological concerns. She concludes that "although they are not members of congregations, their lives contain far more than mere secularism."

Sales further explores whether these dropouts are likely to raise unaffiliated children or whether they will choose to provide their children with the same religious education and experience that they themselves had in childhood. The profiles show a variety of responses to this question, from a positive motivation toward a specific religion (a desire that one's children carry on the religious identity and tradition) to a negative motivation away from religion (an intention to educate one's children about the "dangers" of organized religion).

Part Two includes analysis of large-scale survey data and descriptions of personal cases. Together these describe the range of motivations, beliefs, and life experiences that define varieties of unaffiliation. The understanding which comes from such analysis is critical to our thinking about how the church or synagogue can reach the disaffiliated and whether or not it will be possible to reconnect them to the religious community.

CHAPTER 4

Congregational Involvement of Young Adults Who Grew Up in Protestant Churches

Dean R. Hoge, Benton Johnson, and Donald A. Luidens

An unprecedented period in the life of American Protestantism began in the mid-1960s. For the first time in their history, many major denominations in the United States stopped growing and began to decline; and all have been in decline since. Those with the most educated and most affluent congregants have experienced the greatest losses. Over the past thirty years, the Episcopal Church has lost 29% of its membership, the Presbyterian Church 26%, and the United Church of Christ 21%. Other denominations have also declined, albeit less steeply. What happened? Why now? What can be done to stop the losses?

In 1987, the Lilly Endowment sponsored a symposium on the mainline Protestant decline. By that time, research had produced an important finding: the decline was mainly attributable to a lack of young adults in the denominations. The children of church members, especially offspring born after World War II, were leading the exodus. The problem was not that the older members were walking away, but that large numbers of the young people were failing to replenish the ranks (see Hoge & Roozen, 1979).

At the 1987 meeting, the three authors of this chapter proposed an in-depth study of young adults who grew up in mainline denominations. Our idea was to search out people who were on the confirmation lists of churches in the 1960s and conduct an "alumni study" to see what their views of the church were today. We wanted to talk freely with them in order to explore attitudes about a variety of questions related to religion. The Lilly Endowment provided funding, and work began in 1989. This article discusses some of the findings of the study.[1]

SAMPLING BABY BOOMERS

To make the project manageable, we worked in only six states in different parts of the nation, and we focused on one representative mainline denomination, the Presbyterian. We limited our attention to one age group, to those born between 1947 and 1956 (who were 33 to 42 years of age at the time of the study). This group was mature enough to have arrived at adult decisions about religion. Studying younger persons seemed less useful since they were generally not sufficiently settled down. Our target group had the additional benefit of representing the first ten years of the post-World War II baby boom, so that our results would also help draw a picture of baby boomers.

Although our research is about baby boomers, we were never certain that an understanding of baby boomers per se would be important for explaining the Protestant decline. The baby boom began in about 1946 or 1947, and it ended gradually in the early 1960s. The mainline Protestant decline began in the early 1960s, so it could by no means be attributed to attitudes of baby boomers, who were at most 18 years old in 1965. As we began this research, we also made no assumptions about the uniqueness of baby boomers, and indeed as the study proceeded, we found that they were not very distinct from earlier cohorts. We came to believe that gradual shifts in Protestant life over a half century were more important than the particular experiences of the baby boom generation in explaining the decline in Protestant affiliation.

We sampled the confirmation lists of twenty-three Presbyterian churches, then hired veteran church members to find the individuals who had been confirmed. Overall 73% of those in the target sample were located. The problem of finding the target persons was worst in big city churches where membership was transient and no one knew how to locate families which had moved out of town years before. In four of these churches, we were able to contact fewer than 50% of the target sample.

Approximately 79% of those located were interviewed. In all, five hundred telephone interviews were conducted, mostly in 1990. After completing the telephone survey, we also interviewed forty of the respondents at length in person.

To compare the views of baby boomers with those born before 1947, we interviewed a second sample comprised of 125 persons 43 to 52 years old (born between 1937 and 1946) from the same churches.

WHO ARE THESE YOUNG ADULTS?

Most of these baby boomers are well-educated, vigorous persons. Some 90% have attended college or trade school, and 63% have earned college degrees. These figures are more than double the national averages. Over half are in professional, managerial, or technical occupations. About 79% are currently married, and 76% have children living with them. Of those married, 19% have Presbyterian spouses. Ten percent were never married; about 24% have been divorced; and 14% are in second or third marriages.

Today 62% of our baby boomer sample are members of churches, but only 47% attend worship services as often as twice a month. A fifth never attend church.

It is common knowledge that Protestant young people often drop out of church after leaving home. We found this to be true. In our sample, 75% had dropped out at some time. Of those who had dropped out, 49% have returned. They usually were between the ages of 18 and 22 when they dropped out, and were, on average, 29 years old when they returned. Some 33% have switched denominations at one time or another, and 9% have switched twice. The main reason for switching was the influence of a spouse or relative. The persons who switched are now mostly members of other mainline Protestant denominations.

Comparison of Baby Boomers with Earlier Generations

On the one hand, the baby boomer sample and the pre-baby boomer sample were not as different as we had expected. They were similar in church attendance and youth group participation during their high school years, and later were equally likely to marry a Presbyterian spouse (18% of the pre-baby boomers and 19% of the baby boomers married within the denomination). On the other hand, the baby boomers reported more rebellion against their religious training, more doubt, and more dropping out of church life (75% of baby boomers versus 63% of pre-baby boomers dropped out by age 33). They also told of more counterculture experiences such as attending rock concerts, smoking marijuana, and taking part in demonstrations. Probably the main difference between the baby boomers and pre-baby boomers is seen in the gradually loosening ties to the Presbyterian community. Baby boomers were never as strongly involved in the church as their pre-baby boomer counterparts.

EIGHT RELIGIOUS TYPES

Baby boomers vary in their religious behavior. Based on this behavior, we were able to divide the population into eight distinct religious types. We first sorted the sample into churched and unchurched. We defined a person as churched if he or she was a church member today and also had attended religious services at least six times in the last year. All others were considered unchurched. By these criteria, we found 52% of the baby boomer sample churched, and 48% unchurched.

Figure 4.1
Baby Boomer Sample by Religious Type

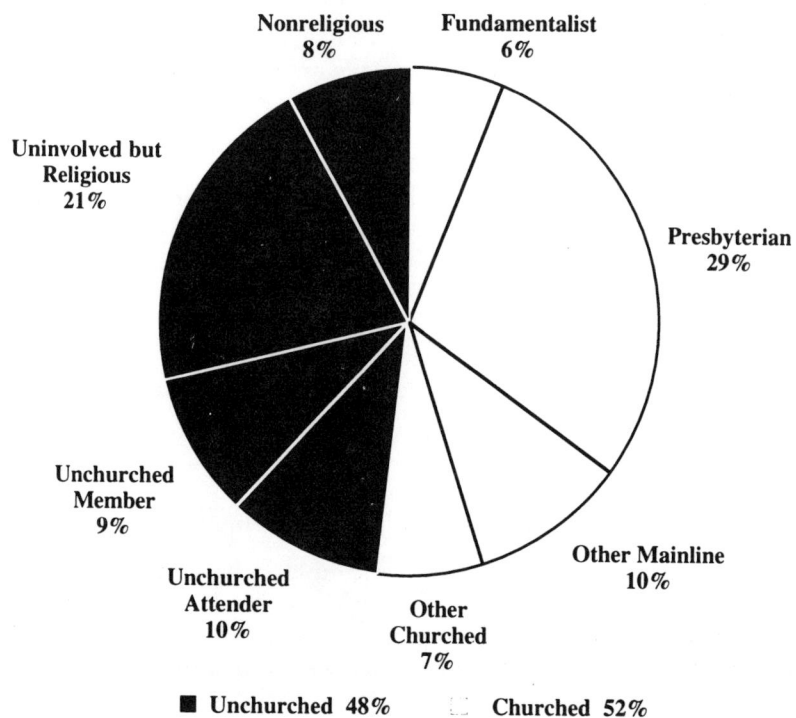

We divided the churched into four types: (1) fundamentalists (including evangelicals); (2) active Presbyterians; (3) active other mainline Protestants; and (4) other churched. The unchurched we also divided into four types: (5) people who are attenders but not members; (6) people who are members but not attenders; (7) people who are neither but see themselves as religious; and (8) people who are inactive and also see themselves as nonreligious.

Let us be clear about the definitions we used. "Church member" means that the person has self-consciously joined a local congregation and now has his or her name on the rolls. If a person stops attending, membership typically lapses only gradually. Protestant churches are tolerant about keeping young adults on membership rolls even if they never come. The term "dropouts" indicates people who have stopped attending entirely, whether or not they have terminated their membership. In most instances, the dropouts did nothing about membership when they stopped going, but gradually the churches removed their names from the rolls.

The percent of our sample in each of the eight types is shown in Figure 4.1.

The Churched

Type 1 (6% of the sample) is composed of persons who left Presbyterianism for a fundamentalist church. Since the imprecise definition of fundamentalist presents a difficult measurement problem, our categorization, which is based on a broad sense of the term, is only approximate. Nonetheless, individuals in this category are active in various denominations, mainly Baptist, Assembly of God, Church of God, and conservative Presbyterian splinter groups; over one-third are members of nondenominational churches. The size of the group (6% of the total sample) is lower than we had expected. Our findings did not bear out the contention of some observers that young adults are deserting the mainline for more conservative churches. On the contrary, the majority in our study who left the Presbyterian Church have stopped church involvement altogether.

Type 1 persons are the most committed of any type to their churches: 97% attend church two to three times a month or more, and 91% are active in a group or committee in their church. At the same time, they are the least involved in secular organizations in their communities. When we asked them about their switch to a fundamentalist church, about two-thirds told of profound religious experiences through which they were saved. The others followed spouses or friends, or simply found the conservative churches more congenial.

Type 2 includes those now active in Presbyterian churches (29% of the sample), and Type 3 includes those active in other mainline churches (10%). Of those now active in other churches, four out of ten are Methodists, two in ten are members of the United Church of Christ, one in ten is Episcopalian, one in ten Lutheran, and one in ten Reformed. At least half of the switches in denomination were a result of interfaith marriage. One-fourth switched after moving from one town to another and shopping around for a church. The other fourth switched for miscellaneous reasons. As individuals involved in mainline churches, people characterized as Types 2 and 3 are similar in beliefs and church involvement, although, as discussed below, some of the Type 3 persons are slightly more orthodox.

Type 4, other churched (7% of the sample), is a residual collection of all the persons active in other churches: Catholics (3% of the total sample); Baptists (1%); members of nonfundamentalist, independent churches (1%); and so on. Only two persons were Jehovah's Witnesses, one was a Mormon, and one a Unitarian. None had become Jewish. None had joined Asian religious movements, the Unification Church, or New Age groups. For these groups, the main reasons for switching had to do with marriage, friendships, effectiveness of ministers, and positive or negative experiences in various churches. But in general the participants in our study did not join groups very different from the Presbyterian churches of their youth; if they departed from the mainline denominations, most dropped out of church life entirely.

The Unchurched

The other four types in Figure 4.1 are unchurched. Type 5 (10% of the sample) is comprised of people who attend church more than six times a year, but are not members. These people tend to be loosely involved in church life. Only 27% attended as often as two or three times a month during the past year (compared with 44% for the Presbyterians in Type 2). They are less likely than churched respondents to be involved in stable marriages and have children. Indeed, 52% have been divorced. From the interviews, we estimate that about one-third of these unchurched attenders go to church only for the sake of their families. Another third attend a church regularly but have misgivings or reservations that prevent them from becoming members.

Type 6, the unchurched members, is composed of people who are members but seldom attend worship services (9% of the sample). About half dropped out years ago, but still keep their names on the rolls for family or social reasons; some of them now have children attending Sunday schools. Others stopped attending more recently for specific reasons, often because they were hurt by or dissatisfied with something related to their church. We suspect that many are candidates for reinvolvement in the future (see Chapter 5).

Type 7, the uninvolved but religious, is important because of its size—21% of the sample. It represents the single largest group of young adults lost to Protestant churches. Most of these people have simply dropped out of churchgoing although they still consider themselves to be religious. They tend to be more universalistic and individualistic than average, and their political and social views are quite liberal. Some told us stories of unhappy experiences in former churches, instances in which they felt unappreciated or snubbed, or in which conflict erupted and was never healed. Many of the Type 7 people are now unmarried or without children; 19% were never married, and 31% have been divorced. As a result they are, on average, less involved in child rearing than are churched people.

Type 8, the non-religious (8% of the sample), is composed of self-described secularists who have essentially given up on religion. The nonreligious report quite frequent early religious rebellion during their upbringing, and most dropped out of church between 15 and 20 years of age. A good many told of long-term religious doubt, although some went through with confirmation for the sake of their parents. Type 8 people describe themselves as liberals who think for themselves. We doubt if any of them will become active in churches in the future.

MOTIVATIONS FOR BECOMING ACTIVE OR INACTIVE

This research provided us a good opportunity to discuss with respondents why they chose to be active or inactive in a church. Remember that everyone in the sample was sufficiently active at age 13 or 14 to be confirmed. And the vast majority were church-involved during high school: 88% reported going to Sunday school or church twice a month or more; and 54% said they were often involved in church youth programs. Yet three-fourths left the church in the following years, generally when they were 18 to 22 years old.

Reasons for Dropping Out

When we asked the dropouts why they had disaffiliated, many of their responses were vague: "left home," "had better things to do," or "I was at college, and no one went." In the interviews, we discerned two main reasons why most people left the church: some lost their faith, and others lost their ties to people in the church. The latter group is the larger. Respondents told us they dropped out when they moved to a new community where they did not know anybody in the church. Or they dropped out when some episode made them feel unwelcome at their church or out of touch with other members. We were reminded by these interviewees many times that "you don't have to go to church to be a good Christian." Respondents in the latter group (who lost personal ties) seem closer to the church than respondents in the former group (who lost faith) and seem more likely to return under proper circumstances in the future.

As already noted, 49% of those who dropped out later returned. When asked why they returned, the main reasons they offered were the presence of children, a feeling of spiritual need or emptiness, a specific crisis or conversion, and the process of settling down geographically or psychologically.

The best way to understand the dynamics of becoming involved or dropping out is to begin with a conception of a network of believers in a church who communicate with each other, affirm each other, and maintain their faith and commitment. This is what Peter Berger calls a "plausibility structure" (Berger, 1979), and it is necessary for the maintenance of any religious community. A plausibility structure must be composed of people in everyday relationships. In Berger's words:

Each conception of the world of whatever character or content can be analyzed in terms of its plausibility structure, because it is only as the individual remains within this structure that the conception of the world in question will remain plausible to him. The strength of this plausibility, ranging from unquestioned certitude through firm probability to mere opinion, will be directly dependent upon the strength of the supporting structure (Berger, 1967, p. 36).

Religious commitment depends on ongoing personal relationships which affirm and support the individual, more than on philosophic demonstration. The interpersonal situation of the individual person is crucial. Strong commitment depends on continual contact with other faithful members, and any experience which damages these relationships will weaken the commitment. The reason a person drops out of church-going for a long period of time more likely concerns interpersonal relationships rather than that person's faith. In our interviews, dropouts told of loss of faith in some cases and loss of personal bonds in others. Although both were probably influential, the problems of personal relationships were emphasized more often by the interviewees.

Why Be Active

The obverse question is why people become, or remain, active in churches. Again we should look at both the personal and social needs of the individual. For a person to be active over a period of time, definite needs must be satisfied. We discerned four needs which church involvement commonly serves. Most prevalent is the need for religious education of children and related support for family life. When we asked everyone in the sample (even those without children) if they would like religious education for their children, 96% said yes—a virtually unanimous response. People want Sunday school or something similar. When we probed for more clarity about what they wanted the Sunday school to do, they talked about moral education, development of character, familiarity with the Bible and Christian tradition, exposure to other churches, and, they hoped, good relationships with exemplary Christian adult teachers. A portion stressed development of faith and piety, but others were cautious, loath to put any pressure on their children.

A second need is for personal support, reassurance, and help in times of difficulties. Respondents told about the need to be certain they are living good lives, the need to reevaluate day-to-day existence, and the need for help getting through the week. The need for support seemed to be stronger when respondents were in troubling situations or felt a need to make changes in their lives. This need was often served by fellowship with other parishioners in situations in which all could talk honestly without fear of rejection.

A third need we heard expressed is for social contacts and a supportive community. Churches provide friendships, social outlets, and chances to work together with good people on worthwhile projects. Everyone seemed to agree that church members tend to be good people—responsible, generous, and charitable.

A fourth need is for inspiration, which respondents often found in worship. Bible readings, sermons, and music all provide refreshment and uplift. Sunday worship can draw a person out of self-absorption or pettiness to remember the greater responsibilities in life. As one woman told us:

I find that when I do go to church—which I am still doing occasionally—it reminds me of things that I need being reminded of, that sometimes I don't think of. You know, sometimes I start feeling sorry for myself for some reason, and I go to church, and say, hey, I don't have any reason to feel sorry. . . . Or maybe reminding me of the larger picture, that there's a lot more out there besides just me that I should be concerned with. It's psychological maybe. Maybe instead of a psychologist sometimes it's good to go to church.

Another woman summed up several of the needs churches serve:

To me, religion could mean a lot in its support. . . . Church is more than just being social. There's a spiritual element that you don't find in a lot of institutions. You can go and play bridge and have a great "in" with a bridge club and have a great time doing it, but you don't have anything spiritual. And you don't have the moral and the ethical underpinnings that create real fellowship.

BELIEFS OF THE UNCHURCHED

The study examined, as well, the extent to which the churched and unchurched believe in Church doctrines, the position they hold on questions of morality, and their criticism of the church.

Doctrinal Beliefs

We asked those who had been confirmed a series of questions about central Christian teachings and from these we devised a summary measure called the Core Belief Index. To score high on this index, a person had to believe in divine inspiration of the Bible, the divinity of Jesus Christ, and life after death. About 80% to 90% of the churched groups (Types 1 through 4) scored high. Among fundamentalists, the score was 100%. Some 51% of the uninvolved but religious (Type 7) scored high on the Core Belief Index, but only 6% of the nonreligious (Type 8) did. Figure 4.2 shows the pattern of belief in Christian doctrine. The length of the bars shows the percentage of each type scoring high on the Core Belief Index.

Another important measure, the Christ Only Index, is the obverse of a measure of religious relativism. To score high on this index, a person has to believe that the only absolute truth for humankind is Jesus Christ and that only followers of Jesus Christ and members of His church can be saved. Presbyterians (Type 2), other mainline church members (Type 3), and other churched (Type 4) averaged about 35% to 45% on the Christ Only Index. The fundamentalists (Type 1) scored 88%. Five percent of the uninvolved but religious (Type 7) and none of the nonreligious (Type 8) scored high on the Christ Only Index (see Figure 4.3). This index highlights the problem of religious relativism that is felt by many of these young adults and is, we believe, a clue to understanding their lukewarm church involvement.

Figure 4.2
Core Belief Index—% Believing in Central Christian Teachings

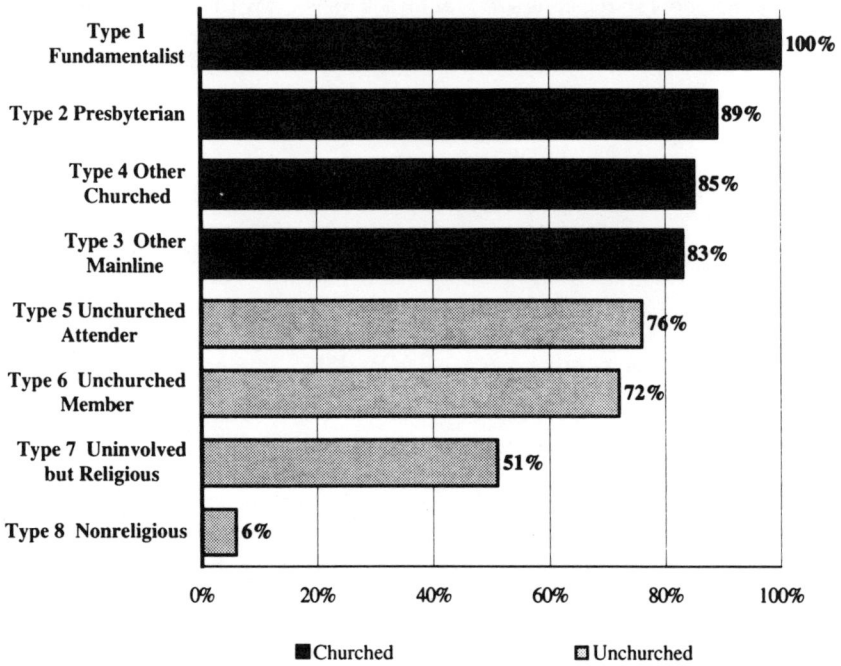

We tried to make some assessment of the depth of religious *relativism* in the sample, as distinguished from religious *universalism*. Relativism maintains that all cultures teach different truths and that nothing is common to all or is the basis for their beliefs. Universalism, in contrast, holds that all religions are expressions of a basic underlying truth. We asked everyone a question which distinguished these two viewpoints and found that 91% believe that "an underlying basic moral and spiritual truth exists for all humanity." To be precise, the common position is religious universalism, not relativism.

In sum, the unchurched are not unbelievers. The majority take Christian teachings seriously although they are also universalistic in outlook. Even though over half do not think Christianity is more true than other religions, its inspiration, moral teachings, and power to form vital community life command their respect.

Views on Morality

The interviews included some questions about the most contentious debates in mainline Protestantism today, those relating to sexuality and gender. From attitudes on three topics we created a Morality Index—attitudes on whether premarital sex between persons committed to each other

Figure 4.3
Christ Only Index—% Believing in Central Christian Teachings

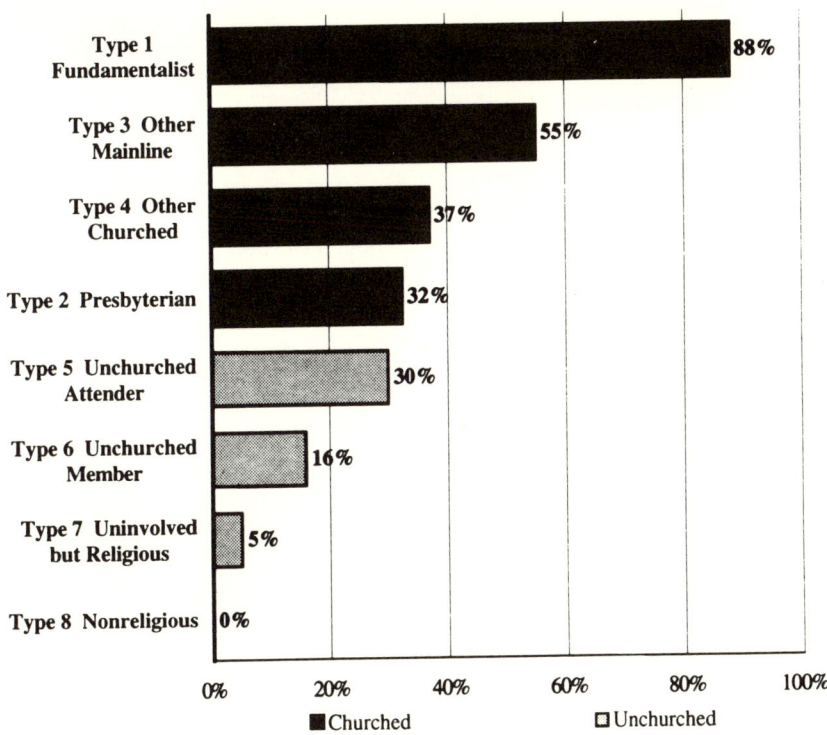

is morally appropriate, on whether abortion should be legal, and on whether an avowed homosexual man should be allowed to be ordained as a Protestant minister. Anyone with consistently conservative views on these topics we labelled a moral conservative; anyone with consistently liberal views we labelled a moral liberal; and anyone with mixed views or uncertainty on one or more of the topics we considered in between these two positions. In all, 14% of our sample were moral conservatives, 35% moral liberals, and 51% in-between. The large number of persons with mixed or uncertain views indicate that, contrary to suggestions by other researchers (Roof & McKinney, 1987; Wuthnow, 1988), the baby boomers are not clearly polarized in these attitudes. The majority are somewhere in the middle.

Moral attitudes are highly correlated with religious beliefs: theological conservatives are usually moral conservatives, and theological liberals are usually moral liberals. The strong correlations tell us that a single polarity underlies beliefs on a number of theological and moral topics. Put simply, the single most telling question for depicting the attitudes of people in our sample would go something like this: "Which of the following statements about religion do you believe? (a) Christ's teachings about God, about heaven, and about how to live are true, and they demand obedience by all humanity; or (b) ultimate religious truth can be found in approximate form in many places, not just the Bible, and since the teachings of different religions are not all the same, we are called upon to be respectful of others." These choices represent the elemental dimension underlying all else.

Criticism of the Church

We asked several questions designed to probe for criticism of churches today, for example that the churches are not concerned enough about social justice or that they have a view of God that is too masculine. In general we did not find widespread criticism. But we did find strong evidence of individualism. Indeed 63% agreed with the statement "An individual should arrive at his or her own religious beliefs independent of any churches or synagogues." To the question "Do you think a person can be a good Christian or Jew if he or she doesn't attend church or synagogue?" 82% said yes. Lack of criticism coupled with high levels of individualism leads us to conclude that when baby boomers leave the church it is due more to indifference than to dissatisfaction.

LIFE EXPERIENCES AND CHURCH INVOLVEMENT

We also asked participants in our study about their life histories and were thus able to calculate statistical correlations between specific life experiences and present-day church involvement. Did any life experience cause them to be active or inactive, to remain in the church or withdraw? Two kinds of influences on the baby boomer population have been widely discussed as possible causes of withdrawal—the counterculture and the greater attainment of higher education. We correlated the extent of each person's involvement with the sixties' counterculture with his or her church involvement today, and we found no significant associations: counterculture participants are not less involved in the church today than others. We also correlated the respondents' type and amount of college education (including no college at all) with church involvement today and found no associations. College may challenge religious faith for some youth, but for the baby boomers in our sample it was not a decisive experience. If education had an impact, it probably happened *before* these people reached college, because they encountered the ideas of relativism and cultural analysis during high school. We have no doubt about the effect of broad education on religious commitment, but we doubt if college education by itself influences people one way or the other.

The most important predictors of church involvement were the person's *religious beliefs* (see Hoge, Johnson & Luidens, 1993, for statistical details). Those who held the most conventional beliefs were the most involved in churches. Beliefs are crucial, and the other motivations for church involvement are far less powerful. As far as we could determine, respondents' beliefs developed gradually throughout life. The second strongest predictor was a series of post-college-age experiences, especially marriage and parenthood. People with children are more church-involved, even apart from their beliefs. Also, several experiences which cause a person to be more, or less embedded in a religious plausibility structure are influential. Divorcing, moving a long distance away from one's hometown, and marrying a person from outside of mainline Protestantism are all predictors of less church involvement. These kinds of experiences pull a person away from the influence of his or her community. A stable marriage with a spouse from inside of mainline Protestantism is a predictor of greater church involvement as it pulls a person closer to the influence of his or her community.

TWO RELIGIOUS ORIENTATIONS: TRADITIONAL FAITH AND LAY LIBERALISM

Overall interview data indicated two main religious orientations in our sample (apart from the roughly 8% who told us they are not religious at all). The first orientation is traditional faith. People in this category believe that the Bible is revealed truth; whether Biblical literalists or not, they are confident that the Bible is authoritative. They have faith in God, and they are strongly committed to church life and to doing God's will. Most of them are loyal and active members of churches. A proportion of these persons are charismatics who believe in speaking in tongues, prophesying, and healing. They often take the religious education of their children into their own hands through home Bible study and family devotions. Almost all of Type 1 persons (fundamentalists) were in this category, as were some respondents from the other churched types (Types 2, 3, and 4) and some from the category of unchurched attenders and unchurched members (Types 5 and 6).

The second, more numerous orientation we call lay liberalism. We refer to people in this category as "lay" because their theological views do not reflect any of the systematic theologies in the writings of today's post-Orthodox Christian intellectuals. The baby boomers do not speak the language of liberation theology, feminist theology, or process theology. Rather, lay liberalism is largely a home-made product, a kind of modern-age folk religion.

Lay liberals comprise about half of our sample, and they deserve further study if only because of their numerical significance. These individuals take a more critical view of the scriptures than do the traditional believers mentioned above, and they are acutely aware of problems of historical and cultural relativity. For this reason, they doubt if Christianity is demonstrably truer than other great world religions. In defending Christianity, they depend on highly personalized reasons to explain why it is true, or better, for them. For example, a 37–year-old man answered our question about whether Christianity is truer than other religions in this way:

For *me* it is. That's just the way I feel. I know I could have a Buddhist sitting here and he would feel that *his* religion is more true. But I feel that's not for me—what I know of it. What I have is what I like.

This problem leaves people in a confusing situation: they feel spiritual needs and aspire to religious certainty, yet they cannot find any religious authority that commands their assent. One 40–year-old woman gave this answer to our question about whether Christianity is preferable to other religions:

No. It doesn't matter. I don't think God is going to punish anyone because they choose the wrong religion, as long as they live a good moral life with good values.

Lay liberals differ in their views of what religious truth might be, but they agree that morality is an essential part. Most lay liberals would probably agree with a 40–year-old active Presbyterian:

I don't think it matters what religion you are in as long as you are comfortable with it and following sound principles, you are raising your kids and spending time with your family, and you are moral. Then it doesn't matter.

Lay liberals are tolerant of doctrinal differences and, with limitations, of differences in moral teachings. They stress personal autonomy and therefore oppose any form of religious coercion or attempts at religious indoctrination. When asked about supporting Christian missions, these people typically say they support humanitarian service and education but not efforts to pull people in other lands away from their native religions. After all, those people have their own religion. The most we should do is tell them about Christianity insofar as they are interested.

Despite their doubts about doctrinal and moral absolutes, lay liberals think religion is a good thing and want it to thrive in its various forms. They have no doubt that religion is beneficial for society and that church people are solid role models for their children. They believe in the life of faith for people who can and wish to have it. For themselves, however, faith comes slowly, and they are determined not to have *blind* faith in anything or anyone. Blind faith is too dangerous. Denominational differences are considered unimportant, as are even differences between Christianity and other ethical non-Christian religions. Such differences are considered merely the products of history and culture.

It has probably struck the reader that lay liberalism is not robust enough to create a vibrant church and community life. We agree. Lay liberals are reluctant to share their faith with others because they cannot assert its truth in relationship to other forms of religion. Some even hesitate to defend their religious views to their children. Their religion has a tentative, unfinished quality, and in general it cannot be expected to produce strong church commitment.

In addition to secularism, traditional faith and lay liberalism describe broad religious orientations seen in our sample. We are not claiming that everyone clearly fits into one of these three categories. Individuals vary too much for such a neat typology. But the two religious orientations are visible, and they are clearly the main ones among the baby boomers we studied. Lay liberals comprise at least half of the sample; traditionalists and secularists are much smaller groups.

RELIGIOUS BOUNDARIES

Above we quoted Peter Berger, who argued that religious faith depends for its maintenance on networks of committed people in constant communication with each other. All religions must nurture their plausibility structures if they are to remain vital. But it seems that mainline Protestantism has not maintained its historic plausibility structure. We say this because the baby boomers we talked with were often outside of the traditional Protestant world view. They were often critical of Biblical authority, sensitive to cultural and historical relativity, and self-consciously independent in the judgments they made about truth and goodness. The Protestant plausibility structure has broken down for them. At least half of the baby boomers we interviewed inhabit a different plausibility structure, one which is much more universalistic and more influenced by twentieth century thought. Put simply, they are lay liberals. We believe that the transformation from historical Protestantism to the more universal plausibility structure has taken place gradually throughout this century. No specific event or historical experience was the cause. Rather, the value commitments central to the faith itself encouraged a loosening of the boundaries and eventually a transformation of the entire structure.

In our interviews, we probed for the kinds of boundaries our respondents were conscious of. Our findings reveal two kinds of boundaries which serve to demarcate what we call the "comfort zone" and the "tolerance zone." The comfort zone includes the religious bodies which the respondents might consider choosing for themselves—in which, to employ their often-used term, they would feel "comfortable." The comfort zone of the sample persons is quite narrow and traditional. For the great majority, it includes all the mainline denominations such as Methodist, Lutheran, and it the United Church of Christ. Some would include Episcopalian, others would not. Catholicism was seldom included, nor was strict fundamentalism or any of the new sectarian movements. This boundary is consciously recognized by most of the people in our sample.

The tolerance zone includes all the religions that merit tolerance and respect. It is much larger and less distinct than the comfort zone. It includes all major Christian denominations, Judaism, and all universalistic ethical world religions. Islam was criticized by some interviewees for its alleged fanaticism and hatred of outsiders. New cults which emerged during the 1960s and 1970s were excluded due to practices that seemed contrary to human rights. In general, religions that teach goodwill, internationalism, integrity, and freedom are considered worthy of tolerance and thus are in the tolerance zone. This zone has expanded vastly among most Protestants in the past half century, at the same time that sources of religious authority have become problematic. The lay liberals tend to say that religious truth is elusive or maybe nonexistent, so we need to respect many kinds of religion—as long as they have a sound moral code.

Why did the respect for many world religions expand in recent decades? It was not because of conquest from outside or weakness of Protestant resolve. Rather, this expansion is a product of the faith itself. American Protestantism as it developed in the twentieth century drove itself beyond its own former boundaries. It has supported scientific work, critical scholarship, and explorations of all kinds and—most important—critical examination of the Bible itself. Protestants have led the world in no-holds-barred Biblical criticism (Berger, 1979). It has stressed communication with outside groups, including cross-cultural experiences, dialogue, goodwill, cooperation, and ecumenism. The dynamic remains in place today, with Protestant families going to great expense to give their children the best liberal education, cross-cultural experiences, openness of mind, and independent personal judgment. Nothing is deemed to be beyond criticism. The faith itself brought about its transformation into something new.

Not many Protestants seem to regret this. Few would like to turn back the clock in an attempt to regain the faith and church life of the last century. On the contrary, they are proud of their heritage of education, cosmopolitan values, individualism, and world-consciousness. Church commitment has weakened in the process, it is true, and the children do not want to go to church. But worse things could happen. This in itself is not a compelling reason to turn back.

The future is destined to be different from the past. The cumulative experiences of this century have had a lasting impact on Protestant churches. Trends now underway are likely to continue, and the old boundaries will disappear.

IMPLICATIONS FOR CHURCHES

The findings of this study provide some clues about the religious life of baby boomers. The baby boomers are different from their elders in one important respect: most feel little obligation to participate in churches. They feel participation is not necessary, either because they are skeptical about church teachings regarding the need to be church-involved, or because they are convinced that "you don't have to go to church to be a good Christian." Therefore, if they participate at all, it will be because they find it worthwhile for themselves. We call theirs a "market" attitude. If the church offers something, a person is free to buy it or not to buy it, as he or she wishes. There is no obligation.

The challenge to churches in this new situation is to minister to baby boomers authentically and successfully. The church involvement of young adults will, for the most part, not be out of family loyalty, obligation, or heritage. Rather, involvement will come through having definite needs genuinely served. In market terms, we can ask what the churches might offer that the baby boomers will want to buy. Earlier we outlined four kinds of needs which motivate this group to become active in a church—religious education for children, personal support and reassurance, a community, and inspiration. These findings imply that to reach the baby boom population, churches will need to pay attention to programs for children and youth, to community-building programs, and to inspiring worship, music, and spiritual life.

One expert on young adults, theologian Tex Sample (1990), has suggested an emphasis on what he calls "journey theology." Such a theology sees life as a spiritual journey, open to new experiences and surprises. The notion of journey is a metaphor for growth and movement. It stresses exploration more than creeds and fixed doctrines, and it assumes that there is no single religious authority and no clear boundary to spiritual life. This metaphor appeals to us as befitting the mentality of the lay liberals we encountered.

Our study provides new information on issues of contention among mainline church leaders. We found that not many mainline young adults have moved from mainline to conservative churches. Also, virtually none have joined Eastern religious groups, cults, or New Age groups. Of those who left, most did not become active in other religious groups. We found that young adults did not leave mainline churches because they were sore at denominational leaders or policies. In reality, few knew about these matters and few cared. The problems lie deeper, at the level of beliefs and questions of religious authority. The majority were confused about where to find religious truth.

The people in our sample were not much interested in denominations. They felt that denominational identity within Protestantism was based on out-of-date struggles, with little meaning for their lives today. This tendency to keep a distance from national denominations is partly a reflection of a broader skepticism about large institutions which is found among young adults today, and partly an acknowledgment that boundaries between mainline denominations have faded and possibly vanished.

Our interviewees stressed the *local church* and how it relates, if at all, to them as individuals. We conclude that local ministries and local experiments hold the most promise for future vitality in mainline denominations; larger structures and institutional authority will be difficult to maintain in their present form. Local experiments in ministry, sensitive to the felt needs of this new generation, are the most promising avenue to the future involvement of young adults in the church.

NOTE

1. See Dean R. Hoge, Benton Johnson, and Donald A. Luidens (1994), *Vanishing Boundaries: The Religion of Mainline Protestant Baby Boomers*, which presents the study's findings in detail.

REFERENCES

Berger, P. L. (1967). *A Rumor of Angels*. Garden City, NY: Doubleday.

Berger, P. L. (1979). *The Heretical Imperative: Contemporary Possibilities of Religious Affirmation*. Garden City, NY: Doubleday.

Hoge, D. R., Johnson, B., & Luidens, D. A. (1994) *Vanishing Boundaries: The Religion of Mainline Protestant Baby Boomers*. Louisville Westminster/John Knox.

Hoge, D. R., Johnson, B., & Luidens, D. A. (1993). Determinants of Church Involvement of Young Adults Who Grew Up in Presbyterian Churches. *Journal for the Scientific Study of Religion. 32*:3 (September) pp.242–255.

Hoge, D. R., & Roozen, D. A. (Eds.). (1979). *Understanding Church Growth and Decline: 1950–1978*. New York: Pilgrim Press.

Roof, W. C., & McKinney, W. (1987). *American Mainline Religion*. New Brunswick, NJ: Rutgers University Press.

Sample, T. (1990). *U.S. Lifestyles and Mainline Churches*. Louisville: Westminster/John Knox.

Wuthnow, R. (1988). *The Restructuring of American Religion*. Princeton: Princeton University Press.

CHAPTER 5

Four Styles of Religious Marginality

Penny Long Marler and C. Kirk Hadaway

About fifteen years ago, the terms churched and unchurched began to be used to distinguish persons who were regular worship attenders from persons who rarely participated (Hale, 1977; Perry, Davis, Doyle, & Dyble, 1980; Princeton Religion Research Center, 1978 and 1988; Roozen 1978). From a church/synagogue perspective, the churched were "in the tent," so to speak, and the unchurched were "outside the tent."

This division between the churched and unchurched may seem like an oversimplification, yet there are some very real reasons for making it. First, frequency of worship attendance is not normally distributed among the American population (Davis & Smith, 1990). That is to say, the largest proportion of Americans do not fall in the middle of the church attendance distribution. People tend to be very active, attending every week or nearly every week, or they tend to be much more sporadic, attending several times a year or even less.[1] Attendance patterns, then, suggest a rough dichotomy between the active and the inactive, or the churched and unchurched.

Another reason for making the division is that persons who are active in churches frequently share similar social characteristics—particularly with regard to religious beliefs and behavior. Active people tend to be religious in every way. They see themselves as religious persons and as spiritual persons. They pray more and typically hold orthodox religious beliefs. They also tend to be socially conservative, particularly in the area of personal morality.

For clear empirical reasons, then, it seems *appropriate* to use terms like churched and unchurched, or as we prefer, active and inactive. Even though some overlap exists (e.g., there are religiously active persons who are socially liberal), the two populations seem quite distinct.

Despite a lot of talk about evangelism and outreach to the inactive or unchurched population, religious professionals spend much of their time and energy making certain that active people remain active. The *inactive* remain mysterious—they are people we *hope* will come back, although we are not sure if they were ever really with us in the first place. As far as we can tell, the only large denominations doing aggressive evangelism are Jehovah's Witnesses and Mormons, and the numbers they attract are not large enough to make much of a dent in the unchurched population.

How many inactive persons are there in the United States? Among adults, about 49% attend religious services several times a year or less (Davis & Smith, 1990). Even though many Americans rarely attend church, the vast majority still claim to be Protestant, Catholic, or Jewish, or affiliated with a specific religious denomination.

WHO ARE THE INACTIVES?

There are *many* types of inactive persons. Actives tend to be religious in most respects, but inactives are not uniformly irreligious and their reasons for inactivity are quite varied. A starting point for dividing the inactive population is to use *religious identity* in addition to frequency of religious participation. We use a three-way division.

(1) *Nones*, persons with no religious preference or identity. Recent survey data indicate that about 8% of the adult population of the United States say they have no religious preference. Not surprisingly, nones do not attend religious services with any regularity (Davis & Smith, 1990).
(2) *Mental affiliates*, persons who claim a religious preference, say they attend religious services several times a year or less, and do not claim to be members of a church or synagogue. Around 24% of the population fit these criteria.
(3) *Marginal members*, persons who claim a religious preference, say they attend religious services several times a year or less, and claim to be church or synagogue members. Using this definition, about 17% of Americans are marginal members.

For the past three years, we have been conducting a major study of the marginal member and mental affiliate populations, a project funded by a grant from the Lilly Endowment, Inc. Our research shows that identification or lack of identification with a religious group and a congregation has very important ramifications for inactive persons (Marler & Hadaway, 1993). Nones, mental affiliates, and marginal members are extremely different in their responses to a wide variety of specific survey questions (Davis & Smith, 1990; Hadaway, 1990). Further, subjective impressions of marginal members and mental affiliates from personal interviewers suggest additional distinctions.

The focus of this report is *marginal members*. This group of inactive Protestant Americans is closest to the church in terms of identification: they continue to claim church membership despite infrequent attendance. If churches and synagogues hope to activate anyone in the broader inactive population, the logical target is persons who still see themselves as connected to *both* a religious denomination and a local congregation.

Our study of marginal members began with two questions: (1) why do marginal members attend so infrequently when they maintain a strong religious identity?; and (2) since they attend so infrequently, why do they maintain a church identity? To help answer these questions and to see if there were certain styles or modes of religious inactivity, a cluster analysis was performed on a sample of 207 Protestants from four states. We identified four groups of marginal members: *traditionalists, critics, liberals*, and *lifelong marginals*. We will introduce them through their individual stories.

DATA AND METHODS

Marginal members were identified through a survey of 2,012 Protestants, age 21 and older, conducted by Southeastern Research Institute in 1991. Respondents were interviewed by phone in four states: Arizona, Connecticut, Georgia, and Ohio. These four states were used as the sampling frame, rather than the entire United States, in order to facilitate face-to-face interviews with selected respondents at a later date. The states represented the four regions of the United States, as defined by the Bureau of the Census (U.S. Bureau of the Census, 1983, p. xvi). The number of interviews conducted in each state varied according to the estimated number of adult Protestants in the corresponding census region. This allowed our sample to approximate a national sample of adult Protestants (see Marler & Hadaway, 1993).

Marginal members are defined as Protestants who attend church several times a year, once or twice a year, or never and who say they are members of a church. A total of 207 respondents, or 10.3% of our sample, fit this definition. This percentage was about 8 percentage points lower than expected, given previous analysis of general social survey data on membership and church attendance among Protestants (Davis & Smith, 1990).

Cluster analysis was used to develop our types of marginal members. This procedure groups respondents according to their similarities and differences, based on responses to a set of survey items (Hair, Anderson, Tatham, & Grablowsky, 1979). These items, or criterion variables, were a series of scales developed through a factor analysis conducted among all items in our survey that related to religion and the church. Our eight scales included: (1) spirituality; (2) traditional religiosity; (3) cultural liberalism; (4) religious experimentation; (5) church criticism; (6) church support; (7) childhood religious socialization; and (8) geographical mobility/distance from the church. The full text of the items used to create the scales are included in the appendix to this chapter. Four types of marginal members were indicated by a dendrogram produced by the clustering procedure (see Aldenderfer & Blashfield, 1984; Hadaway, 1989).[2] The meaning and interpretability of the clusters were determined by examining responses of cluster members to a wide range of questions from the survey. This is also how we gave names to our clusters.

Multiple discriminant analysis was performed on the cluster solution to measure the degree of separation between the clusters—in other words, to determine the degree to which each type of marginal member was distinguishable from the other three types. Using multiple discriminant analysis, we were able to accurately classify 93% of cluster members. This indicated that the clusters were quite distinct.

FOUR PROTESTANT MARGINAL MEMBERS

Four marginal members are described below: Horace, a traditionalist; Janet, a liberal; Carlos, a critic; and Mark, a lifelong marginal. Each represents his or her type very well, but it should be noted that no individual is likely to have *all* of the characteristics that define the type. No two traditionalists are exactly alike, for instance, but they do share a common orientation toward religion and the church.[3]

Traditionalists are religious persons by most measures and are typically members of conservative Protestant denominations. They are conservative in every way and feel guilty when they miss church. Many are inactive because of chronic health problems, old age, work schedules, or a spouse who will not attend. Liberals are religious and social liberals. They are not antagonistic toward the church, nor do they see themselves as disconnected from the church. They do not feel guilty when they miss church because they do not believe that regular worship attendance is necessary. Critics are, as their name suggests, very critical of the church. They view church worship services as boring, and most feel that the church is unconcerned about social justice. Over half give their church a grade of "C" or less. Critics also hold very nontraditional religious values, and few feel guilty when they miss church. They have rejected the church and in some cases replaced it with alternative forms of religious expression. Lifelong marginals grew up on the periphery of the church. They have a vague sense that the church is a good thing, and feel that they should attend, but this feeling does not provide the motivation for attendance. They are not religious seekers, nor are they privately religious in any way. They hold fairly conservative (though vague) religious views, but very liberal social attitudes.

Horace—A Traditionalist

Horace is a 79-year-old Southern Baptist. He lives in Georgia and has been Southern Baptist all his life. As a young boy, Horace's parents took him to Sunday school and church, although he says they never *made* him go. His parents sometimes had family devotions. Horace played "picnic baseball" at the church, and in general felt that "adults in the church cared about him." He enjoyed going to church. Even during his teenage years, Horace was fairly active: he was in the church youth group; read the Bible and prayed by himself; and sometimes "took things to the church for the needy." He adds, even if there were "times as a teenager that I didn't attend, I never questioned the teachings of the church."

Horace's father died before Horace turned 20. Horace did not go to college, but he was in the navy during the Second World War. Before he retired, Horace was a retail manager in a jewelry store. He lived most of his life within thirty-five miles of his birthplace. And he is a member of the Masons.

Horace's wife claimed "no religious preference" when they were married, but she was eventually converted, apparently by Horace. She is a Southern Baptist church member, too.

Horace was most active in the church in his early 40s to early 50s. He was a Sunday school teacher, led training union, and was a deacon. The church he attended was a "small" one where people "knew everyone." When asked to describe the most meaningful experience he ever had at a church, he said, "I was a Sunday school teacher, and a little boy in our class—a rascal—I told him Jesus loved him. One Sunday morning, he joined the church after I had been working with him for a year. I didn't know he had been listening. Took a lot of patience but it was worth it."

Things were not always rosy between Horace and the church, however. There was a time when Horace quit going altogether. The small church in which he was active had, in his words, "difficulties, there was a strong division." Horace recalls, "It took as much out of me as the little boy put in me. The church destroyed itself."

Then Horace joined the next nearest Southern Baptist church, which was much larger and had a less friendly feel. Still, he thinks that belonging to a church is "very important." He says, "When we outgrow the need for churches, we won't be around!" Even at his age, Horace feels he has a lot to learn about Christianity. Finally, he thinks that the best place to worship God is "in church," not in private, "because that's what the Lord wanted."

Horace holds traditional views on most social and religious issues: he prefers to call God "Father"; he holds a literal view of the Bible; he sees premarital sex, homosexuality, abortion, income tax evasion, and marijuana use as wrong. He would not lie under any circumstances. He does not support the ordination of women as ministers, but he does believe that

"Christians should be more involved in promoting racial equality, women's rights, and economic reform."

As traditional as he is, why is Horace a marginal member? Simply because he and his wife are in poor health. Horace has chronic heart and lung conditions, and because of hearing difficulties, his concentration is not what it used to be. Horace feels "cut off" from his church because of these problems. When asked if someone from his church visits or calls regularly, Horace said "no, only when we're in the hospital." He concludes that "the church is not that involved [with us] anymore. But it don't bother me. The church has a lot to do."

Horace would like to attend church more often. In fact, he feels guilty when he does not go. Physical barriers like steep stairways make it difficult for him. He says that he and his wife would attend services more often if it were easier to get around.

Horace and his wife *do* watch worship services on television and listen to religious programming on the radio. He prays about twice a day. Horace expresses interest in receiving communion at home, but he would clearly rather be in church if possible. Despite the fact that it is hard to attend and no one visits, Horace continues to give generously. Although he lives on a very modest fixed income, he gives about $1,500 a year to his church.

Traditionalists like Horace are our oldest and largest cluster (about 38% of all marginal members are traditionalists). They are disproportionately Southerners, conservative socially and religiously, highly socialized in the church, and religiously "serious." This group of marginals is separated from the church because of poor health or chronic disabilities, some severe, most merely "nagging."

Traditionalists could and would participate in church if it were more accessible to them. Many are lonely, and some are depressed. Nevertheless, they still value the church—even if they are cut off from it—and most continue to give money. With the graying of the baby boomers, there will be an increasing number of these kinds of marginals in and around the church. These "Horaces" and "Ednas," if you will, still have religious and spiritual needs—and many have personal and financial resources to contribute.

Also among traditionalists are a number of younger persons who hold strong, traditional church values but cannot go to services because of work, school, or obligations to care for someone who is sick or elderly. These individuals would definitely come to church if worship was held at other times or if someone would provide respite for them.

Janet—A Liberal

Janet is a 41-year-old woman from Connecticut. She lives about 45 miles from the community where she grew up, and her best friends are her neighbors. She was raised a Congregationalist and was very active in her local church. While her parents encouraged her to attend, they rarely made her go to church. As a child, she frequently talked to her parents about religious faith and regularly attended church school, choir, and fellowship activities. As a teen, she was active in the youth group and sometimes she read the Bible or prayed privately. Like Horace, Janet enjoyed going to church.

Janet went to a Quaker college and, for a time, "switched" to a Quaker congregation. Her most powerful religious experience occurred during a Quaker service when she literally "saw the light." Also during her college years, Janet supported the anti-Vietnam war movement. She even joined in a peace march. After college, Janet moved and joined a Presbyterian church "because it was closer." Her husband is presently a lapsed member of a Congregationalist church—although the rare times he does attend church, he goes with Janet.

Janet is liberal: she prefers to describe God as "a higher power," and she believes all the great religions of the world are equally true and good; she sees premarital sex, homosexuality, and abortion as "morally gray" and tax evasion and marijuana use as morally "wrong"; and she would be willing to lie in some situations. Janet speaks out for women and minorities, and she would not be concerned if a non-Christian were elected president of the United States. She is not in favor of prayer in public schools. She does favor the ordination of women as ministers.

Janet is supportive of the church as an institution. She values the church's potential as an agent of social and political change. She values its power as a moral teacher and a shaper of faith. She encourages her children to attend. Janet warmly recalls the prayers and help of church members when her twins were born prematurely and needed a long hospitalization. But while Janet appreciates the prayers of others, she rarely engages in personal prayer herself.

Janet does spend some personal time in church activity. She volunteers a couple of hours a month to do graphics for the church, and on occasion, she provides help with child care. Yet her worship attendance is very sporadic. And despite a $50,000 annual family income, her church contributions were only around $200 last year.

Unlike most liberal marginals, she feels a bit guilty when she does not attend, but not too much. What keeps her away? Frankly, she admits, "The fact that Sunday is one of the few times that our family has free time together." What would it take for her to become more involved? "Well," Janet says, "just a conscious decision to do it—to make time for it. Also having other family members want to do it."

Liberal marginals are predominantly middle-aged to older adults, oldline Protestant, very liberal, and committed to the enduring social and moral value of the church. Since liberal Protestants view conversion as a process of moral nurture, "bringing up the child in the way he or she should go" is critical. That is why the church is viewed principally as a "children's school" and not as a necessary activity for adults.

Janet, and other liberal marginals, are open to more church involvement, but the bottom line is that most liberal marginals we have talked to are satisfied with their attendance. In fact, most (unlike Janet) say they do not feel guilty when they miss. Many do not see a need to attend more often than they do. These marginal members seem to feel that they "got all the church they needed" between their baptism and confirmation.

Ironically, there is one thing that seems to motivate many liberal marginals: their families. Most agree that church is necessary for their children because it was very important for them. Still, their children go less frequently than they did simply because "Janets" go less often than their own parents did. In the balance of busy lives, even liberal marginals who are convinced that it is important to "go for the sake of the family" are content with a smaller—though in their minds no less important—piece of the church pie.

Carlos—A Critic

Carlos is a 43-year-old native of Texas who moved to Atlanta, Georgia, ten years ago. As the son of an Assemblies of God preacher, Carlos spent most of his formative years in church or in some kind of church activity. Carlos talked to his parents about faith all the time, participated in regular family devotions, sang in the church choir, and attended Sunday school, vacation Bible school, and church camp. Carlos adds that his parents were "very strict" and made him go to church when he really did not want to. When asked at what age his parents stopped making him attend, Carlos laughed and said, "Never . . . not until I was drafted into the army."

When Carlos was about 22 years old, he joined a Christian church (Disciples of Christ). He explains that he switched because he "wanted to learn a new religious discipline." Carlos is still somewhat of a religious seeker. He explains that he visits many other churches including "Mormons and Jehovah's Witness," and he adds that he has even "talked to Buddhists and Hindus." He says that he has "powerful religious insights" almost daily.

Carlos's wife was a Lutheran prior to their marriage. Afterward, she joined her husband's church. When the family moved to Atlanta, they became members of a local Christian Church congregation. Despite the fact that Carlos feels that "belonging to a church" is "very important," he has not been to church in four or five years. And despite the fact that he was very active in the church as a child and feels that religious instruction is important, none of his children have gone to church school. What happened?

Four Styles of Religious Marginality

According to Carlos, he went through a period of searching "for answers on my own." He says, "There are some very hard Christians now, that is, a lot of church people who are not willing to listen; they are more into interpreting their own issues. The Bible is not living, but Christian people today see it as an object." Carlos insists that no particularly "bad experience" pushed him away from the church. "More," he says, "the group method of thinking scares me." What Carlos is looking for now is a local church that is "honest . . . and loves the individual."

Carlos may not be very involved with the local church, but he is experimenting with alternatives. Carlos sometimes attends home Bible studies, prayer groups, and spiritual growth retreats. He also listens to religious programming on the radio. On top of that, last year Carlos gave about $1,500 to churches or church-related organizations. Carlos engages in personal prayer at least four times a day. And he admits that he would like to be more active in church. Still, he says "it depends on whether or not I could feel some respect for individuals."

All in all, Carlos is fairly liberal in his views of God and the Bible: he prefers to describe God as "a higher power" and believes the "Bible is inspired by God, but contains human error." He thinks that women should be ordained as ministers. Like Janet, he believes that all the great religions of the world are equally true and good. Still, Carlos would be "bothered if there were no churches" in his community, and he does feel guilty whenever he misses church—which poses a problem, as he is chronically absent.

What can we say, then, about Carlos and other critics? These marginal members are primarily older baby boomers. They are disproportionately Southerners with a lot of church involvement in their backgrounds. Not surprisingly, however, you can find critical marginal members in almost any denomination. After heavy doses of church life, many are clear about what the church "ought" to be, and equally clear that it rarely measures up to those standards. Concerns are most frequently raised about "hypocrisy," "pressuring" tactics, and constant requests for money.

Critics' anti-institutional penchant (a trait that is in part a legacy of this cohort's sixties' involvement) contributes to their liberality on religious issues. Still, a hard anti-institutional edge does not tell the whole story. About a quarter of marginal critics do not have specific complaints about the church; they have simply decided it is really not for them.

In general, critics have left, or drifted away from, the church because it does not measure up. But that does not mean that they have found religion totally bankrupt. It is just not palatable to them in its present institutional form. Many critics experiment with alternative religious expressions, both corporate and individual. Not surprisingly, most critics do not feel guilty when they miss church.

What will bring critics back? A change in the church is what most suggest. The church should "quit pressuring me to get deeply involved" and yet also "show a little bit of interest in me." One woman notes that there should be "greater effort and open-mindedness to accept beliefs outside of official church doctrine."

Most critics are looking for love, personal comfort, and even a renewal of belief. Others, however, claim that there is nothing the church can do to get them more involved. The hardest to reach have drifted away. One woman noted, "My beliefs have evolved, and church [just] doesn't fit me anymore." When asked what it would take for her to become more involved, she simply said, "I don't know."

Mark—A Lifelong Marginal

Mark is a 35-year-old Episcopalian. He lives in Connecticut and is married to another lifelong Episcopalian. Mark is a young man on the move. Since school, he has changed jobs about eight times. To support their family, which includes four children, Mark works six days a week and his wife works nights.

As a child, Mark seldom talked to his parents about religious faith and never went to church school, church camp, or participated on any church-related athletic teams. Mark's parents rarely attended themselves. And on the few occasions when Mark went to church, his parents "made him go." Still, his "somewhat permissive" parents never made him go to church after the age of 11. Mark does not have particularly good memories of church. Something clicked somewhere, however, because Mark recalls that he did read the Bible and pray privately as a teenager.

Despite Mark's lack of involvement in the church on any regular basis, he has turned to the church for the "big events" in his life. He, and his children, were christened in the Episcopal Church. Somehow he managed to become confirmed as an Episcopalian, and his wedding was performed by a minister in a church. In fact, Mark's most meaningful experiences in church include his wedding and the baptisms of his children. Mark and his wife joined the church they currently belong to about eight years ago. But neither has been to that church in a year. Mark rarely feels guilty when he cannot attend, yet says that belonging to a church is "somewhat important."

All in all, Mark is supportive of the *idea* of church. He thinks that churches are important, and he would rather worship God with others than alone. He says that he would like to go more often and thinks that an increase in involvement is "possible" in the future. Nevertheless, Mark admits that "sometimes I get the feeling that people who are active in the church live in a different world from my own."

In general, Mark is vague about "things religious." When asked to think about books in the Bible and name those most familiar, Mark replied, "Oh Jeez—Genesis, Exodus. I've read quite a few. Tell you the truth, I should pull it out and look at it." Mark thinks he could recite some of the Ten

Commandments, but he cannot tell you the story of the good samaritan. One other lifelong marginal said, "Which good samaritan? There are lots of Good samaritans in the Bible."

Mark's most powerful religious experience sounds so much like musings from a popular film about baby boomer angst that it is almost cliché. Mark says, "I was on vacation in Arizona, at the Grand Canyon. I realized how small and insignificant we really are . . . that God is really the only answer to things in life . . . there are things more important than self-gain . . . it really humbles you."

Mark is a fairly liberal person. He sees premarital sex, abortion, income tax evasion, and marijuana use as "morally gray." Mark would lie to protect himself. When asked whether he has a "real sense that God is guiding him in his daily life," Mark responded, "Jeez, sometimes I hope not." Mark believes in life after death and in the devil, but he is very unclear about the practical consequences of both.

About eight years ago, Mark was slightly more involved in the church than he is now. He said, "I felt obligated because I just joined. They asked me to do some things like come to meetings." This involvement did not last for long, however. Other pressures, such as work and personal debt, took priority over church in Mark's life.

According to Mark, the main thing that keeps him away from the church now is his children. Sunday is "the one day to ourselves." Because he and his wife work so much, and because "church is 10 miles away," "getting the children up and getting them dressed [is too much trouble]; they're cranky and cry." Moreover, Mark is bothered by the fact that the church "asks for money. They send things in the mail . . . they treat you like an account, a bank account. They've got percentages of what you should give." He adds, "I give when I can give freely."

What would it take to become more involved? Mark responds, "If I had a lot of pressures in my life off my shoulders . . . personal debt, etc. Once the burden of outside forces are gone, I can see myself going back on a regular basis." He adds, "I refrain from swearing when I go to church regularly and strive to be better."

Like Mark, other lifelong marginals are predominantly younger baby boomers. Most are Northerners, and generally unsettled. They tend to move a lot and change jobs frequently. They are culturally liberal and are generally positive about the church. After all, lifelong marginals have not really gone to church enough to be too critical. But they have attended enough to feel that it is at least marginally important. Major life events are still properly marked by church rituals.

Because they are marginally connected, many things keep these "lifers" away, although most of the reasons they list are, as one lifelong marginal admitted, "more of an excuse than a real reason." Everything from "work" to "laziness" to "children" to "no children" to "distance" to "nothing at all" are mentioned. Our favorite quote is from the lifer who said, "Sundays come and something says . . . 'no.' "

Lifelong marginals are equally vague about "what would bring them back." They speculate that "starting a family" might help or, conversely, that "maybe when my children get older, I'll come back." Some say "maybe a smaller church with younger people." Many say "nothing" or "I don't know." One thing is certain: being marginal in the past means being marginal in the present (and probably the future). This lifer concludes: "I don't know. The church has nothing to do with going to heaven, hell. . . . What's the church got to do with anything? What's important is believing in God. You can be saved without going to church. I see myself like my daddy. My daddy didn't go inside churches much, but I knew he was moral, enjoyed life, and didn't tell you what to do and what not to do."

SOME OBSERVATIONS

We are convinced that marginal members are a too-long neglected group among American Protestants. We are equally convinced that their tribe has been and still is increasing. What do you think of Horace, Janet, Carlos, and Mark? Have you met them before? Do you know others like them? These types should add names and faces to the larger unchurched population.

One weekend we met with the interviewers who talked at length to these 207 marginal members. We wanted to hear their impressions of these people. The overwhelming consensus of the group was that marginal members are still interested in the church, fairly positive about its past influence on their lives, and a little bothered by the fact that they are not more involved. Interviewers told stories of lonely and depressed traditionalists who cried during the interviews. They told stories of lifelong marginals who were so interested in the interview itself that they asked for copies. Finally, they told stories of a few marginals who stated at the end of the interview that they thought they would try church again. One interviewer joked, "I think the interview is going to end up making regulars out of some of these marginals."

We discovered that the strongest source of an enduring church identity and persistent religious practice is a strong baseline church experience. Marginal members say they are church members and continue to feel the church is important mainly because they went to church frequently when they were growing up and their parents did too. This is especially true of traditionalists, liberals, and critics. In a sense, they are now "banking off" previous reserves, although no one knows how long those reserves will remain effective resources for the increasing social and spiritual challenges of daily life.

If the strength of a church identity persists because of the intensity of earlier experiences, without the benefit of continuing involvement, what is the prospect for the children of current marginals? For example, the children of critics and liberals attend church less frequently than their parents did when they were growing up. This amounts to a kind of legacy effect that has serious implications for the second and third generations. Critics and liberals (the wayward children of active members) are rearing lifelong marginals. On the other hand, lifelong marginals, who are the least active and least religiously-sensitive group, are rearing children whose contact with the church is minimal. They identify with a church primarily because they were baptized or christened there and because they may occasionally attend a Christmas or Easter service with their families. Lifelong marginals are likely to be rearing persons with the religious profiles of our mental affiliates—persons with a vague sense of denominational affiliation, no church membership, and very infrequent attendance.

What approaches will bring marginal members back to the church (or to active membership for the first time)? Traditionalists are marginal to the local church because of logistics. If church buildings were more accessible, if church programming was more creative and flexible, these persons would increase their involvement almost instantly. The results would not only enrich the life of the church, but most certainly the lives of these marginal members as well. Traditionalists are easily dismissed; if they cannot come, it is more their problem than ours. We should not forget, however, that as this nation grays, the ranks of these marginal members will swell. If for no other reason, their investment, demands, and sheer numbers will finally call them to their churches' attention. But churches should not wait that long to reach out to traditionalists.

Liberal marginals are peripheral to the church because marginal attendance is expected and generally acceptable in many of their churches. Liberal marginals have heard the message that church attendance is optional. Regular adult education, for example, was all but phased out in many mainline churches over the last twenty years. The message is that church involvement is primarily "for the children." Denominational norms should change. Liberals must be reeducated about the demands (and the potential fruits) of active church membership. This task is critical for mainline denominations in which conversion is more a matter of nurture. If our hunch about the strong legacy effect of church marginality holds, the children of mainline marginal members seem most at risk.

Carlos and other critics are disillusioned with the church. Few are embittered because of bad experiences, but most are still very skeptical. Critics are looking for a low-pressure, nurturing congregation. They do not, however, spend much time and energy church shopping. These marginals admit that personal contact with church members who are caring, open, and honest might "woo them back" to church more often.

Lifelong marginals like Mark are barely churched. Their knowledge, understanding, and experience of church is minimal and episodic. Consequently, activating lifelong marginals calls for a major change in their understanding of and orientation to the church—something akin to a conversion experience. Outreach strategies that are low-pressure, personal, and compatible with their culturally liberal values and tastes may be most appealing. Such approaches may bring lifelong marginals "through the front door" more frequently.

Unlike critics, lifelong marginals feel positive about the church (although vaguely so). That positive regard and the fact that they are likely to show up at church on holidays and for big events provides a good place to start with them. In addition, lifetime marginality means that they "sometimes feel like people in the church live in a different world" from their own. Therefore, it is essential that reentry be accompanied by reeducation to church traditions, doctrine, and practice. Nevertheless, like traditionalists, liberals, and critics, lifelong marginals do see themselves as churched, and as Christians, and should be approached on that basis.

All marginal members have a tenuous connection to the church. Some became disconnected at some point in their lives, whereas others were never connected in the first place. The dilemma for the church is how to establish or reestablish that connection, so that church attendance and involvement in a church community become a part of their lives. The key to this is interest and effort—without pressure. Our interviews rekindled an interest in the church on the part of a few marginal members, and others felt grateful that someone finally was willing to hear what they had to say. Being heard should not be such a new experience, but for many church members it is. Would marginal members welcome such interest and effort? Most would because few marginal members are antagonistic toward the church. And even many critics would welcome the opportunity to express their opinions if someone was willing to listen.

In conclusion, if we are truly to "be the church" today, we must take an account of all those who are in our fold and all those who have strayed away. Simply hoping that new additions will balance out inevitable losses is not enough. It is, after all, more than a game of numbers. Holding and nurturing the whole community of faith—that comprises the local church— is necessary for making the journey and for keeping the promise.

Appendix

CRITERION VARIABLE DEFINITIONS FOR CLUSTER ANALYSIS

1. *Spirituality Scale* (Alpha = .69)
    A. Closeness to God: "How close do you feel to God most of the time? Would you say extremely close, somewhat close, not very close, or not close at all?"
    B. Spiritual Person: "Do you consider yourself to be a spiritual person?" (Yes, No)
    C. Regular Prayer: "Do you sometimes engage in a regular discipline of prayer and meditation?" (Yes, No; persons who never pray coded "no")
    D. Grace: "Do you sometimes say grace before meals?" (Options same as C)
    E. Pray Aloud: "Do you sometimes pray aloud in public?" (Options same as C)
    F. Regular Devotions: "Do you sometimes read devotional literature (such as daily devotional guides, prayers of the saints, etc.)?" (Options same as C)

2. *Traditional Religiosity Scale* (Alpha = .55)
    A. Name for God: "I am going to read a short list of words which are often used to describe God. Which *one* are *you* most likely to use?" (Options: Father, Creator, Mother, higher power)
    B. View of Bible: "Which of the following statements best describes your feelings about the Bible?" (Options: (a) the Bible is God's word and all it says is true; (b) the Bible was written by people inspired by God, but it contains human errors; (c) the Bible is a good book, but God had little or nothing to do with it)
    C. Guilt: "I feel guilty when I do not attend church." (Options: agree, uncertain, disagree)

3. *Cultural Liberalism Scale* (Alpha = .67)
    A. Universalism: "All the great religions of the world are equally true and good." (Options: agree, uncertain, disagree)
    B. No Church: "I think a person can still be a good Christian even if he or she doesn't attend church." (Same options as A)
    C. No Money: "I think a person can still be a good Christian without giving money to the church." (Same options as A)

D. Premarital Sex: "If a man and woman have sexual relations before marriage, do you think it is: (a) always wrong; (b) almost always wrong; (c) sometimes wrong; (d) not wrong at all."

4. *Religious Experimentation Scale* (Alpha = .52)
   A. Reincarnation: "Have you ever read books about reincarnation or near-death experiences?" (Yes, No)
   B. Crystals: "Have you ever experimented with astrology, psychic healing, or crystals?" (Yes, No)
   C. Native American Spirituality: "Have you ever explored Native American spirituality or religion?" (Yes, No)
   D. Commune through Nature: "Do you sometimes commune with God or a higher power through nature?" (Yes, No)

5. *Church Criticism Scale* (Alpha = .56)
   A. Too Much Business: "Churches put too much time and energy into committees and business meetings." (Options: agree, uncertain, disagree)
   B. Boring: "Church worship services are often boring." (Same options as A)
   C. Social Justice: "Most churches today are not concerned enough with social justice." (Same options as A)
   D. Unresponsive to Women: "Many churches are insensitive and unresponsive to the concerns of women." (Same options as A)

6. *Church Support Scale* (Alpha = .58)
   A. Church Warm: "Most churches today are warm and accepting of outsiders." (Options: agree, uncertain, disagree)
   B. Meaning: "Most churches today are effective in helping people find meaning in life." (Same options as A)
   C. Clear: "Most churches today are clear about what they stand for." (Same options as A)
   D. Church Grade: "What grade would you give that (church where respondent is a member) church? Would you give it an A, B, C, D, or F?"

7. *Baseline Experience Scale* (Alpha = .76)
   A. Youth Camps: "When you were in high school, how often did you take part in church-related youth programs, such as fellowships, retreats, or camps?" (Options: often, occasionally, seldom, or never)
   B. Mother's Attendance: "When you were in high school, how often did your mother attend church worship services?" (options: every week, two or three times a month, once a month or less, or never)
   C. Father's Attendance: (Substitute father for mother in B)

D. Attendance in High School: "When you were in your last year of high school, how often did you attend Sunday school or church? (Options same as B)

8. *Mobility/Distance Composite Variable*
   A. Moved: "How many times have you changed residences (that is, moved) in the past ten years?"
   B. Distance to Church: "About how many miles is that church (where respondent is a member) from your home?"

NOTES

1. This pattern was also seen in our 1991 survey of 2,012 Protestant Americans and in Hoge, Johnson, and Luiden's (Chapter 4) survey of Presbyterian baby boomers.
2. A dendrogram is a graphic, resembling an organizational chart, that allows visual identification of clusters and their degree of separation from other clusters.
3. A more complete description of the clusters and their statistical characteristics can be found in an earlier paper (Marler & Hadaway, 1993).

REFERENCES

Aldenderfer, M. S., & Blashfield, R. K. (1984). *Cluster Analysis.* Newbury Park, CA: Sage Publications.
Davis, J. A., & Smith, T. W. (1990). *General Social Surveys, 1972–1990* [Machine-readable data file]. Chicago: National Opinion Research Center.
Hadaway, C. K. (1989). Identifying American Apostates: A Cluster Analysis. *Journal for the Scientific Study of Religion, 29*(2), 201–215.
Hadaway, C. K. (1990). *What Can We Do About Church Dropouts?* Nashville: Abingdon.
Hair, J. F. Jr., Anderson, R. E., Tatham, R. L., & Grablowsky, B. J. (1979). *Multivariate Data Analysis.* Tulsa: Petroleum Publishing Company.
Hale, J. R. (1977). *Who Are the Unchurched?* Washington, D.C.: Glenmary Research Center.
Marler, P. L., & Hadaway, C. K. (1993). Toward a Typology of Protestant "Marginal Members." *Review of Religious Research, 35*(1), 34–54.
Perry, E., Davis, J. H., Doyle, R. T., & Dyble, J. E. (1980). Toward a Typology of Unchurched Protestants. *Review of Religious Research, 21*(4), 388–404.
Princeton Religion Research Center. (1978). *The Unchurched American.* Princeton: Author.
Princeton Religion Research Center. (1988). *The Unchurched American—10 Years Later.* Princeton: Author.
Roozen, D. A. (1978). *The Churched and the Unchurched: A Comparative Profile.* Washington, D.C.: Glenmary Research Center.
U.S. Bureau of the Census. (1983). *County and City Data Book, 1993.* Washington, D.C.: U.S. Government Printing Office.

CHAPTER 6

Profiles of the Disaffiliated: Four Case Studies

Amy L. Sales

Dropout has several denotations in the discussion of congregational affiliation (Chapter 3). Basically, a person might be considered a dropout by no longer identifying as a member of a religious tradition, by a lapse of faith, by ceasing to attend or participate actively, and/or by dropping his or her formal membership in the church or synagogue. This chapter examines the experiences of individuals who, for one reason or another, gave up their formal affiliation and had their names deleted from the membership rolls of the church or synagogue. Presented are the profiles of four dropouts:

1. Carol, a 53-year-old retail salesperson who was brought up in an Orthodox Jewish household
2. Bill, a 42-year-old management consultant who was raised Presbyterian
3. Steve, a 25-year-old director of a community service organization who was raised Catholic
4. Paula, a 25-year-old secretary who was baptized Methodist

Although distinct in many ways, the profiles portray a common experience. All four individuals were raised in a mainstream religion. In all cases, both parents were members of the same faith tradition and were thus able to offer their children a single, unambiguous religious affiliation and identity. (In Paula's case, this unity was obtained through the conversion of one parent.) They all reached a point in adulthood when the church or synagogue no longer served their needs, ceased to be "worth" it, or became anathema to deeply felt values. Although that point occurred for each at a different stage in life, all four have dropped out, suspending their affiliation with a congregation and filling their lives with alternative sources of community and meaning. Still, each maintains some connection to the childhood religion—be it respect for the education received, a sentimental bond to holiday celebrations, or a longing for the spirituality of the church.

This chapter begins by tracing the backgrounds of these individuals, from childhood to their separation from the church or synagogue. It next presents their attitudes toward the future—their own possible reaffiliation and their intentions for the religious upbringing of their children or grandchildren. The final section considers the implications of the four profiles for our understanding of affiliation and disaffiliation.

BACKGROUND

The personal histories that follow describe the routes people have taken from their native families and the religion bequeathed to them by their parents, to their grown-up lives and the choices they have made as adults—how they have confronted the decision of affiliation or allowed the decision to be made by default.

Carol—A Jewish Dropout

Carol grew up in a typically Orthodox family in Roxbury, Massachusetts, the heart of Boston's Jewish community in the 1940s. Her family belonged to a small neighborhood *shul*, and she has clear memories of her father and grandfather walking to Sabbath services each Saturday morning. When Roxbury underwent a transition from a Jewish neighborhood to a black ghetto, Carol's family, along with thousands of other Jewish families, moved outside the city proper. With the move away from the old center of Jewish life came membership in a Conservative synagogue. However—whether Orthodox or Conservative, old-world *shul* or modern synagogue—her father was always a model of the observant Jew and the actively involved congregant.

Carol married a Jewish man. Her husband, however, was not a Jew in the tradition of her father. He fully accepted his Jewish identity, but religiously had no connection to Judaism. His childhood family had only marginal ties to organized religion. As a young boy in Sunday school, he was wont to spend the coins intended for *tzedakah* on pinball machines. He did manage to celebrate his bar mitzvah, but beyond that, he never went to services.

The couple followed the centrifugal movement of Boston's Jews still further out from the old center. Carol and her husband moved to the suburbs and joined a Conservative synagogue. As their primary concern was religious education for their two daughters, they chose the congregation where the "in crowd" went to Hebrew school. The girls received their Jewish education, and they celebrated their bat mitzvah in the synagogue.

Meanwhile, Carol's husband, true to his upbringing, remained distant from the synagogue religiously and socially. Carol, a woman who tends to be active in organizations, never managed to become involved in the synagogue. The times she tried she was rebuffed by those in the temple's "inner circle." She could not "break in," and she never felt comfortable there. Her involvement in organized Jewish life centered not on her local synagogue but on ORT (Organization for Rehabilitation through Training) a philanthropic organization dedicated to providing training and education to young Jews in the United States, Israel, and elsewhere around the globe.

The children were Carol and her husband's reason for affiliation and their connection to the congregation. Understandably then, when their daughters went off to college, ties to the synagogue became noticeably thinned. The invoice for that year's dues arrived in the mail. Taking out his checkbook to pay the bill, her husband began to complain: "I really resent this. If any one of us was using the temple, OK." But no one was "using" the temple, so the dues became insupportable to this family.

Carol wrote a letter of resignation. The year was 1980. Twelve years later, recalling the event, her voice took on a touching mix of sadness and anger: "Nobody ever called to ask me why we dropped out." The slip from marginal member to dropout was simple and was not noted by the congregation.

Bill—A Presbyterian Dropout

Bill was raised in a Presbyterian household in Dallas, Texas. As a child, he went to Sunday school every week, an activity he remembers not as a burden or a family requirement, but as a positive experience. By high school, his connection to the church was very strong, and indeed, in those adolescent years, he found the church to be "more real than school."

Unlike school, the church was a place where Bill felt encouraged to say what was on his mind, an institution which valued self-discovery and honesty. Bill was receptive to the religion and deeply involved in a number of activities through the church. His parents, too, had strong religious faith and devotion to the Presbyterian church. There was only the slightest hint of a less than perfect match between the individual and the institution. The young Bill "never understood how theology was to connect to me personally. I was confirmed, and I learned the catechism. I said it, did it, but never really was sure how it was supposed to change my life."

Despite this gap, when he was an undergraduate at Southern Methodist University, Bill considered entering the ministry. He was motivated primarily by a Presbyterian minister with whom he had formed a "counseling relationship." This minister was someone Bill could talk to, a guide, a role model. His most important contribution to Bill's development was teaching him "that I could love myself the way I was because God loved me." From this critical learning, Bill derived a strong sense of self, within a Christian framework.

Bill read a great deal through college and graduate school; his religious horizons were wide. He both joined in the Human Potential Movement and became an elder in an experimental Presbyterian church. This experiment was dedicated to exploring and validating the religious feeling that attends the words said in prayer. The elders designed experiential worship services with active participation from congregants and opportunities for expressing reactions to themes in the service and the emotions they evoked.

About this time, Bill learned transcendental meditation (TM) as a stress-reduction technique. TM's premise is that twenty minutes of meditation twice a day helps to calm the inner noise, relax the senses, and allow for a more peaceful and harmonious existence. As Bill's interest turned toward Eastern religion, he came to see the spiritual dimension of such meditation. Once again, a teacher with great "presence and purposefulness" provided him inspiration. Guided by this master, he taught himself Zen meditation, a practice he has continued regularly since that time.

The members of Bill's Presbyterian church, although good and caring people, had had no exposure to Eastern religion or meditation. Finding amongst them no support for this path, he inevitably gravitated to other sources of support. Moreover, his new experience of spirituality "went beyond" anything he had known before, and he now found the Christian church "too limited" in its approach to worship. It made no sense to him to stay with the Presbyterian Church merely because he had been born into it. He decided to drop out.

The question of religious identity was raised only years later when Bill was to marry. His bride and her family were practicing Reform Jews, his parents and his own happy childhood were rooted in the Presbyterian tradition, and his current spiritual life was being carried out through Zen meditation and other practices of the Eastern religions. Under what religious tent would Bill and his wife be wed? With great care and innovation, the ceremony was designed to be true to the beliefs of the bride and groom *and* to respect the traditions of both families.

Steve—A Catholic Dropout

Steve grew up in the Catholic Church in the Midwest. When he was a young child, his parents "dragged" him to church, and even when they themselves stopped going, they still made their children attend. The church, nonetheless, eventually came to have meaning for Steve. In that community, it was the only institution actively addressing social issues. Steve, who was always concerned with threats to equal rights and social justice, was ultimately attracted to the church and its good work. From junior high school on, he was an active participant in church activities.

Steve went off to college at Boston University. When he arrived on campus, the first entity with which he affiliated was the Catholic Center. In the context of a large urban university, the Catholic Center provided a setting where the new student felt "connected" and at home. While an undergraduate, Steve came out as a gay man. The Catholic community, a warm and caring group, was "fairly accepting" of him, and the Catholic Center provided a structure through which he was able to continue his work for social justice. Given only the immediate context, he would have remained a practicing Catholic.

Newspapers and television, however, provided constant reminders that everything he stood for on social issues, and gay rights in particular, was anathema to church dogma. "Every time I picked up the Boston *Globe*, I felt slammed by the Catholic Church." For example, he felt enveloped by the suffering and devastation brought on by the AIDS epidemic, but saw that "the church still says no condoms." For two years, he struggled with the conflict between his personal views and those of the church, remaining throughout this time strongly affiliated and active. After all, the Catholic Center was his source of community. "I didn't know about the gay community yet. I thought they only hung out in bars."

In the end, it was social politics that drove him out of the church. The congregation accepted him for who he was, but the institution did not. Now he is no longer religiously affiliated. He derives his support and sense of belonging from the gay community, and he engages in action for social justice through his professional work. His needs remain unchanged, except now they are no longer fulfilled by the church. They are, richly and fully, being met elsewhere.

Paula—A Methodist Dropout

"The last ten times I was in church I got paid," says Paula somewhat flippantly. Paula is a musician who is sometimes hired to play for a church service or event. Unlike Bill, Carol, and Steve, she has never had strong ties to the church. In Paula's words, "church never really did anything for me."

Paula's father, a Catholic, converted to the Methodist Church to marry her mother, a "*very* devout" woman who unfailingly went to church every Sunday. They belonged to a Methodist church in Portland, Maine, the town where Paula was born, but when they later moved to Bangor, they did not affiliate anew. They continued for years to receive mailings from their former church in Portland and always thought of that as "their church."

Early on, church became, at best, an inconvenience for Paula. She was often out late on Saturday nights baby-sitting and getting up on Sunday morning to attend worship services was literally "a pain" to the young girl.

Moreover, the family lived on a farm, and Sunday was the only time for family chores, the day, as Paula recalls it, "to weed the beans." The pattern continued into high school, when Paula became seriously involved in music and determined that she wanted to be a musician. She joined a small band which frequently played "gigs" on Saturday night. Once more, Sunday mornings at church were not particularly appealing to the young teenager.

Although not personally attracted to church worship, Paula would occasionally go to Methodist services to appease her grandmother, and sometimes she would go to Catholic mass to please her grandfather (even though she was "the only one there who could not take communion"). Her neighbors were Catholic, and she would at times go with them on Catholic retreats. She never "believed everything the church was saying" and, as an adult, finds herself increasingly in disagreement with the church's stand on social issues like abortion and the role of women. At the same time she says that she "had felt a lot of connection" with Catholicism.

Nonetheless, she "resented" church, and she resented giving money to the church when she was getting nothing out of it and when she could think of "better things to spend the money on." When she arrived as a freshman at the University of New Hampshire, she checked "unaffiliated" on her registration form so that she would not be bothered with calls or mail from any of the religious groups at the school. She wanted no part of religion on campus.

Now a young adult living on her own, Paula feels completely removed from any congregation or denomination and wonders at the power these exert in others' lives. One of her current roommates visited several Catholic churches before choosing the one she would join, and the other roommate, about to marry, had to find "the perfect Congregational church" for the wedding ceremony. Paula's own orientation differs strikingly from that of her roommates. "I would be just as happy," she suggests, "getting married by a justice of the peace at the Holiday Inn."

Paula's fiancé, it should be noted, is an identified Methodist. When told that the probability of her finding a Methodist boyfriend is suspiciously small, she retorts that his being the same denomination as her family of origin is "just coincidence." They are both musicians, she explains, and met through a jazz band at the university. The connection, in her view, is purely musical and not religious.

CURRENT BELIEFS AND PRACTICES

Each of these individuals—considering their backgrounds and individual needs, personal relationship to God, and religious and political sentiments—has arrived at a *modus vivendi* with the church or synagogue and with organized religion.

Carol's religious identity is firm and unambivalent: "I am Jewish to the core," she declares without hesitation. "I do everything except go to services." In her view, her Jewishness is as spiritual as it is ethnic. Her observance of Jewish practices in the home is motivated by a clear religious sense and not mere nostalgia for a childhood home. She keeps a kosher home. She observes the holidays with her relatives. On Rosh Hashanah and Passover, her older daughter comes home, and Carol prepares traditional meals and seders. She neither eats nor drinks on Yom Kippur for "as long as I can," and she experiences this as a fast of atonement. On the anniversary of her parents' death, she says Yiskor. Indeed, intoning the memorial prayer alone at home is the only moment in which she feels "discomfort" with her solitary practice of Judaism and her lack of contact with a religious community.

She wonders if the family had affiliated with a Reform synagogue rather than a Conservative one if things would have worked out differently. Maybe they would have felt more comfortable and would not have dropped out. She thinks that she might affiliate again, possibly when life is not as busy as it is now. She would need both the time to be involved and a setting in which her participation would be invited. At the present, she does not have the time; earlier in life when she had the time, the congregation did not welcome her contribution.

Bill feels that he does not need a religion per se. Indeed, when he filled out the registration form for his graduate program at Harvard University, he faced the question of his religious affiliation. "I debated between 'nothing' and 'Buddhist,'" he recalls. Ultimately, however, Bill rejected religious labels. "If someone wants to know what I am into, I will tell them."

His religious practice, particularly the Zen meditation, is deeply personal and spiritual, and yet he sees that "the path I am on is compatible with all the great religions." Christianity, in his view, has much of value and is complementary to Buddhism, not in competition with it. A primary difference for him is that the meditative tradition, which is at the core of all religions, is less accessible in Christianity or Judaism than it is in the Eastern religions. He thus feels there is "something missing" in Western religion which he wishes were present.

Asked if he feels the need for ritual observance, Bill says that he cannot imagine giving up the celebration of Christmas, largely because he has so many memories and feelings connected with the holiday. He eschews empty ritual, however, and insists that those he embraces be relevant to his personal experience and meaningful to him. For example, he attends Jewish high holiday services with his wife and finds nuggets of meaning in the prayers. He has to admit, however, that he is there for his wife; his own needs do not draw him to Jewish observance.

Steve says, "I know where I'm headed and what I'm committed to." His values in life—selflessness, generosity, identification with those who suffer poverty or injustice—parallel Franciscan ideology, and he clearly embodies some Christian teachings. His community and social activism, however, the core of his life and his identity, are not connected to the spiritual and the transcendent. He recognizes that theology is missing from his life. "The who or what is God is still important to me," he acknowledges, even though he has ceased to associate with a religious community. On the inside, Steve is still concerned with the religious, "but not enough for me to affiliate."

Paula, in contrast to Steve, is not certain if there is a God or a higher power in the universe. Regardless, she says that this is not an important issue to her since she is "in control of my own life." She says that if she were to wake up tomorrow and find the church gone, it would make no difference to her whatsoever.

With respect to ritual observance, Paula regards Christmas as a family event, the only time her extended family comes together. She, like Bill, is drawn to this holiday and would be loath to give up its personal meaning. Her spirituality, however, "comes through the music." The relationships she has formed with other musicians provide her with community, and the music they play is a source of transcendent experience. In essence, music has replaced religion in Paula's life.

These profiles highlight the importance of conceptually distinguishing between affiliation and identification. Carol and Steve intentionally disaffiliated from the synagogue and the church, yet their identification as Jew and Catholic is clear and unquestioned. Paula and Bill, also unaffiliated, retain an essential identification with their Protestant backgrounds, particularly in the celebration of holidays. Important, too, is the distinction between affiliation, on the one hand, and faith or religious sentiment, on the other. Despite having dropped out from organized religion, all four, to one degree or another, continue to engage in religious practices and dwell on theological concerns. Although they are not members of congregations, their lives contain far more than mere secularism.

THE NEXT GENERATION

The first section looked at the religious development of four individuals, at how they were raised and how they moved away from formal congregational affiliation in their adult years. This next section looks at their views and practices vis-à-vis their own children. We examine whether these dropouts, once active members of a church, are likely to raise unaffiliated children or whether they will choose to provide their children with the same religious education and experiences they themselves had in childhood. The religious institution, at least at the moment, has lost these people. Has it necessarily lost their children as well?

Carol: Concern with Jewish Continuity

Carol's older daughter has married a Christian, and from this union Carol has a fifteen-month-old granddaughter. She does not know if the grandchild will be raised Jewish and is loath to insinuate herself in the parents' decision making. "I tell myself to shut my mouth. I have to remember that I am the grandmother, not the mother." At Christmastime, her daughter and son-in-law have a Christmas tree. Carol bites her tongue and says nothing. She consoles herself by noting, "It's a decorator's tree. There's nothing religious on it."

Carol is hopeful, however, that she will have an impact on choices made for the grandchild. She looks at possible signs and notes, for example, that the child spends more time with her than she does with her non-Jewish grandmother. She agonizes over her ability to influence the child's identity and affiliation. She would like to buy a Jewish star for her granddaughter, a small silver star she could wear on a chain around her neck, but she is fearful of insulting her son-in-law. She acknowledges that she is sending a "mixed message" to her daughter and granddaughter. She is not affiliated with the synagogue, yet wants this grandchild raised as a Jew. As the baby gets older and the question of religious education comes to the forefront, Carol plans to talk with her daughter about all of this. In the meantime, waiting, she says nothing.

Bill: Decision Deferred

Bill has a two-year-old son. He firmly believes it is important the child be raised "in some kind of religious tradition," not so much for the child's identity as for his education. Bill treasures the teachings of the great religions and wants to assure that his son has every opportunity to learn of this history and wisdom. The specific tradition in which the child will be raised, however, is unresolved. There is "slim chance" that Bill would affiliate with a Protestant church, and a greater possibility that his wife and son would affiliate with a Jewish temple. At the same time, although he feels there are "wonderful things" in many religious traditions, he would not want his son to have only the Jewish perspective on Christianity. Bill's discomfort with these choices is obvious. He understands his own spiritual path and relationship to the church, but decisions concerning his wife and son remain confused. The general value on religion is agreed upon in the family; the specifics of how to raise the child is, at this time, undetermined.

Like Carol, Bill maintains that these decisions concern the child's religious education and, therefore, are not pressing. Asked when religious education or identity begins, Bill admits that even by age two it has already started. The son, for example, goes to temple and observes the lighting of the Sabbath candles in the home on Friday night. There is, after all, an immediacy as such events take on a momentum of their own. Bill wishes he were further along in answering the question of his son's religion, but for now admits, "I haven't thought it through."

Steve: Catholicism Rejected

Steve at this point does not have a child, but is adamant that any child of his will not be brought up in the Catholic Church and that any exposure the child has to Catholicism will be from "a critical perspective." Children, Steve argues, need to know about the influence on their lives "of oppressive institutions," including the church. "Theoretically my children will know where I stand," explains Steve. "I will actively discourage them from affiliating with groups I think are destructive to my peers and to me."

Although he would not allow the church into his child's life, he would still maintain the holidays. At home he would talk with his child about the meaning of the holidays, and together they would celebrate them as a "cultural" event, a time for family to come together to share a joyous occasion.

Paula: Laissez Faire—Let the Children Decide

Paula, as seen above, has the loosest connection to the church of any of the four individuals presented here. It is not surprising then that her notion of how her children would be raised is the least defined and the least grounded in a particular religious tradition or sentiment.

When she has children, Paula says she will bring them to church because "it is the right thing" to do and because it carries on what she and her boyfriend experienced in their own childhood. "You know, religion," she says, "it's like a tradition." She intends to "expose" her children to religion so that they will have the choice of whether to accept it into their lives or not. To her, exposure means taking her children to Sunday school so they can learn the Ten Commandments and the Bible. Given the simplicity of her choice, she was asked why she would not merely teach her children at home. Her answer was an honest one: "My beliefs are not strong enough to do that."

Despite her own background mix of Methodism and Catholicism, Paula would probably bring her children to a Congregational church. Why? It is a "little more liberal," and she feels "a little more welcome there." Her decision is not powerfully motivated as we see in her language. She admits that she knows little about the Congregational church, that her one exposure was a candlelight service she attended last year.

Ultimately she says her children can do whatever they want with regard to religion. "If they come home and say they want to be Jewish, that would be OK with me." Her only hesitation concerns evangelical Christianity. She has some sense that she would be uncomfortable with her children's involvement in a fundamentalist Christian group. Aside from that, her children can convert to any religion they like, as long as they are serious and well informed about it. With her own weak beliefs and her vague notions of what denomination would be suitable for her family, Carol still allows the possibility of religion in her children's lives.

Four Orientations

Four patterns in the transmission of religion to the next generation are evidenced in these profiles.

1. *Positive motivation toward a specific religion.* Carol has a strong attachment to Judaism and desires for her granddaughter not religion in general but very specifically a Jewish identity and affiliation.
2. *Positive motivation toward religion in general.* Bill wants his son to be as educated as he himself is in world religion, to have a spiritual life, and to enjoy the wonders and richness of religion, without becoming enmeshed in any particular faith tradition.
3. *Value neutrality, which neither approaches nor avoids religion.* Paula would merely expose her children to religion. Note the choice of words: she would not insist, urge, or encourage them to affiliate, but would expose them so that they might choose for themselves. Her drive is not toward a specific religion. Indeed, she seems quite open to the possibility of *any* religion, or none at all. While hers is not a strong investment in or commitment to religion, it is also not an antireligious stance. She does allow for the possibility of her children being religiously affiliated.
4. *Negative motivation away from religion.* Steve, in contrast, is more solidly antichurch. He would educate his children in the oppression of the church, in the dangers of organized religion and its attack on personal liberties and freedom.

In sum, the mere disaffiliation of the parent does not predict intentions toward the religious upbringing of the children. Dropouts will locate themselves somewhere on the continuum from positive motivation toward a specific religion (undoubtedly the one they enjoyed as a child), to negative motivation away from religion (in general and in its manifestation in a particular church or faith tradition).

IMPLICATIONS FOR AFFILIATION AND DROPPING OUT

Although Carol, Bill, Steve, and Paula are not statistically representative of the population, their choices, motivations, and rationalizations exemplify principles discussed elsewhere in this volume. Most notably, these profiles illustrate three phases which may be entailed in congregational affiliation and dropping out: ties to organized religion, separation, and personal religion.

Ties to Organized Religion

There were significant personal and communal ties which brought Carol, Bill, and Steve close to the church or synagogue and bound them in some fashion to the institution. At one time, these ties gave the church or synagogue a special place in their lives and particular relevance to their needs.

Personal Needs. Through his counseling relationship with a minister, Bill learned self-acceptance. As this critical learning occurred in a religious context (the teacher was a cleric, the message was enfolded in a message of God's love), there developed for Bill a link between the church and his own ability to love himself. For Steve, the early tie was between his political consciousness and the church. In the community where he grew up, the church's offering a platform for social action appealed to Steve's personally felt need to engage issues of social justice. Carol's tie appears to have been less an inner-driven need, as it was for Bill and Steve, and more an outer-driven need concerned with her children. Carol's affiliation was tightly coupled with her daughters' religious education and, presumably, with her sense of personal responsibility for Jewish continuity. Her tie to the synagogue, an institution uniquely posed to transmit Judaism to the next generation, was a necessary and inevitable consequence of her parental role.

In Paula's case, we see little evidence of an early tie to the church. She attended prayer services merely to "appease" her grandparents. In essence, her connection to her grandparents was her connection to the church. She participated strictly for others and not for herself.

Social Needs. Need for community and relationship also ties the individual to the church or synagogue. Individual religion, many would argue, does not work. Rather, our religious identity emanates from community, and the call to service and to prayer comes most powerfully from a congregation.

Bill, for example, experienced a strong connection to the minister who served as guide, teacher, and therapist. This relationship was a critical element in his earlier tie to the Presbyterian Church. Steve experienced the possibility of engaging in concerted social action through the community of his childhood church. In both instances, leaving the church has involved finding replacements for the teachers and communities left behind. Bill has identified other teachers to guide him in his spiritual path, and Steve has found a supportive community more compatible with his politics.

Carol, too, is concerned with the social aspect of affiliation. She initially chose to join the synagogue where the "in-crowd" went, a decision motivated in some measure by an attraction to desirable, popular members of the community. Her sadness today is evoked by remembering that at the time of her disaffiliation, the community did not respond.

For Paula, there is no sense of religious community, and there are no prominent teachers or guides. Having never sought or established such connections, she never experienced their loss or the need to find replacements for them.

Separation

We further see in each case conditions which drew attention away from the religious setting and separated the individual from the church or synagogue. Once these conditions grew stronger than the countervailing ties, they became a rationale for disaffiliation.

Bill was pulled away from the church by his exploration of Eastern religions and his dedication to meditation. The spiritual path to which he was drawn was foreign to the Presbyterian tradition (whether mainstream or experimental) and neither appreciated nor understood by the members of his congregation. Steve was drawn into involvement in the gay community, a situation in which he felt comfortable and at home. His homosexuality, an important aspect of his personal and social identity, was condemned by the Catholic Church. Beginning in adolescence, Paula's identity took root in her music. Experiencing music and organized religion as mutually exclusive, she moved toward music and away from the church.

In Carol's case, the separation was the loss of a positive pull toward synagogue affiliation rather than an attraction toward some outside alternative. Her motivation for affiliation was the education of her children. Once that need was met, the positive tie was gone and the break occurred.

We might think about the separation as some combination of "push" and "pull" factors. People may feel pushed away from the church or synagogue, and simultaneously they may feel a pull toward an alternative. As seen in the four profiles, the pull-push mix might be quite different for each individual. In any event, the forces which move people to drop out from the church or synagogue eventually exceed the forces which draw them toward it. Steve has ardently rejected the church for its position on homosexuality and other social issues of deep importance to him—a strong "push" factor. Bill has been powerfully drawn into a spiritual search which has taken him beyond the church—a strong "pull" factor. In both cases, the total forces away from the childhood religion were strong enough to outweigh whatever ties remained.

Personal Religion

It is a serious error to assume that congregational dropouts are bereft of religious impulses. Indeed, some nonattenders are quite religious. Disaffiliation did not leave Carol, Bill, Steve, and Paula with vacuous lives devoid of significance or of connection to the transcendent. On the contrary, they have continued to create meaning in their lives and to focus on observances or practices which elevate them beyond mundane concerns. Marler and Hadaway (Chapter 5) offer the metaphor of a spiritual bank where funds deposited during the early years of affiliation are available for withdrawal later on as needed. Our dropouts, however, do not appear to be touching the principal in their spiritual banks. Rather, they have embraced alternatives for replenishing their accounts—if not by adding to the capital at least by allowing themselves to live off the interest alone.

Carol has filled her life with Jewish practices. She maintains a kosher home; she observes the ritual calendar in her home, even fasting on Yom Kippur; she lights a candle on the anniversary of her parents' death and says Yiskor. She has left the synagogue and community prayer, but she has maintained personal Jewish observance in her home. Bill meditates on a regular basis at the Buddhist center and over the years has attached himself to teachers who could guide him toward a deeper and more meaningful practice of meditation. He continues to explore other New Age avenues to raise his consciousness and to enrich his connection to his inner self and to the enduring in the universe. Steve transcends the petty concerns of the everyday by immersing himself in social action, obeying some inner command to create a just and peaceable world. Paula, finally, has her music and recognizes that therein lies her religion. Music takes her beyond words into the realm of the aesthetic. Never able to appreciate the church, she readily feels and responds to the beauty and power of music.

Future Possibilities

The profiles show us the complexity of the disaffiliateds' motivations: (1) their resistance to organized religion; (2) their continuing acceptance of alternatives; and (3) their ongoing search for significance and meaning in life. These are people whose relationship with the institution of religion failed. They could not reconcile financial, personal, developmental, or sociopolitical issues with the institution. Still, they have religious feelings, and they are struggling with religious concepts. In the process of searching for what works for them, they have developed *personal religions*. This is not relativism but individualism, the attempt of each to create his or her own religion. To recapture the dropout, the church and synagogue are thus challenged to compete with life interests, alternative sources of spirituality and meaning, and the individualistic belief that a life of faith is possible without religious community.

PART THREE

Programs and Practices

Part Three presents church/synagogue programs and practices that have been successful in promoting congregational affiliation.

In Chapter 7, Rabbi Steven E. Foster enumerates the motivations for synagogue affiliation and disaffiliation which he has observed as a practicing rabbi and as the chairman of the Task Force on the Unaffiliated (Union of American Hebrew Congregations). Employing a market analysis, Foster notes that people join the synagogue when they want or need to purchase services which the synagogue has to offer. Some join for religious education for their children or for access to religious services on the high holy days. Others join seeking community or compelled by a feeling of responsibility for the maintenance of Jewish life. At some point in their lives, individuals may drop their membership citing the expense or some dissatisfaction they have with the synagogue. Their disaffiliation may be connected to a life event or to the feeling that they no longer need the services provided by the synagogue.

Foster goes on to describe an experimental program which targets a specific group in the unaffiliated population—interfaith families. This program, "Stepping Stones—To A Jewish ME," was developed in response to the current reality in the Jewish community that 52% of Jews are marrying non-Jews who do not convert to Judaism. Most of these interfaith families do not affiliate with synagogues, and few provide Jewish education to their children. The majority of these families decide to raise their children in both traditions under the potentially false assumption that when the children are grown they can (happily and successfully) choose their own religious identity. Stepping Stones offers free religious education to the children, giving the parents time to grapple with the deeper issues entailed in intermarriage and to make necessary choices. About half of the families in the program eventually join the synagogue or actively enter the Jewish community in some way. Generalizing from Stepping Stones' success, Foster concludes with a set of principles to guide outreach programming.

In the next chapters, three clergymen describe how their churches or synagogue reverted from greatly diminished conditions to notable growth. These profiles of congregational growth are a valuable source of insight into affiliation dynamics.

In Chapter 8, Reverend John F. Steinbruck tells how Luther Place Memorial Church in Washington, D.C., was transformed when it opened its doors as a refuge and sanctuary to the homeless. In Chapter 9, Dr. James A. Scott explains the growth which occurred at Bethany Baptist Church in Newark, New Jersey, as a result of long-range planning and a commitment to social action, which is a critical component of the church's mission. In Chapter 10, Rabbi Marshall T. Meyer recounts the remarkable story of growth which took place at Congregation B'nai Jeshurun in New York City. Building an inclusive community, encouraging passion in prayer, and embracing social action are elements which renewed this congregation.

These three institutions have important similarities. First, all are urban congregations located in the center of major metropolitan areas. As such, they had access to large populations with significant numbers of potential members. At the same time, none could deny nor avoid the realities of urban life, the social ills and injustices which are so clearly seen in the inner city. The urban setting of the three congregations proved advantageous for both numerical growth and incarnational growth (Chapter 2).

Moreover, these were old congregations with long histories and with memories of former prestige. Although not necessarily "playing by the rules" of their national organizations, each is clearly identified with a national denomination (the Lutheran Church, American Baptist Churches USA, United Synagogue of Conservative Judaism). These profiles, therefore, do not describe the creation of new institutions, but rather tell of the resurrection of long-standing but dying institutions. They show how new life can be breathed into old systems which have ceased to be effective in attracting, exciting, and involving members. In particular, they demonstrate the possibility of liberal churches and synagogues achieving high commitment and membership gains without compromising their ideological orientation.

The key to growth for all three congregations was in achieving clarity about their mission (their purpose for being) and their message (what it is they have to offer their congregants). They all recognized that they could not exist without directly engaging the issues literally lying on their doorsteps (homelessness, poverty, discrimination, and so on). In each case, clergy recount opening their churches and synagogues to the world—setting up shelters and services for ministering to people, incorporating social action with religious purpose, living the words of the faith. The "opened doors" attracted large numbers of new members drawn to the deeper experience of faith offered by a congregation whose mission was relevant and meaningful to their lives.

Part Three is not intended as a "cook book" with recipes for making vital congregations. Rather, it presents models from the world of practice—some aspects of which corroborate affiliation theory and research, and other aspects which challenge common notions. A critical ingredient in these models is the dedication, charisma, devotion, and leadership of the authors. Although this is not explicitly noted in any of the chapters, we would suggest that any analysis of congregational stories must also include the essential role played by clergy in the renewal and growth of the congregation.

CHAPTER 7

Reaching Out to the Unaffiliated

Rabbi Steven E. Foster

Clergy who serve "on the front lines" in congregations are charged with developing programs to reach out to the unaffiliated and bring more of them into the religious fold. These outreach efforts cannot be conceived in a vacuum, but must be rooted in a clear understanding of the unaffiliated, the target audience. This chapter describes, from the rabbi's perspective, the motivations that impel individuals and families to affiliate with a synagogue at some times in their lives and to drop out at other times. Structures and programs for helping people successfully cross the threshold into synagogue membership and remain an active part of the congregation must be designed with these motivations in mind.

The chapter next presents an outreach program created in response to a contemporary issue in the Jewish community—a high and increasing rate of intermarriage. Although this outreach program is concerned with a specific subpopulation (intermarried families), the principles underlying it have general relevance for the practical side of congregational growth, as they inform the specific actions that can be taken to reach out to the unaffiliated.

SYNAGOGUE AFFILIATION RATES

The 1990 National Jewish Population Survey[1] (NJPS) shows that synagogue affiliation rates vary significantly by region of the country, age, length of time in the community, income, maturity of family, and years of Jewish education (Tobin & Berger, 1993). Regardless of how they are analyzed, the data consistently show that only a minority of Jewish households

Table 7.1
Synagogue Affiliation by Region

REGION	Current Synagogue Affiliation %	Synagogue Dropout %
Northeast	43	30
Midwest	48	24
South	35	45
West	29	42

Table reprinted from Tobin and Berger (1993)

are currently affiliated with a synagogue. The percentage of affiliated families varies from 29% in the West to 48% in the Midwest (see Table 7.1).

Notably, more than half of American Jews have at one time or another been members of congregations. The majority of Jews in the United States join a synagogue at some point in their lives, making a commitment to the institution and becoming, for some period of time, dues-paying members of a congregation. As we see in the NJPS data, however, the synagogue in many instances is like a vacuum cleaner (Chapter 2): it draws people in, but without a bag on the other end, it allows them to leave once they are "done" with what the synagogue has to offer. The resulting dropout rate is substantial.

The percentage of true unaffiliates is probably rather small. I would estimate 15% of Jews are "hard core" unaffiliated: they want no involvement in synagogue life; and conversely, they want the synagogue to have no involvement in their lives. The hard core have never been affiliated and probably never will be. Again, given the distinction between Jewish identity, religious ideology, and congregational affiliation, it may be that some of the unaffiliated are attached to other parts of the Jewish community. They may be actively involved in the Jewish Community Center, the Anti-Defamation League, the Federation, or other secular communal agencies, but they have no meaningful connection to the religious institution of the synagogue.

MOTIVATIONS FOR SYNAGOGUE AFFILIATION

People choose to affiliate with a synagogue out of diverse motivations. Some are undoubtedly single-issue members who join to fulfill a specific need; others may be motivated by a complex set of needs and desires.

A marketplace analysis would suggest, first of all, that people join synagogues when they want or need to purchase services which are unavailable or less desirable elsewhere. For example, some congregations offer excellent preschool programs with extended hours of day care, well-qualified staff, and an environment which is safe, loving and—whether the customer cares or not—Jewish. Synagogue membership may grant the family priority in preschool registration or a welcome discount on tuition. These advantages may be sufficient to compel some young families to become dues-paying members of the congregation.

A related motivation is the desire of families to provide religious education for their children. The education they seek generally entails Sunday school a couple of hours a week and/or afternoon Hebrew school two to four hours a week. Although this education may be minimal in comparison with serious study of Judaism and the Torah, parents believe it is important and feel that it gives the whole family a connection to the Jewish community. These parents do not necessarily provide any religious education in the home. Some feel their own knowledge is inadequate for them to cast themselves in the role of teacher; others lack a sufficiently deep commitment to Jewish education to bother bringing it into the home; and still others, I suspect, feel that because they had to "put up with" Sunday school when they were children, their children should now have to do the same. Whatever feelings parents have about religious education, it is generally accepted that the synagogue should be the locus of Jewish learning and the agency responsible for transmitting it to their children.

Some people affiliate with a synagogue because they identify with other members of the congregation. They join because their friends are members or because their parents or grandparents belonged. Indeed, in stable, mid-sized communities like Kansas City, Denver, or Cincinnati there is frequently a family history which motivates affiliation. Present families can look back on three or four generations of membership in the congregation—reason enough to make a commitment to the temple.

A fourth reason people join a congregation is for access to the synagogue on the high holy days, Rosh Hashanah and Yom Kippur. Virtually every Jew, whether affiliated or not (including, perhaps, even some of the hard core unaffiliated), wants to come to services for these holy days. They may not necessarily want to have access to God, but they do want to be with the community and, for whatever reasons (guilt, family or personal tradition, fear of negative consequences for not attending, spiritual longing, and so forth), seem drawn to the synagogue at this point in the Jewish calendar. If every Jew who wanted access to the synagogue were allowed in without any regulation, there would not be sufficient seats for the people who pay their dues, the bona fide members who have been responsible for the upkeep of the institution. As a result, most synagogues issue tickets to manage the extraordinary number who would come to worship services on these days. Tickets, which are either included in the annual dues or charged for separately, are a commodity in high demand, a benefit of membership.

Another motivational factor is a sense of responsibility that some feel to maintain Jewish life and to assure that it not go out of existence. Survival, a topic of continual discussion in the Jewish community, is a very real concern for the Jewish people. As a result of assimilation, intermarriage, and low birth rates, the Jewish community is diminishing in terms of absolute numbers and percentage. Jews today comprise less than 2.5% of the population of the United States, and as the country grows, this percentage is likely to become even smaller. Worldwide there are only 13 million Jews. Small and declining numbers highlight the need for Jewish continuity. Some Jews respond to the question of survival by joining a synagogue to show their solidarity with Jewish people everywhere and to demonstrate their desire to help the community survive.

A final consideration is the unique motivation of converts to Judaism, Jews by choice. Some converts have come to Judaism through a personal search for a faith tradition they find meaningful and fulfilling. Most, however, were introduced to Judaism through their partnership or marriage to a Jewish person. In many cases, these individuals were raised with the notion that the church is the place where one's religious identity is nurtured. After conversion to Judaism, they join the synagogue because they assume that being part of a faith community means membership in a congregation.

The congregation is thus comprised of individuals and families who come to the religious institution out of diverse motivations. Members include Jews by birth and Jews by choice. Their relationship to the institution ranges from marginal affiliation to deep commitment to the principles and values which the synagogue represents.

REASONS FOR DROPPING OUT

The motivations of those who disaffiliate are equally complex. Dropping out is a widespread phenomenon in synagogues across the country; at least a third of those who have ever been synagogue members at some time drop their membership (Tobin, Milder, Sternberg, & Seltzer, 1989). When asked in community surveys why they are not a member of a synagogue, respondents most often say that belonging to a temple or synagogue is not very important to them. This explanation usually includes such responses as "I do not have the time," "I'm not a religious or observant Jew," or "It's not important in my everyday life." Such reasons are particularly common among those who have never belonged.

Other reasons given by those who have dropped out or never affiliated are, in descending order of frequency of mention (Tobin, Milder, Sternberg, & Seltzer, 1989):

- The expense. (Some consider the dues prohibitive; others do not believe that what they are purchasing justifies the cost.)
- Dissatisfaction with the synagogue. (Former members complain about the rabbi, particular programs at the synagogue, aspects of their child's Jewish education, and so on.)
- Ideology. (Those who have never affiliated express a dislike for organized religion or a preference for personal religious observance over the traditional communal form.)

Other motivations for disaffiliation are noted by clergy. Rabbis find that people most often drop out when they go through certain life transitions and life events. They leave the synagogue when positive life events (e.g., their children's weddings) have passed and there is no longer a felt need for a congregation, or when negative life events, such as a divorce or death of a loved one, drive them away from religion and/or the religious institution.

Disaffiliation is sometimes tied to a life stage. Some centers of Jewish population have shifted from the Northeast to the South or Southwest. When people (generally middle-aged couples or retirees) move to the Sunbelt, their commitment to a religious community is attenuated. The New Yorker down South says, "I belong up North," while up North he says, "Well, I go to temple down South." In that way, he avoids a financial commitment in either place.

For those who joined the synagogue primarily for the religious education of their children or for the various needs of their young family, dropping out becomes a predictable step when the family grows older. If people do not feel a personal commitment to the values of synagogue life, the institution ceases to be a priority for them once their children have left home. They remain synagogue members for their children's bar/bat mitzvah celebrations, confirmations, and weddings, but feel free to leave the congregation once these life-cycle events have passed.

Rabbis know that when people say, "I don't belong to the synagogue because I don't need it," there is often a conditional quality to the rejection. What they mean is they do not need the synagogue *now* but when they do, they want the synagogue to be there for them. The need is usually felt when a family member dies: "Rabbi, you remember me," the former member says. "I used to belong to the temple. My mother died." These people take it for granted that the temple will always be there for their needs. However, if they have no immediate needs, they discontinue their support.

Disaffiliation can also be motivated by negative emotions. Some drop out of the synagogue because life has dealt them a cruel blow—the death of a loved one, a serious illness, a business failure, and so on. Faced with such a tragedy, a person might ask, "How come I'm such a good person and such terrible things have happened to me?" Unlike Job, some who face this question lose what little faith they might have had and displace frustration with their life circumstances onto the synagogue. Their rationale is quid pro quo: "Since the synagogue has not done anything for me lately, I do not have to do anything for it and I can drop my membership. If God has not done anything for me lately, I am also free to reject God."

It is not unusual for individuals to disaffiliate when the expectations they had of the congregation are not met (see Chapter 2). I recently received a letter from a long-time member of the congregation who is now on the verge of dropping out. She complains that the synagogue does not meet her spiritual needs. She does not want to hear about social action on the high holidays (although "repairing the world" is a central tenet in the religion), and she does not want to hear about international politics (although support of Israel is a fundamental commitment in Judaism). Because she comes to services only on Rosh Hashanah and Yom Kippur, she deems it essential that the spirituality of those days transcend the other fifty weeks of the year. When she does not get what she has come for, she blames the synagogue: the synagogue has become too large, she complains; it has lost its intimacy. Clergy find a certain sadness in such stories. We cannot meet every person's needs, and yet we are reluctant to admit failures in our attempts to serve our congregants.

Sometimes the disaffiliation is accompanied by intense anger and frustration. Perhaps the expression of such emotions is directed to the synagogue because it is seen as a safe place in which to express anger, or because clergy are supposed to be compassionate and understanding figures who will not retaliate in anger. Regardless, clergy can well testify to the commonality of the phenomenon, of a group of people who leave the synagogue out of anger and frustration.

Finally, there are those who leave the synagogue because they do not "know the ropes." They are not schooled in Hebrew, they do not know the liturgy, and they lack familiarity and comfort with the rituals of Jewish prayer. They feel inadequate in the synagogue, embarrassed or frustrated by their own lack of knowledge. Rather than confront their inadequacy and take remedial action on their lack of Jewish education, they withdraw from the synagogue and drop out.

INTERMARRIAGE AND SYNAGOGUE AFFILIATION

The 1990 National Jewish Population Survey issued a "wake up" call to the Jewish community: its findings reveal that 52% of young Jews are marrying non-Jews who do not convert to Judaism. As a result, two-thirds of all new households formed by Jews are mixed-married households, and few of these appear to be raising their children as Jews. If this trend continues, the Jewish community faces the possibility that most of its children will live in other faiths or with no faith at all.

Research indicates that mixed-married families are significantly less likely to affiliate with a synagogue than are in-married or conversionary married families. A recent study of eight Jewish communities in the United States found that 60% of in-married families and 56% of conversionary married families belong to synagogues, but only 15% of mixed-marriage families do (Medding, Tobin, Fishman, & Rimor, 1992).

Not surprisingly, mixed-married families were also shown to be lower on a host of measures related to Jewish observance and practices. They are significantly less likely to attend religious services regularly (over half *never* attend), to participate in Passover seders, to fast on Yom Kippur, or to light Sabbath candles. They are also less likely to hold membership in other Jewish organizations, to visit Israel, or to contribute to Jewish philanthropies.

The likelihood that the children of mixed-married families will become members of a religious community depends in large measure on the religious identification of the family. Two points are of relevance to outreach:

1. Most mixed-married families provide no Jewish education for their children (but virtually all in-married Jewish families do).
2. Mixed-married households can resolve religious identity in one of several ways. They can be unambiguously Jewish or Christian; they can take on a secular identity (one that is religiously and ethnically neutral); or they can be dual-identity households (in which both Jewish and Christian symbols and identification are maintained side by side). Almost two-thirds of mixed-marriage households (62%) are dual-identity households. The percentage is even greater among Reform Jews, particularly among those under age 45 (Medding, Tobin, Fishman, & Rimor, 1992).

It should be noted that denominational identification has a significant influence on these overall results. The Jewish partners in mixed-marriages who identify with a denomination are more likely than those who consider themselves "just Jewish" to affiliate with a synagogue (Tobin, Milder, Sternberg, & Seltzer, 1989), and they are much more likely to provide Jewish education to their children (Medding, Tobin, Fishman, & Rimor, 1992).

Rather than respond to these demographic studies with depression or outrage, many of us in the liberal community believe the research points us to where opportunity lies. Mixed-married families with children are the fastest-growing household type; they represent large and growing numbers of families in the community. These families may not be affiliated with any religious institution because they have not resolved the personal and family issues which attend interfaith marriages. They may feel marginal to both religious groups and unable to commit to either. Under these circumstances, outreach can provide an important service to this segment of the community's population. At the same time, it increases the possibility that the families will affiliate religiously. Our synagogue has, therefore, targeted the mixed-married population as an important group for outreach programming.

OUTREACH TO MIXED-MARRIED FAMILIES

Outreach to interfaith couples, as to other populations, is most often understood as an attempt to encourage greater Jewish involvement by making Jewish life more accessible (Wasserman, 1990). In recent years, both the Reform and Conservative movements have made efforts to facilitate the conversion of Gentile spouses married to Jews and, short of that, to help interfaith couples raise their children as Jews. Admittedly, outreach to interfaith families is a highly controversial topic in the American Jewish community. Nonetheless, the Reform movement has chosen to reach out to interfaith couples—to those who wish to become members of our congregations as well as to those who are not yet ready to make a commitment to Judaism.

To the latter group, those not yet ready for religious involvement, we offer help in making fundamental decisions about religion in their lives. We believe these uncommitted, often confused families merit our time and resources because their ability to resolve basic issues related to religious identity is a necessary (albeit insufficient) precondition for their taking the next steps, embracing the religion, and affiliating with the synagogue.

"Stepping Stones—To a Jewish ME"

"Stepping Stones—To a Jewish ME" is a program designed to provide knowledge of the basic elements of Jewish life, traditions, and history to children of interfaith families and their unaffiliated parents. Studies conducted by Egon Mayer (1979, 1990) suggest that it is the assimilation of Jews into mainstream American society that causes intermarriage (rather than intermarriage being the source of assimilation). Mayer argues that: those who have a weakly grounded Jewish identity are more likely to intermarry than are those who have deep roots in Judaism; given their own weak Jewish background, they are less able to create a Jewish home, and the interfaith family they have formed is thus less able to transmit Jewish identity to the children. Our program thus focuses primarily on the children, but includes educational support for the parents as well.

The program is described in detail elsewhere (Heller, 1990). Presented here is a summary of the program's goals, its criteria for participation, the methods used to publicize it, its content, and the results which demonstrate the effectiveness of the program in reaching out to the unaffiliated.

Goals of the Program. The program encourages and supports all children and parents who would like to know more about Judaism. Its goals are to strengthen Jewish identity, to foster a sense of acceptance in the Jewish community, and ultimately to increase rates of affiliation among the intermarried. Unlike standard educational programs in the synagogue, Stepping Stones does not assume that its clients are Jewish. Rather, its major goal is to create that awareness and develop a desire for involvement in Jewish life.

Criteria for Participation. In order to take part in the Stepping Stones program, a family has to meet the following criteria: (1) one partner in the marriage must be Jewish and the other not; (2) the family must not have a Jewish or Christian congregational affiliation; and (3) it must have an explicitly expressed interest in Judaism. Both parents have to be willing for their children to come to the program, and they have to agree not to send the children to church on Sunday morning and to Stepping Stones that same afternoon. Such dual practices are proscribed as a source of confusion and weakness in the children's religious identity (Bayme, 1990) and an obstacle to the program's attempts to strengthen Jewish identity.

Publicity Campaign. The first challenge in implementing the Stepping Stones program was to reach unaffiliated interfaith families who, by their very nature, did not have their own organization, were not on any Jewish agency mailing lists, and rarely read the Jewish press. The publicity campaign had several thrusts, but the most successful was a high-quality brochure describing the program. This was sent to individuals on the Jewish Federation [the central fund-raising organization] mailing list, who were instructed to read the folder and pass it on to an interfaith family. The networking proved highly effective: a large number of interfaith families were reached; at the same time, the general Jewish community was made more aware of and informed about the interfaith population.

Program Content. The content of the Stepping Stones program includes educational units on the Jewish holidays, the synagogue (synagogue symbols, the Torah, services, and prayers), the Jewish home, Shabbat, the life cycle in Judaism, and the state of Israel. In addition to providing classroom and experiential activities, the program gives participants several books on Jewish themes in order to prime them to begin building a Jewish library at home. Family programs which coincide with classroom activities bring parents, siblings, and grandparents together with the children for holiday celebrations, special worship services, and Jewish cultural events.

Beyond imparting knowledge, the curriculum encourages the children to share their feelings and interests, and it nurtures the formation of a social connection to peers and to the synagogue. The design of the sessions incorporates an opportunity for the young participants to examine their own identities more closely, to talk about themselves, to develop deeper relationships with their classmates, to learn from and support one another, and thereby to feel part of their own small community within the synagogue.

During the first sharing time, a teacher may ask, "How many children have a Jewish parent?" All the children raise their hands in response. She then asks, "How many have a Christian or non-Jewish parent?" Again, all the children raise their hands. Invariably, they look around in amazement, excited to find themselves in a room—indeed in an entire school—full of others like themselves.

Given the program's emphasis not only on the cognitive aspects (acquiring knowledge about Judaism) but also on the affective and social elements of the children's development, it is important for the instructors to be proficient as Jewish educators and also to be attuned to their own attitudes about interfaith families. In preparing each unit, the teachers, individually and together in faculty meetings, consider the content of the material at the same time they carefully examine their own biases and beliefs.

Ultimately the aim of each teacher is to create a classroom atmosphere that will achieve the following:

- encourage the children to take risks in answering questions and sharing ideas
- promote the acceptance of differences and the unique value of each person
- teach critical thinking and problem-solving skills
- help clarify values through structured exercises and discussion
- provide opportunities for students to share their concerns, commonalities, and differences
- provide opportunities for children to have fun together, to enjoy each other, and to build a sense of community (Heller, 1990)

Although the children were initially conceived of as the clients of Stepping Stones, it soon became evident that family dynamics had a critical influence on the children's learning and development. Parental involvement was clearly essential to Stepping Stones' success, so, in the second year of the program, a parent track was initiated. Each week, different rabbis present information on basic Judaism; they also describe the branch of Judaism they represent and the activities offered by their congregation. An information table set up at these sessions has descriptions of programs and events in the Jewish community which might appeal to parents and help to draw them into participation in Jewish life. Parents are also given the opportunity to participate in interfaith support groups. These groups, which meet weekly for eight sessions, provide a valuable forum for examining issues of religious identity and working toward heightened self-awareness and improved communication about these issues.

Results. Each year approximately sixty children enroll in Stepping Stones, and thirty or forty parents take advantage of the parent track. After the program had been in operation for five years, about 50% of the participating families had either joined congregations, were attending Jewish schools, or had entered the Jewish community actively in some way.

A formal evaluation of Stepping Stones[2] found that most people are quite positive about their experience in the program and that, given participants' needs, the program obviously fills an important gap in services. Stepping Stones is seen to affect people's lives by promoting family unity and strength, personal celebrations, a sense of tradition, a Jewish experience, a sense of community, and friendships with other interfaith families. Participants also report that the program provided support to children, acquainted them with Judaism, broadened their understanding of their Jewish heritage, and perhaps most importantly, encouraged parents and children to enter into the Jewish community.

The program had a marked influence on families' accepting a Jewish lifestyle. Some 74% felt that change occurred in their families as a result of Stepping Stones. A majority (67%) of the participants chose to continue their Jewish education, and many (48%) increased observance of the Jewish holidays as a result of the program.

In terms of identity, a majority of the children (72%) reported a better sense of religious identification after having gone through the program. Through teaching children Hebrew words and Jewish symbols, concepts, and prayers, Stepping Stones helped them become familiar with and comfortable in a congregational setting.

The program provides opportunities for families to make informed decisions about their religious future. Often new meaning in Judaism is found by the Jewish parent, and the non-Jewish parent is given information about and experiences with the religion. Notably, about 40% of the Stepping Stones families have subsequently joined a temple or synagogue.

Individual case histories provide further testimony to the positive effects of the program. One former Stepping Stones family tells how they have transformed their household into a Jewish home, observing Shabbat and enjoying Judaism together. Another talks about their son who has clarified his identity and now proudly recognizes himself as Jewish. A third reports that their daughter, who has gone off to college, has sought out an active involvement in Jewish groups on campus and continued Jewish learning. We plan our outreach programs for a generally defined target audience, but the effect of our work is etched on the lives of individuals.

CONCLUSION

The Jewish community has traditionally been a closed community with limited outreach. The increase in mixed marriages has precipitated the need for programs such as Stepping Stones which open the door to interfaith families. Indeed, hundreds of thousands of children who would be defined as Jews by Jewish law are today living in households in which only one parent is Jewish (Kosmin, 1990). These children and their families represent a vital opportunity for synagogues if they can but design and implement effective outreach programs. These programs need to incorporate a dual mission—the transmission of basic knowledge about Judaism and the formation of a clear religious identity. Mixed-married families that are reached by these programs are more likely to affiliate with a congregation and to become seriously involved in the religious community.

Extrapolating from our experience with Stepping Stones, we would suggest the following general principles to guide outreach programming.

1. *Target the outreach program to a distinct, carefully defined population.* While it is possible to direct outreach efforts toward specific individuals, it is quite costly to seek out potential members one by one, particularly in light of the possible payoff to the congregation. Our congregation, for example, has established a variety of outreach programs, each geared toward a specific group in the community: Mixed-married families, Jewish singles, unaffiliated young adults, and so on.

2. *Understand the motivations of the target group—what would attract them to the congregation and what would serve to alienate them further or hinder them from joining.* If we understand the motivations of affiliation—the negative ones (lack of comfort in the synagogue, no felt need for the institution, and so on.) and the positive ones (identification with the Jewish people and concern for their survival, life-cycle events, the desire for Jewish education for one's children, and so on)—we can begin to see the linkage between outreach and affiliation. Outreach through such programs as Stepping Stones helps to strengthen identity, increase comfort in the synagogue environment, and build toward commitment. After these have taken place, affiliation often follows.

3. *Develop structures and programs that literally reach the target group.* Our first challenge in implementing Stepping Stones was to figure out how to market to a population which had no group organization and whose individual members had weak or nonexistent ties to the Jewish community. Networking (the snowball approach) was most successful. Beyond publicity, there exists the need to create a quality program which touches on the specific needs, interests, and motivations of the target group.

4. *Staff need to be not only professional and well trained in their particular area of expertise (e.g., Jewish education), but also to be sensitive to the special issues presented by the target group.* Audiences for outreach differ in important ways from the population to which synagogue professionals are most accustomed. As noted above, for example, Jewish education is largely based on the premise that the students who come to us have some commitment to the religion and an unambiguous identity as Jews. In contrast, the outreach

program for the children of interfaith families brought in individuals who were presumably coming for education but who fundamentally needed to resolve complex and troubling identity issues. Unless faculty were aware of these issues and had the skills and tools for dealing with them, the educational program would have had little impact on the students.

5. *The congregation needs to be willing to make an investment in outreach programs or to generate resources for supporting such programs.* Stepping Stones was offered free to participants. Although we received outside funding to help defray the costs of the program, the program was not fee supported. The congregation has to undertake such outreach programming on good faith. If it does not, it will never reap the benefits that outreach can produce. Indeed, for this particular program we found that the increased affiliation which eventually resulted more than offset program costs.

6. *We need to accept whatever outcomes result from our outreach efforts.* In the case of Stepping Stones, we could not ask program participants for a quid pro quo—a commitment to conversion, synagogue affiliation, or a Jewish upbringing for their children—as a condition for entering the program. As Rabbi Michael Wasserman (1990) wisely points out, we ought not judge the success of our programs on such outcomes, for then we make ourselves overly dependent on the personal decisions these families will make. Assessment of our efforts needs to based on a broader sense of what an outreach program can accomplish. We need to accept and be satisfied with a variety of outcomes—participants' greater knowledge about our faith tradition, increased goodwill toward Judaism, a clearer sense of self, or a more harmonious family life, to name a few. Casting our outreach programs in this way, as a service to the unaffiliated, does not preclude our constant hope that those we reach will choose to join us and become active members of our congregation.

NOTES

1. The National Jewish Population Survey (NJPS) was conducted by the Council of Jewish Federations and the North American Jewish Data Bank. The study is based on a sample of 2,441 interviews conducted during 1990, after a year-long process of screening over 125,000 randomly selected adult Americans. The NJPS is currently the main source of sociological analysis of American Jewry. Results of the study can be found in Goldstein, S. (1992). Profile of American Jewry: Insights from the 1990 National Jewish Population Survey. In D. Singer (Ed.), *American Jewish Year Book* (vol. 92, pp. 77–177). NY: The American Jewish Committee and the Jewish Publication Society.

2. The evaluation was conducted in 1991 by the Graduate School of Social Work at the University of Denver and supported by a grant from the Nathan Cummings Foundation. It was based on questionnaires sent to both parents and children, focus groups, and case studies.

REFERENCES

Bayme, S. (1990). Changing Perceptions of Intermarriage. *Journal of Jewish Communal Service, 66* (3), 212–223.

Goldstein, S. (1992). Profile of American Jewry: Insights from the 1990 National Jewish Population Survey. In D. Singer (Ed.). *American Jewish Year Book* (vol. 92, pp. 77–173). NY: The American Jewish Committee and the Jewish Publication Society.

Heller, S. (1990). Case Study: Stepping Stones . . . to a Jewish ME. *Journal of Jewish Communal Service, 66* (3), 298–305.

Kosmin, B. (1990). The Demographic Imperative of Outreach. *Journal of Jewish Communal Service, 66* (3), 208–211.

Mayer, E. (1990). Intermarriage, Outreach and a New Agenda for Jewish Survival: A Perspective on the Contemporary American Jewish Community. *Journal of Jewish Communal Service, 66* (3), 202–207.

Mayer, E. (1979). *Intermarriage and the Jewish Future.* New York: The American Jewish Committee.

Medding, P. Y., Tobin, G. A., Fishman, S. B., & Rimor, M. (1992). *Jewish Identity in Conversionary and Mixed Marriages* (Jewish Sociology Paper No. 7). New York: The American Jewish Committee.

Tobin, G. A., & Berger, G. (1993). *Synagogue Affiliation: Implications for the 1990s* (Research Report 9). Waltham, MA: Brandeis University, Cohen Center for Modern Jewish Studies.

Tobin, G. A., Milder, L.K.E., Sternberg, L., & Seltzer, S. (1989). *Synagogue Affiliation Among Reform Jews.* Brookline, MA: Union of American Hebrew Congregations, Committee on the Jewish Family.

Wasserman, M. (1990). Outreach to Interfaith Couples: A Conceptual Approach. *Journal of Jewish Communal Service, 66* (3), 235–243.

CHAPTER 8

Luther Place Memorial Church: A Church as Refuge/Sanctuary

Rev. John F. Steinbruck

Luther Place Memorial Church is in the heart of Washington, D.C., not far from the White House. It stands at a major urban intersection (of Massachusetts and Vermont Avenues and 14th and N Streets) through which people of every class and background pass—a crossroads of the good, the bad, the ugly, and often the beautiful. Sometimes the church is referred to metaphorically as an "oasis in the asphalt desert of the city."

HISTORY OF LUTHER PLACE

Luther Place was founded at the close of the Civil War in memory of the fallen of the North and the South, and in celebration of freedom from slavery. Like many metropolitan churches, Luther Place for many years led a quiet existence as a racially segregated downtown congregation. Its restful history, however, began to change after World War II. With massive migrations of Southern blacks to the cities of the North, Washington became, as it is now, a predominantly African American city, with blacks comprising nearly 70% of the population. The black liberation movement, which began to take shape during the 1950s, often turned Washington into a focal point where the civil rights struggle was dramatized for all the nation to see. Deinstitutionalization of the mentally ill (without provision of adequate services and facilities for their treatment and assistance) and intractable urban poverty were swelling the population of the homeless. All the while, suburbs were developing rapidly, enticing residents from the crowded and turbulent city.

The result of these social changes was significant membership decline for Luther Place as many congregants opted for suburban security and stability. Throughout the early 1970s, the remaining worshippers agonized over the church's reason for being. Fortunately, those who had stayed in the city were at least open and tolerant and, at best, willing to reach out and embrace the new age that had erupted about them with volcanic intensity. Their attitude seemed to be one of confidence in God's future, even if that future should mean the death of the traditionally conceived congregation.

GROWTH THROUGH MINISTRY

One January during the time of this struggle, there was a bitter cold spell in Washington, D.C., and people on the streets began to die from the freezing cold. Every day the *Washington Post* carried a story of somebody found in an abandoned car or an abandoned house or wrapped in cardboard under a bridge or under the Whitehurst Freeway. An emergency meeting was called at Luther Place Church. Three groups from the radical edges of the Christian spectrum responded: Community for Creative Non-Violence (a group derived from the Pax Christi and Dorothy Day Catholic Worker movement), The Sojourners Community (an evangelical group from Chicago with deep concern for civil and human rights), and Luther Place. As a result of the meeting, letters were sent to every congregation of every persuasion around the Washington Beltway, inviting them to participate in a response to this highly visible, immediate crisis of homelessness. To the 1,300 letters that were sent out, we received not one reply.

At that point, I appealed to the church council of Luther Place, the congregation's leaders, to open the doors of the church to the homeless. The lay leaders of Luther Place are admirable: they are able to take risks and to imagine alternatives to normal operating procedures for a religious institution. Such leadership is a critical resource for congregations in the inner city. They asked the usual questions, such as whether our insurance would cover the proposed project. Why, we answered, should it bother the insurance company whether people are in the church at eleven o'clock Saturday night or eleven o'clock Sunday morning? But once the preliminaries were dispatched with, the decision was made.

The doors of the church were opened and within hours the building was filled to capacity, wall-to-wall. People came in out of the night, taking a few square feet of floor space in the social hall and falling asleep. We kept hot tea going and served baked potatoes, about as nutritious a snack as we could offer. Luther Place was thus transformed into a hospice/refuge, in response to the need for hospitality in the hostile urban environment. It has continued to be so twenty-four hours a day, seven days a week, since the night it first opened its doors.

Out of this transformation came congregational learning and church growth. Opening the doors of our church made us look at things very differently. It made us consider what it means to try to be faithful, to be a congregation, to be a refuge, to be a place of hospitality. We have learned always to leave a space for the stranger—if not a pew then at least some room in the social hall or in the classrooms.

Once our doors were opened, the numbers began to swell. The social hall was filled. People spilled up the stairways, onto the landings, into the classrooms, and now, literally, we have had to go through the roof and have added a fourth floor for a new emergency shelter for homeless women. Twenty years ago, when we were wondering how we were going to cover the simple costs of opening the doors, no one would have believed such growth possible. The congregation, which was in fast decline and seemed to have no future whatsoever, magnanimously opened its doors to provide hospice to strangers who had no place and were in danger in the bitter cold. Miraculously, this congregation now cannot die. It has no right to think terminally, and absolutely must survive for the sake of those who need refuge. When a congregation has a reason to be, it will live.

Growth and Development of Luther Place Facilities and Services

In the end, the key to our situation was our space and its usage. Luther Place happens to be abundant in real estate—it owns a parcel of land 36,000 square feet in area. Much of the property is occupied by a block of townhouses contiguous to the church. When I came to Luther Place, the townhouses were occupied by a Chinese laundry, a McDonald's, a fortune teller, and a row of brothels. After a woman was scandalously injured in one of the houses, the church council decided to tear down all the houses at once, pay for new asphalt, and expand the parking lot. Thankfully, cooler heads prevailed: if the property could be used so basely, it was reasoned, it could also be used inspirationally.

We initiated an immediate transition and founded N Street Village, Inc., a nonprofit organization which would convert the townhouses into facilities for housing and treatment for homeless women. The full complement of services today includes:

The Women's Night Shelter, which provides shelter, dinner, and breakfast for women, many of whom are struggling with chronic physical and mental health issues

Bethany Women's Center, a community center which provides day services, including lunch, individual counseling, support groups, job counseling, literacy programs, fitness and art therapy

Harriet Tubman House and Sarah House, townhouses for women recovering from substance abuse which provide pre- and post-residential treatment programs, counseling for substance abuse, and life skills counseling (job training, employment searches, money management, and so on)

Raoul Wallenberg House, a residence for mentally ill senior citizens who are capable of living partially independent lives within a caring and supportive community

Carol Holmes House, a residence for mentally ill women capable of living independently with a minimum of supervision

Albert Schweitzer House, the Health Care for the Homeless Project Outreach Center, a center that offers medical testing and follow-up consultation to homeless women and respite (long-term) care

Anna Center, a twenty-four-hour-a-day program which provides a temporary place of rest for women who are recovering from an illness or surgery

Zacchaeus Medical Clinic, which provides free prenatal and primary health care to those unable to pay

Bread for the City, a project to collect and distribute food and clothing to those who are elderly, disabled, or have dependent children, and whose incomes are below the poverty line

Dietrich Bonhoeffer House, Emmaus House, and Dag Hamarskjold House, buildings that are leased as community houses for voluntary organizations affiliated with the church (such as the Lutheran Volunteer Corps)

In 1991, N Street Village's shelter and housing programs served more than 1,800 women, providing 30,000 nights of shelter and 100,000 meals.

The development of Luther Place and N Street Village has included as well the organization of a volunteer corps and concerted efforts in the realm of social advocacy. The Lutheran Volunteer Corps (based on the Mennonite and the Jesuit Volunteer Corps) was organized in 1979. It now recruits more than seventy full-time volunteers each year to work for social service organizations in Washington and five other cities. Over 46,000 hours of volunteer service are contributed each year. Most of the volunteers provide direct services through shelters, medical clinics, and children's programs.

At some point, it became the conviction of our congregation that we must ask the White House, Congress, and City Hall: "From whence come these homeless and why?" We are not here merely to bind up the wounded, but to advocate on their behalf. Unfortunately, we have not been all that successful in this task; homelessness remains a growth industry in our society. Still, I do not know who is going to speak out for those who are voiceless if it is not us, the interfaith community: Jews, Christians, and others committed to promoting the agenda of justice.

Our services and advocacy for the homeless essentially help me fulfill my basic role as pastor to the congregation. What is established on our block is the enactment of Matthew 25: "I was hungry and you fed me, thirsty and you gave me drink; I was a stranger and you received me in your homes, naked and you clothed me; I was sick and you took care of me, in prison and you visited me." Such actions ironically result in our own enrichment and salvation. Always as we host, the tables are turned and we are blessed.

THE MISSION OF THE CHURCH: HOSPITALITY

The call to hospitality is rooted in the Biblical stories of the Hebrew Scriptures. In the nomadic world of the Torah, people wandered with their flocks and their tribes, always in need of places in the desert where there was water and vegetation. Certain values evolved at that time, I imagine, which were critical to survival, including the absolutely bedrock moral principle that we are always to welcome and be protective of the stranger, the sojourner, the refugee in our midst.

The Biblical Teachings of Hospitality

The motif of hospitality is emphasized throughout the Bible. In Genesis 18, Abraham and Sarah, encamped at the Oaks of Mamry, see three strangers approaching. This story offers a formula for survival not just for the strangers, but for Abraham and Sarah as well. Abraham rushes to the strangers and beseeches them to come under his tent to rest and be refreshed. Abraham and Sarah wait upon the strangers and give them something to eat. The strangers then tell Abraham who they are and proceed to confirm God's promise that he is to be the father of a great nation and that his wife, Sarah, is to conceive a child. Here, as so frequently in the host-guest relationship, the roles are reversed: Abraham and Sarah become the guests, and their guests become the hosts.

In 2 Kings 4:8–37, Elisha was shown hospitality by the Shumenite woman who had a small room built for his use whenever he was passing through that area of the country. She, his hostess, was blessed with a son through the prayers of Elisha. He, her guest, became her host through his act of concern. Each was guest of the other. Hospitality, too, was implicitly commanded by God when he gave the law that harvesters were not to be too efficient in their job so as to leave some of the crop for the poor and the needy (Deut. 24:19; Lev. 19:9–10, 23:22; Ruth 2:1–3).

The Christian Story

Hospitality is best exemplified in the life of Jesus, who was both the supreme host *and* guest of all who came in contact with him. The Christian story begins with a family forced to go to Bethlehem to meet the requirements of the oppressive Roman occupiers. Mary was about to deliver. The one thing the family needed was refuge for her. The innkeeper said, "No room at the inn, but there's a stable out there. You can use that." The child was born, and what we know in the Christian tradition was salvation not just for the innkeeper but for humankind.

The story tells us to protect the stranger, to provide refuge, to offer the homeless what they need to survive in the asphalt desert of our cities today.

Jesus' parables, stories, and teachings repeatedly emphasize the dual themes of hospitality and justice to the poor. In the Gospel of Matthew, Jesus insists that to host the hungry, the thirsty, the stranger, the prisoner, the sick, and the naked is to host Christ himself (Matt. 25:31–46). In his instructions as to who is to be hosted, Jesus says not to invite friends, relatives, or rich neighbors, for they will only ask you back again. Rather, ask the poor, the crippled, the lame, and the blind, and find happiness, not repayment. The poor have no means of repaying, but hosting them brings salvation to the giver. Indeed, hospitality and refuge bring all kinds of surprises, not the least of which is the miracle that we who presume to save the homeless are often saved by them.

HOSPICE AS EVANGELISM

You should not have to go to seminary for five years to know the appropriate Biblical/theological response to a knock on the door. But opening the door to our church was not easy. In fact, in the late 1960s and early 1970s, we worked harder at eluding the homeless on the streets than at trying to provide a place of refuge for them. I can remember checking to see who was on the other side of the door before opening it because I did not want to have to deal with all the difficulties involved in what was obviously a homeless person, a disturbed person, and in those days, a mentally ill individual. I call that time our God-wrestling period. Wrestling, although difficult and painful, is critically important for any congregation. But if you wrestle through the night, finally dawn comes and the light shows you the direction you have to go—often as not the very direction you did not want to take.

The obvious was simply to open the door, to welcome and provide for these people who were not what the congregation had hoped for—card-carrying Lutherans who were reasonably affluent, who could fill offering envelopes, make the budgets, and keep the roof repaired. Here instead were people who ostensibly had nothing to offer, the poorest of the poor, the wretched of the earth, the sick and suffering, who smelled bad and had scabies and lice. Yet they became the ones who unexpectedly gave that church the most precious gift, its own survival.

We had to relearn our whole theology from those who came to us as homeless, to begin to understand the Scriptures from the underside rather than from the top down, and to rediscover a God who is the God of the homeless. We in the Christian tradition had to make the amazing discovery (as we should have known all along) that we worship and follow a homeless messiah.

I do not know of any better way to teach the people I serve, to help them understand the Biblical word, than through this kind of immersion experience. Through the experience, we begin to see the miracles of redemption and resurrection as they happen every day on our city block. The experience brings alive the Biblical exodus and the people that Jesus encountered. The Scriptures take on a reality that could not possibly be achieved by studying them in an abstract way, by reading abstruse texts prepared by scholars and theologians who write books to each other. The situation we have created is a tremendous resource for growth and personal fulfillment, for finding one's own identity. It is amazing how many other problems pale and evaporate as individual congregants begin to concentrate on responding to people who are in crisis. It is amazing what this does for their own personal well-being.

Through our work, we have begun to fulfill our purpose as a congregation and to evangelize. The Hebrew concept for such actions is *Kiddush Hashem*—to sanctify God's name by bearing witness in body, mind, soul, and spirit to the difference that faith makes in the world. This is not a conquest-oriented expedition, like those of the television evangelists. Rather, it is enough for us simply to do our work, to provide refuge for those who do not get invited to White House banquets, those who are not the priority of our society. In the Christian tradition and in the worship of Luther Place, it is enough for us simply to expand our communion circle around the altar on Sunday mornings so that it is all-inclusive of God's people—especially those who do not have access to the abundant feast of this society.

CHAPTER 9

Bethany Baptist Church: Growth through Planning and Social Action

Dr. James A. Scott

Bethany Baptist Church, in the heart of Newark, New Jersey, has a predominantly African American membership. Today Bethany is thriving, but in 1963, the year I arrived, a mere 200 worshippers attended Easter services and far fewer participated on the average Sunday. Our congregation today numbers about 2,700 resident members, who come from the entire metropolitan area. On a typical Sunday, between 1,100 and 1,300 attend our two worship services. Bethany has grown because it engaged in a strategic planning process, seriously involved its membership in community action, and deliberately promoted discussion about critical issues affecting the community.

HISTORY OF BETHANY BAPTIST CHURCH

Bethany is the oldest black Baptist church in Newark. It originally considered itself a "silk stocking" church, a place of worship for high-class blacks. It has always had a trained pastoral leadership, and until World War II, it was a strong, vibrant church boasting some 3,000 members. The church was both successful and effective because it was connected to a "natural affinity community." Segregation forced blacks to live in the ghetto, and the church served as a *general purpose* institution, providing identity and status as well as social control and advocacy for greater opportunity.

After World War II, blacks moved from the ghetto and membership dwindled. Only the old or least economically viable persons remained in Newark. All of the churches in the ghetto—an Episcopal church, a Roman Catholic church that served blacks, and another within three blocks that served Irish—were withering on the vine.

Newark gradually was transformed into a black city. Although blacks gained political power, the city became a "sandbox," that is, its importance was as a commercial, governmental, and recreational center—not a place of residence. Shifts in concern within the African American community, from maintenance and survival to protest and advocacy for equality (as represented in civil rights efforts), diminished the importance of churches. Like the rest of Protestantism, black churches experienced decline.

In 1963, when I began my ministry, Bethany was dying. Its life centered on worship, and it had few programs beyond the worship services. Most resources were consumed in maintenance of the building or support of the pastor. We had no target population and few priorities.

PLANNING FOR NUMERICAL GROWTH

Bethany wanted to remain in the city, and the congregation was willing to accept innovation and take risks. The congregation committed to undertaking a strategic planning process. We prioritized goals and objectives, measured costs and benefits, and monitored results. We soon recognized that unexpected consequences often skew plans. If the church had not been convinced that it had a future in the city and if lay leadership had not been receptive to new ways to minister, planning would have been ineffectual.

Goal Setting

One of the first decisions the congregation made was to develop a solid membership base. We set numerical goals, and the entire congregation set about to win adherents. We understood that new members required systems for training and integration. Attitudes had to be stretched, and changes in structure and style had to be put into place. We set goals for middle-range growth, over a three- or four-year period.

Integration of New Members

It is necessary to hold newcomers long enough so that they taste the flavor of the church and experience a compatibility with others in the congregation. Instead of launching into community-oriented programs, energy and attention were devoted to integrating new members. We implemented intensive new member training, using as a model the training experience of the early Christian church. It was necessary to modify the program, as the ancients required as much as two years of preparation. Initially, we had a twelve-week program, now reduced to about six weeks. We also instituted a corollary program for longtime members, built around examining the Biblical and doctrinal purposes of the church. About three hundred members were involved in this program during the past year.

The first year of membership is critical. We developed several redundant systems to assure the integration of new members into the congregation. Each new member is assigned to a "buddy." Polaroid photographs of newcomers are posted in the narthex. Several dinners are held throughout the year so that newcomers and longtime members can meet. Worship is intentionally celebratory, and persons are encouraged to move about and meet one another at planned intervals. Newcomers are also encouraged to join one of our small groups—either clubs that service jails or homes for the aged and other agencies, or committees that assist families with AIDS, work with the emotionally disturbed, disburse scholarship awards, and so on.

We serve a region, not a neighborhood. Some members travel as much as forty miles to come to church. We have, therefore, developed numerous communication mechanisms to stay in touch with a scattered membership. A sophisticated newsletter, a detailed bulletin replete with membership news and reports on community issues, and a parish zone plan that brings people in the same geographical area together for social and spiritual, as well as supportive purposes—all knit the congregation together.

Requirements of Membership

People join Bethany because there is a great deal of activity, and programs for diverse tastes and interests are offered by the three full-time ministers. Programs are continuously reexamined, and some activities are phased out as new interests surface. Even when congregants move away, they remain loyal to the church and continue to support it financially. In fact, about 35% of our members pay their dues by mail.

The church offers much, but it also expects much. We expect members to make a commitment of time, intellectual engagement, and financial support.

Commitment of Time. When people join the church, they often protest how busy they are, and some have reminded me that the average American has only sixteen hours of leisure time a week. My response to this argument is "So what?" If you come to our church, you are expected to give time. If newcomers do not want to give time, then we do not need them. Ultimately, if the church does not demand anything of its members, it may get just that—nothing.

Many people drive long distances to get to Bethany. But they come several times a week directly from work because what happens at the church is significant, satisfying, and challenging for them. Our computer database tells a lot about our membership, and we build on this information. We found, for example, that there were over sixty public school teachers in our congregation, but they had never assembled to talk about connections between their professional values and their understanding of faith. Now there is an annual retreat for teachers, and we refuse to accept notions such as "burnout." Lawyers are enlisted to help the poor obtain better housing. Financial planners give talks about saving and budgets, how to buy a starter home, and how people with limited means can pool resources to invest.

Requirement to Give of One's Intellect. We start from the premise that every person, regardless of class or training, has skills or insights to offer others. We celebrate intellect, while not depreciating faith. We discuss issues, approach black ideology critically and analytically, prepare members for political involvement, offer lectures dealing with world affairs, and talk about art and music. We intentionally appeal to creative persons, who often use art or music to celebrate their alienation from the church.

Controversy is encouraged in our church. We do not take a monolithic stand on issues. Whether discussing abortion, affirmative action, or the United Nations, members strongly contest one another. We do not invite politicians to speak Sunday mornings because that is a time for worship, but we have planned discussions and invited outstanding speakers to share their views about South Africa, Eastern Europe, relations with Cuba (we financially support a "sister" church in Cuba), and feminism. Mayors, senators, welfare rights advocates, and tenant rights advocates come and share. No pastor or board member plays the role of authority figure; congregants are urged to make up their own minds about these challenging issues.

Requirement of Financial Commitment. Bethany needs a lot of money to support itself—more than a million dollars each year. We decided to stop wasting energy on fashion shows, rummage sales, baby contests, and other fund-raisers and instead emphasize tithing. Tithing depends on people understanding the purposes of the church and willingly sharing in its concern for building community. Members are encouraged to give according to their means. No one is turned away because he or she cannot give. In order to serve a community, a local church must have financial resources. In the early 1980s, we set a financial goal for an endowment fund that would secure the church for our children's children. We had hoped to raise the money in thirty years, but reached our goal within ten years.

We take a low-key approach to soliciting. About 20% of the membership is poor and lives in public or subsidized housing; 10% are blue-collar working class; perhaps 30% fall in the middle class; and some 40% are affluent suburbanites. It is the position of the church that the affluent are responsible for doing more than paying their own way. They are expected to contribute at a level that will enable Bethany to offer programs that serve both its constituents and the wider community.

SOCIAL ACTION AS CHURCH MISSION

If our local parish was to grow and influence the city, action structured into forms of mission would have to thrive and dominate, replacing worship as the focus of concern. By no means did this mean that worship was denigrated—worship in African American churches tends to excite—but worship became preparation for action. The church existed to do something, to engage in redemptive acts, not simply to be something or report about events that had already happened.

During the 1960s, black churches were struggling to establish claims to relevance. Challenge was frontal and ideological. Often it stemmed from nationalistic organizations which claimed to be more able than the church to deal effectively with racism and social injustice. Children of many of our church members were attracted to these groups. When they joined a civil rights organization, they saw this not simply as a substitute for religious activity, but the equivalent, and in some cases a superior kind of affiliation.

Across the street from our church, CORE (Congress on Racial Equality) rented a storefront. Soon as many as 175 to 200 young adults were attending CORE meetings. At best, we attracted no more than 20 young people to any activities at the church. One evening, I took the board, the lay leaders, for a walk across the street. They looked at the young people there and asked, "What's wrong with us?" As they struggled to define and answer that question, they began to see the direction in which the church needed to move.

Issues Tackled

We could not attack all the important issues affecting our community, so we selected a few and stayed with them. We did not expect to solve complex, deep-seated problems overnight. Although there have obviously been many foci to our mission during the past thirty years, I will discuss only three—redlining, advocacy, and community ministry.

Redlining. Unfair real estate and lending practices were strangling our community. To tackle these, we did not need bankers sitting in the choir. Rather, members who were bankers were able to help us by divulging financial institution secrets, and real estate brokers helped by sharing experiences (while admitting complicity). Knowledge about savings patterns, as well as the intricacies of obtaining mortgages, and state and federal roles in regulatory activities, could only be obtained from "insiders." Congregants from the investment world, real estate brokers, and regulators joined together to help the church change what all agreed was an unfair system.

Rather than picket or boycott, we developed a strategy that would demonstrate power. The church bought stock in one bank and dropped the word to a major stockbroker that a group of churches was interested in buying bank stocks and wanted first shot as any shares became available. We sat back and waited. Within a few days, a group of clergy was invited to discuss community reinvestment. With minimum effort on our part, the banks turned away from redlining. They sought advice for membership on reinvestment committees, and several set up advisory boards for community input.

Advocacy. Our congregation uses two distinctive strategies for advocacy: direct and indirect. Direct advocacy is the intentional and ongoing alignment of church members with the interests and activities of a group. Strangely, direct advocacy means church members will play a supporting role and stand behind community persons who are major actors and spokespersons. Indirect advocacy tilts policy and program toward a group and prepares church members to become participants on boards or exercise authority as bureaucrats to foster desired change.

We have tackled black racism (while acknowledging the pervasive influence of white racism). We have penetrated a number of community organizations, shared with them the church's perspective, and encouraged them to speak firmly and plainly about black racism. There was considerable danger in this enterprise because many self-help programs were fueled by black racism. We wanted to be certain that decisions were guided by a citywide perspective (not just that of our neighborhood) and an inclusive portrait of needs (not just one based on African American claims).

We have also tackled public education in Newark, which was mired in politics and patronage. A poor city with an eroding tax base and shrinking revenues could offer few patronage jobs. The largest number were found in schools. We have done substantial research, but have made little progress in overhauling schools. A coalition of churches managed to elect school board members, but the idealism of these candidates was no match for the cronyism and political hardball of others on the board. Despite failure, the congregation continues to engage in dialogue and plan for educational change. Our latest move involves launching a major capital funds drive to build our own school. We have not abandoned public school reform, but know dependence on a single approach will be fatal.

Community Ministry. Bethany is committed to giving away at least 10% of its revenues. The church also urges members to give at least a tenth of their time to community service.

Two broad principles guide community service. The first is that the church cannot and should not control all of the services or activities it is involved in or supports. We work with a homeless program, the largest in the city, that is sponsored by a Pentecostal church. Our service is limited to providing exit counseling for those about to enter the job market. Ecumenism is based on need and opportunity, not on doctrinal consensus or payoffs for church growth. The second principle is that the church cannot do everything and often cannot change public or organizational policy. In most instances, we can only empower recipients of our services to press for change from the outside or infiltrate the agencies they deal with and work for change from the inside.

Community is broadly interpreted. One member, a retired social worker, journeyed to Kenya and in a remote village, with assistance from the church, started a school, taught residents how to govern themselves, and persuaded the elders to make room for women in governance. Another member, a professional photographer, volunteered to use her skills as a photojournalist among a neglected group in Central America.

After surveying how to relate to the burgeoning problem of AIDS in our city, the church decided to train a corps of members who would go to persons and families facing this affliction and not only minister to them where they were, but also invite them to share with us in worship and community service. Our food and clothing closet closes a gap between what is needed in the community and what is provided by social welfare agencies, and we provide essential services on an emergency basis upon recommendation by an accredited agency. We serve almost five thousand persons annually. It is important to bring those whom we serve close and not conduct long distance ministry. Each day, seniors meet for arts and crafts, lectures, health examinations, occasional trips, sports, and lunch. We reach out to two disintegrating public housing communities and offer after-school tutorials, recreation, scouting, and enrichment programs for children, GED (General Equivalency Diploma) classes for adults, and classes in parenting.

CHALLENGES TO CHURCH GROWTH THROUGH PLANNING, PROGRAMMING, AND SOCIAL ACTION

Planning itself may deceive a church into thinking that it is doing something to change the context in which ministry is conducted. We began hoping that planning conducted in a democratic mode would involve congregants and continually ask, "Why is this church in business?"

Planning is contextual to the extent that action flows from the congregation's concept of mission and purpose. There is a constant interplay of what the congregation sees in the world, the effect this has on persons and groups, and the determination of appropriate actions. We are not totally altruistic, but are candid about why we adopt a strategy and recognize that not all actions will provide payoffs for our church.

Bethany Church has grown as a result of its involvement in social action in the community. Its approach is neither paternalistic nor self-serving, and there are many who criticize its refusal to identify fully with any ideological position or group. There is an unsettled condition within the congregation, and there are serious challenges to future development.

1. *The church's successes lock it into demand for more success-oriented programs.* Members have not accepted failure, and tolerance for risk decreases as successes increase. Institutional attitudes and expectations are often

impervious to ideals, the planning process, or critical examination of purpose.

2. *The church's programming needs to be diversified so that it reaches and provides meaningful engagement for all groups in the congregation.* There is an unending struggle to allocate resources and balance programs so that all age groups and genders are served. For example, because we have nineteen non-American groups in our church, programs must be broader than those that satisfy African Americans alone. Many graduate students attend our church, but we have no programs explicitly for them. Demand by members for programs outstrips our capability to provide.

3. *There are enormous financial costs when a church engages in social action and community ministry.* Our church is open daily from 7:30 A.M. until 10:00 P.M. and incurs staggering utility bills. The cost of community programs escalates and creates guilt that we are not doing more. Administering diverse programs is very time-consuming.

4. *Church programming cannot be self-referencing and must be tuned to real issues and needs.* Some members feel we neglect their personal and spiritual needs because of our outward perspective. We address many personal needs, but mainly to prepare members to share with others. When we deal with grief or divorce, for instance, it is to enable our members to provide support for others.

5. *A church that involves itself in community action has to deal with public conflict as it interacts with other agencies.* No agency is immune from criticism. Bethany church has fought with the political establishment, chamber of commerce, social workers, and housing agencies. It is never comfortable to be reviled, but we are learning to face the consequences of speaking out for our values.

6. *We need to continue to hammer away at racism in American society.* Bethany Church has tried to establish relationships with white churches in the community. Whites tend to know little about African Americans; in fact, it was disconcerting to us to learn that many white people have never spent an evening or a weekend in the home of a black person. We have tried, with mixed results, to break down the walls of separation. Our community is undergoing gentrification, and whites, Asian Americans, and Hispanics are moving in. We have been more successful in encouraging Asian Americans and Hispanics to visit and become members (although still only a trickle have joined with us) than whites. Many members do not want to open "their" church to others, so we must continue to combat racism both within and outside the walls of the church.

CHAPTER 10

Congregation B'nai Jeshurun: The Power of a Relevant Message

Rabbi Marshall T. Meyer

B'nai Jeshurun was the first Ashkenazic synagogue established in New York City and the third Conservative synagogue in the United States. It was founded in 1825 when a group of Ashkenazic Jews broke away from the Sephardic congregation of Shearith Israel, until then the only place of Jewish worship in New York City. The new congregation was housed in a series of buildings before it built, during World War I, a magnificent synagogue on its present site on West 88th Street on the Upper West Side of Manhattan.

In the early 1980s, this once-prestigious synagogue was in decline. The building was in shambles, and the congregation on the verge of extinction. There was no heat in the synagogue. Rooms were piled high with trash and broken furniture. The roof leaked and the vestry was flooded. The congregation, in bankruptcy, had sold one of its buildings. Only eight paying members remained, not even enough for a *minyan* (the 10 Jews required for prayer) without counting the rabbi and his wife.

In 1959, my own life took me to Argentina, where, for twenty-six years, I worked within the Jewish community of Buenos Aires. I founded a synagogue, Bet El, which grew from a handful of members who met in a private home to an institution with more than a thousand families and its own school system and summer camp. In 1984, the board of trustees of B'nai Jeshurun, hopeful the same congregational growth might be possible in New York, invited me to assume their vacant pulpit.

I was attracted to B'nai Jeshurun in part because there was not anyone or anything to fight against and, literally, the only way to go was up. There was no need for politicking because there were virtually no members of the congregation. There was a board, but it presided over virtually nothing. When I assumed the rabbinate in September 1985, there was no office and no telephone. I had a bridge table, a folding chair, and a public pay phone in the hallway downstairs in what once was the community center of the congregation.

Today B'nai Jeshurun has 3,200 congregants—over 1,000 member units (both families and singles). Some 600 to 700 worshipers attend Friday night services, and 250 to 300 come for Saturday morning services. The annual budget has increased from $100,000 to over $1 million. This growth was achieved by sending forth a message which appealed to a large number of unaffiliated Jews.

ATTRACTING A TARGET POPULATION

When we began our work in the mid-1980s, we faced an establishment Jewish community which had moved to the right. To many Jews, the Orthodox stream seemed unable to deal effectively with the modern world, and a congealing, deadening process in Judaism had turned many liberals and social activists away from the synagogue. The synagogue, in large measure, had become a reactionary institution—Jewishly, politically, and economically. In contrast, at B'nai Jeshurun we proposed that taking Judaism seriously required having a *relevant message*—a community to which people could relate seriously, a liturgical experience relevant to their feelings and lives, and social action which provided a meaningful response to the world in which they lived.

Our message attracted a population distanced by previous congregational experiences and by the current social, political, and religious climate in the Jewish community. Many had never been in a synagogue or had left twenty to thirty years ago vowing never to return. Our message spoke to those repelled by congregations in which one's wealth and social status were of utmost importance, to those who disagreed with rightist politics in Israel and similar policies of much of the American Jewish establishment, and to those who rejected the positions of the right-wing Orthodox and their almost exclusive concern with ritual law at the expense of dealing, Jewishly, with the existential exigencies of contemporary society. Intellectual Jews, liberals and social activists, were attracted to B'nai Jeshurun. We did not attract the very wealthy because there is no social status in being a member here. Rather we have a highly volatile group of people, passionately interested and mostly creative—writers, artists, scholars, university professors, and people in creative endeavors in business. Our membership is young (on average, members are around 40 years of age) and highly educated (most have advanced degrees). The majority share liberal views and find within our synagogue an outlet for their social-political leanings, although there are many who come for the rich liturgical experience they find regardless of all politics.

The following sections detail the ways in which we have developed a religious institution relevant and meaningful to the lives of our congregants.

BUILDING COMMUNITY

We do not talk about "building a congregation" at B'nai Jeshurun; rather our work is *building community*. I have heard it said that it is not possible to build a community of New Yorkers, a people who cherish anonymity. That, however, is simply not true. In my experience, New York can be a lonely, cold city, and many of its citizens want to reach out to others. We have seen many lives changed in the synagogue because people have engaged other human beings, because they have enlarged their support group, because they have responded emotionally to a service in which people dying with AIDS were called to the Torah. When people desire to belong to a real community—one that cares, one that allows them to cry in a service, laugh, sing, dance, or sit quietly and meditate—a spiritual electricity is generated which energizes the rabbi and the entire congregation.

Inclusion of All

In building community, we have striven to be an inclusive body. We have no fixed membership dues, but rather have established a system in which dues are determined according to self-declared income. We do not have tickets for the high holidays. Our doors are open and there is no charge. Should our congregation grow so large that tickets become necessary, we will still manage to find a place for those without tickets to join us in prayer. (N.B. An open door policy is highly unusual in the Jewish community. Given space limitations, the importance of the holidays to so many Jews [even those who do not practice their Judaism during the rest of the year], and the resulting fund-raising potential, the vast majority of synagogues admit worshippers to high holiday services only if they have a ticket. In some cases tickets are included in the annual membership dues; in other cases there is an additional assessment for high holiday seats.)

We welcome diverse groups. For example, we hold a special gay/lesbian Shabbat dinner, and we perform the *brit ahavah* (covenant of love) for homosexual couples. When the first lesbian couple engaged in this ceremony, the congregation embraced them and danced about them in a fulfilling and emotional moment of community.

Once a month, B'nai Jeshurun has a spiritual gathering of Jewish people with AIDS and their loved ones (who may be Jewish or Christian, white, black, or Asian). During Passover, the temple sponsors an AIDS seder attended by over one hundred people. The congregation provides meals which our members serve to AIDS patients in one of the local hospitals.

Reaching out to those with AIDS is a quintessentially Jewish act. We learn in the Midrash that God himself visits the sick and that God himself accompanies the dead. The imitation of God (*imitatio dei*) in Judaism is the *Kedoshim TiHyu*, "You shall be holy." Just as God is full of loving kindness, so shall you be full of loving kindness. Just as God is compassionate and full of mercy, so shall you be.

Intimacy and Egalitarian Forms

A great intimacy was struck up from the beginning. We all knew each others' names and the names of each others' spouses and children. After services on Saturday morning, worshipers were invited to the rabbi's house for *kiddush* (the blessing over the wine), something to eat and conversation. As new members joined the congregation, they were invited to a meeting at the rabbi's house where they would hear what the congregation was trying to accomplish and have the opportunity to ask questions and feel "ownership" in the congregation.

We have striven to eradicate hierarchy in the synagogue, and our membership has been highly responsive to egalitarian forms. Everyone in the congregation, including the rabbi, is addressed on a first name basis. My former student, Rolando Matalon, joined me in the synagogue when he graduated from the seminary. We have a cooperative rabbinate; there is not a "senior" and a "junior" rabbi. We changed the geography of the sanctuary. In most synagogues, there are chairs placed on the *bimah* (pulpit) where the president, cantor, and rabbi sit looking out at the congregation. We removed these chairs so that worshipers would look at the ark and the eternal light, not at the rabbi. The rabbis lead services; they do not sit or chat, and they rarely look up during prayer. It is not theater: there is no performance and there is no audience.

We did away with other formalities which interfere with intimacy and community. There is a social element in many synagogues in which a person does not fit if he or she does not have money or he or she is not dressed properly. How could seriously searching moderns identify with that type of religious expression? People come to B'nai Jeshurun in blue jeans or whatever clothing suits them. The rabbis wear *kipot* (skullcaps), but never robes (except on the high holy days). In summer, they stand on the pulpit on Shabbat without a tie or jacket.

At services, debates outnumber sermons. The rabbis do not sermonize; we hold dialogues with each other or with the congregation. Something new happens at each service. The congregation is challenged: a question is posed before the reading of the Torah and those assembled respond, or in the midst of the service, the rabbi will stop to ask "What does this prayer mean?" We discuss with the congregation the many meanings of the Torah portion. People raise their hands, and they are free to speak into one of the microphones passed around the sanctuary. And they listen to each other. We might read an article, for example "Principles and Procedures of Jewish Law" (Robert Gordis, 1979) or Abraham Joshua Heschel's *Man's Quest for God: Studies in Prayer and Symbolism* (1954). These are not easy pieces, and we spend a number of services on them, a half hour each session, five hundred to seven hundred people studying together.

The message of community is found in these simple acts—that the rabbis are called by their first names, that they do not set themselves apart with robes and chairs on the dais, that they speak spontaneously from the pulpit and hold dialogues with the congregation. In this community/congregation, everybody, in cooperative partnership, is called upon to do something. We sing together, pray together, and invite those with musical instruments to come and play for the congregation. As we approach community in this way, so do we enhance the passion and vigor of our prayers.

PASSION IN PRAYER

The liturgical drama is of overwhelming beauty in Judaism. It is destroyed, however, when we confuse pomposity with esthetics and solemnity with passion. At B'nai Jeshurun, we have created a liturgical experience that, while truthful to the traditional text, invites spontaneity, melody, and dance.

We have no formal cantor but rely on the congregation itself to make music. We have a variety of musical instruments, including an organ. Our musical director, Ari Priven, sings from the organ and only assumes the formal role of cantor on high holy days. (N.B. In many Conservative synagogues, prayers are chanted unaccompanied; the organ is often viewed as an assimilationist form imported from Christian churches.) How did we get the people to accept all the instruments? We took the *Kabbalat Shabbat* service (Welcoming the Sabbath) and went psalm by psalm to show how many instruments were mentioned. Evidently the cymbals, strings, drums, and other instruments were played in the temple—every reason to bring them into our worship services now.

Freedom of liturgy in the synagogue is a hallmark of Jewish growth. It allows for passion, for music, for dance. Indeed, we dance in our services. On Friday night, hundreds dance *L'cha dodi* just as they did in Safed in the sixteenth century.

We want and need a faith experience that spurs us to commitment, to living testimony, to passionate witness through encounter with reality. It is a necessity for us to pray. It is a joy to sing praises to God. But praying and singing are simply not enough. We must translate our prayers into action.

SOCIAL ACTION

Abraham Joshua Heschel used to say that the most tragic figure is the messenger who has forgotten his message. And so we began by asking, what is the message of our synagogue? What do we stand for? In response to this question, we challenged the congregation to accept its social responsibility. A congregation cannot pray on Shabbat and not have a position with regard to the hungry and homeless on the street. The less fortunate may be black or Latino, but they are our brothers and sisters. If the synagogue does not say anything about them or to them, how can we engage in authentic Torah? Where is the message of compassion and justice? Where is Isaiah's prophetic message: "Share your bread with the hungry. Take the homeless into your home. Clothe the naked when you see him. Do not turn away from people in need"? There are tens of thousands of homeless families in New York City. If this is not a Jewish problem, then I do not know what Judaism is all about.

Such was the message that came from the pulpit. We never preached what people wanted to hear. We never avoided difficult issues. Personally, I do not believe in a neutral Judaism, nor a gastronomic Judaism where people gather for lox and bagels. Synagogues, I find, have frequently become settings for sterile exercises in ritual, gathering places with a country club atmosphere, or arenas to enjoy culture. We proposed, instead, a Jewish liberation theology, a prophetic Judaism that informs a relevant message about how we relate to the world and to other human beings.

Establishing a Shelter

The first step we took at B'nai Jeshurun, therefore, was to establish a shelter for the homeless and to feed the hungry people in the street. We cleaned out the vestibule, previously flooded and full of trash, to create a space for people to eat and sleep. We instituted a weekly meal for the hungry. This is not a soup kitchen. At the meal, flowers grace the tables, a Barnard professor plays the piano, and members of the congregation join the people they term their "guests" for food and conversation. Other congregants sleep overnight at the shelter or come in the morning to serve breakfast.

The synagogue has always been a trifold institution—a house of gathering, of study, and of prayer. The fact that there should also be a shelter in the synagogue goes back at least to the medieval period, when the wayfarer slept in the synagogue. The role of social action within Judaism dates from the eighth century B.C.E., although one might also say that it began with Moses himself. Despite these historical traditions in Judaism, it is a rare synagogue that opens its doors to the homeless and the poor.

Eco-Kashrut

Only kosher food is allowed in the synagogue because *kashrut* (the code of Jewish dietary laws) is a tenet of the Conservative movement that we believe in and maintain. Kashrut is a highly valuable concept which teaches reverence for life. But kashrut as generally practiced today is not meaningful enough and it often devolves into a competition to see who can be more kosher than the next. In response, we want to extend the concept of kashrut to make it more relevant to the congregation. We have been working for a number of years with the Jewish Renewal Group on the concept of eco-kashrut, a new sense of kashrut geared toward ecology and what is appropriate to use without defiling the planet. It is inconceivable to us that *piku-ah nefesh*, the saving of human life, not be extended to include fauna and flora, the water we drink, the air we breathe, the refuse we leave, the products we manufacture, the destruction we wreak upon God's creation, and the economic resources that we plunder. We believe that within Judaism are found the tenets to support the concept of kashrut as applied to the environment.

For example, is nonrecycled paper kosher? Can you or should you eat grapes picked in California by migrant agricultural workers who are treated inhumanely and are dying by the thousands because of the pesticides and other chemicals used in the vineyards? Perhaps those grapes should not be *kasher*. Our children, the next generation, are probably more sensitive to ecology than we are. If we can show them that Judaism has a relevant message on this topic—that we should not have some item in the house because it is not ecologically kasher—kashrut would become an important and worthwhile concept to them.

Role of Women

The structure of Judaism is male-dominated and patriarchal. Women, for example, have been largely read out of Jewish history. There is Golda Meir in modern Israeli history, and Deborah and a few others in the Bible, but overwhelmingly women are ignored in rabbinic, medieval, or modern literature. As with other elements in Judaism, gender roles have become fossilized.

B'nai Jeshurun, to the extent possible, has created a nonsexist liturgy. In the Hebrew blessing (of Abraham, Isaac, and Jacob), for example, we add the blessing of the matriarchs (Sarah, Rachel, Rebecca, and Leah). In the wedding ceremony, we use an egalitarian *ketubah* (Jewish marriage contract). Women have been given a role in the congregation equal to that of men. They recite the blessings at the Torah and perform all the other functions traditionally fulfilled only by men. This egalitarian approach attracts both men and women who neither understand nor tolerate the inequality of women in some other congregations.

Education and Discussion

B'nai Jeshurun has become identified as a place where all shades of social politics are presented and discussed amidst the traditional functioning of the synagogue (worship services, bar/bat mitzvahs, the naming of newborns, and so on). After services, we might have a speaker who represents a hotline for the protection of workers' rights in Israel, prominent members of the peace camp (representing both Israeli and Arab perspectives), someone from the Israel Religious Action Center concerned with religious freedom, social action, government accountability, and civil rights in Israel, or a local activist educating the congregation on how to keep the religious right from taking over the public school system.

This programming is an important part of realizing the potential for taking action in the world as a Jew. Our theology suggests that the congregation address the world through its Judaism, but not limit itself to the Jewish world. We Judaize our understanding of the human condition by passing the elements of human wisdom and knowledge through the filter of Judaism. We find when we do this that many social and political problems marked by suffering and injustice are religious, spiritual issues. We emphasize this perspective in the liturgy at B'nai Jeshurun, changing the text so that prayers are not offered exclusively for Israel. For example, as we conclude the *Kaddish* ("God who makes peace in the high places, may God grant peace to us, to all Israel"), we add, "May God grant peace to *all* the inhabitants of this planet."

RELEVANCE AND CONTINUITY

Judaism is not a fundamentalist religion based on the literal understanding of the Biblical text. Rather, it is an ongoing search for the meaning of God's revelation and the adaptation of that revelation to the exigencies of an ever-changing world. Thus Jews believe in the oral law as well as in the written law. The oral law's basic text is the Talmud and its exegesis according to certain hermeneutic laws. The dynamic, organic process of its development, which occurs throughout history, reflects Judaism's endless search for the relevance and merit of its message in history and its search for God's presence in time.

In the aftermath of the 1990 National Jewish Population Survey, which showed increased rates of intermarriage and declining rates of affiliation (Kosmin, Goldstein, Waksberg, Lerer, Keysar, and Scheckner, 1991), there has been deep concern with Jewish continuity and with the survival of the Jewish people. Let us begin by asking, survival as what? Is Judaism a relic from antiquity, a fossil, or does it have something to say to the world? Does it have something to say to our own children? If we have a message, the unaffiliated will come to us and our children will remain with us.

If Judaism is only about whether or not swordfish is kosher or whether men and women sit together or separately, the vast majority of young Jews will not be interested. Most intelligent, sensitive, well-educated Jews have questions. The richness of life—spiritual, psychological, and emotional—is bound up not so much with answers but with the formulation of the questions. The synagogue should be the place where people are in quest of a meaningful encounter with God, and with the reality of their lives and their world.

NOTE

This chapter is a compilation of previous writing, speeches, and interviews on Congregation B'nai Jeshurun. During 1993, the editors worked with Rabbi Marshall Meyer to prepare this piece.

REFERENCES

Gordis R. (1979). A Dynamic Halakhah: Principles and Procedures of Jewish Law. *Judaism, 28*, 263–282.

Heschel, A. J. (1954). *Man's Quest for God: Studies in Prayer and Symbolism*. NY: Scribner.

Kosmin, B.A., Goldstein, S., Waksberg, J., Lerer, N., Keysar, A., and Scheckner, J. (1991). *Highlights of the CJF 1990 National Jewish Population Survey*. NY: Council of Jewish Federations.

PART FOUR

The Institutional Context of Affiliation

Explanations of congregational affiliation depend, in part, on institutional factors (Chapter 1). Part Four is concerned with the local institutional issue of the roles of clergy and laity and the national institutional question of the role of the denomination.

In discussions about congregations, we increasingly hear the words "empowerment," "ownership," "stakeholders," and other terms that indicate giving ordinary people a central role in the life of the church. Not only do we see congregants take a growing part in managing the institution or making policy, but also in the religious realm, in setting spiritual direction for the church or synagogue.

In Chapter 11, James R. Wood notes that lay people often provide expertise, experience, and practical wisdom which are valuable supplements to the training and experience of clergy. He contends, however, that clergy have a distinctive leadership role that they may share with laity but must not surrender. No matter how democratic or how expanded the role of the laity, congregations still need leadership that is spiritual. As knowledge, sophistication, and consciousness grow among the laity (perhaps along with increased demands, expectations, and levels of criticism), the clergy must adjust their leadership style and methods, but they cannot abandon their leadership roles. It is the job of the clergy to vitalize the faith of the laity, to raise the consciousness of the scared values of the religious tradition, and to connect transcendent truth with everyday life. It is the unique work of clergy to help the congregation achieve maturational growth (Chapter 2) by educating the laity and leading them to deeper faith.

In Chapter 12, William McKinney calls for a reexamination of the role of denominations in helping local congregations. He begins with a standard equation: people come into religious organizations through birth, transfer from another tradition, or conversion from unaffiliation. They leave because they die, transfer out into another tradition, or drop out into the ranks of the unaffiliated. Congregations grow when births, transfers in, and conversions exceed deaths, transfers out, and dropouts. This model suggests three arenas of activity which can be undertaken by congregations and supported by their national religious organization: education, for those born into a religious tradition; extension (interdenominational recruitment) for those who transfer into the tradition; and evangelism, for those who are on the outside. Of these, McKinney believes evangelism is the area in which the greatest national-level attention is needed. He suggests that the national organizations should be concentrating on "sharing faith" with the unaffiliated population and identifying entry or reentry points to help transform occasional "inquirers" into "applicants."

Overall, McKinney proposes that the most important contribution a national denomination can make to congregational growth is establishing an organizational culture that values and supports growth. His call for a revitalization of the national religious institutions parallels the calls elsewhere in this volume for a reawakening of the local congregations.

Wood and McKinney remind us that affiliation, a relationship which is established between an individual and a congregation, occurs within a local and national institutional context. We must take account of these institutional factors as we strive to achieve a full understanding of congregational affiliation, chart our future research in this field, and design strategies to enhance congregational affiliation and growth in the 1990s and beyond.

CHAPTER 11

Leadership, Ministry, and Integrity Amid Changing Roles for Clergy and Laity

James R. Wood

Pervasive changes in clergy and laity roles and, especially, in the relationships between them pose both opportunities and dangers. American laity are seeking, and often gaining, increased voice in churches and synagogues and an expanded role in their administration, counselling, community outreach, and teaching. Clergy can (and under some conditions must) share much of traditional ministry with the laity. In our complex world, lay people often provide expertise, experience, and practical wisdom that are essential supplements to the training and experience of the clergy. Increased reliance on laity in ministry will strengthen lay people's faith and provide them a powerful motive for participation in a synagogue or church. Just as important, the mobilization of the laity can enrich and energize the churches' and synagogues' ministries to their members and to their communities. Though clergy encouragement of an expanding role of the laity in ministry strengthens the ministry of synagogues and churches, hence contributing to those institutions' spiritual (and often their numerical) growth, *there is a distinctive leadership role that clergy may share but must not surrender.*

CLERGY'S DISTINCTIVE ROLE

The clergy's distinctive leadership responsibility is what we Methodists call preaching—some other traditions call it teaching. In sharing thoughts about the importance of preaching as the basis of clergy leadership, I will draw both on my experience as a minister in Alabama and on my research as an organizational sociologist.

In 1910, a Methodist bishop named William Quayle painted a word picture of the task of preaching: when the preacher stands before them on Sunday morning, the people ask,

> "Preacherman, where were you and what saw you while the workdays were sweating at their toil?" And then of this preacher we may say reverently, "He opened his mouth and taught them, saying:" and there will be another though lesser Sermon on the Mount. And the listeners sit and sob and shout under their breath, and say with their helped hearts, "Preacher, saw you and heard you that? You were well employed. Go out and listen and look another week; but be very sure to come back and tell us what you heard and saw." (quoted in Martin, 1949, pp. 63–64)

The above picture of preaching powerfully affirms that the distinctive task of the clergy is to connect transcendent truth with everyday life. That is the core of the clergy role: to teach and interpret the faith, applying it to everyday life—for example, as it relates to such secular values and behaviors as materialism, consumerism, Americanism, self-centeredness, insensitivity to the poor, and lack of acceptance of minorities. Clergy need to find ways to vitalize their ministry to the laity and incorporate the laity into the ministry of churches and synagogues, yet retain their own distinctive leadership role.

Clergy are trained to interpret the Scriptures, and where church and synagogue have their priorities straight, clergy are given time to study the Scriptures and to reflect on them. In addition, within mainstream American religion, most clergy are enmeshed in networks of interaction with other clergy, religious leaders, and scholars which insulate them from some of the deep cultural biases that affect many lay people's views of religion and society. Clergy have regular opportunities to speak with the members and constituents affiliated with their synagogues and churches, and they have some claim for their attention. In this sense, the affiliated are points of connection between transcendent truth and everyday life. Herein lies both danger—that the transcendent truth will become diluted—and opportunity—for applying that truth in a way more insightful and more extensive than clergy alone can apply it.

My studies have shown that clergy attitudes toward public issues are much more affected by religious values than are the attitudes of members of the laity. By contrast members of the laity bring values and commitments of social networks outside the religious community that can undermine the core values of the faith. Lay people draw their views of life's important issues more from other organizations and social networks. To use Peter Berger's (1967) term, clergy have different plausibility structures than lay people. For Berger, that network of people we interact with on a regular basis—including those we interact with through books—helps make certain beliefs and thoughts more or less plausible to us. He speaks of a plausibility structure as a conversational fabric. The conversations we carry on throughout the week tend to make some ways of thinking more plausible than others.

In our intensive study of twelve Protestant ministers' ability to press for positions on public issues that were dissident from those of their congregations, Anson Shupe and I found that socialization and social interactions within the clergy's denomination helped to anchor the ideologies (theology and attitudes toward church polity) that sustained their dissidence (Shupe & Wood, 1973). In a later study of fifty-eight Indianapolis clergy and their congregations (Wood, 1981), I also found that clergy's attitudes toward social issues (and the church's involvement) were influenced more by values and interactions within the church than were the attitudes of church members. About 66% of clergy, for example, but only 30% of church members, agreed that the denomination had influenced their attitudes toward social issues. Also, 91% of the clergy, compared with 62% of church members, said that the central interests of their lives were related to the church. Overall, clergy's attitudes were more influenced by the plausibility structure they found within the church while members were more influenced by those outside the church, such as membership in conservative organizations, including Masonic lodges, Republican party organizations, and the American Legion.

As a consequence of their plausibility structures, clergy often see what is going on in our society from a broader perspective than laity. Just one example: laity tend to be less aware of structural causes of social problems. A national survey has shown that the causes of poverty seen as most important are those (such as lack of thrift, lack of effort) that place blame on the individual for his or her poverty (Feagin, 1975). Similar responses have been obtained from a large sample of members of mainline churches. Clergy, however, appear much more socially conscious than church members. The causes of poverty which clergy rated most important were all structural causes (prejudice and discrimination, low wages in some businesses and industries, and the failure of society to provide good schools). An indication of how sharp the difference is between laity and clergy is the fact that the cause of poverty ranked first by the laity (lack of effort by the poor themselves) was ranked tenth (out of eleven choices) by the clergy, while the cause ranked first by the clergy (prejudice and discrimination against blacks) was ranked eighth by the laity (Wood, 1981).

The tendency for laity more than clergy to blame the poor for their own poverty, hence to avoid becoming involved with the problem of poverty, highlights the importance of the clergy's role of teaching God's transcendent truth. Though both Hebrew and Christian scriptures champion the poor, apparently most laity are not prepared to lead their churches and synagogues in sympathetic ministry to the increasing numbers of poor people in America. Certainly few laity are prepared to lead in efforts to reduce poverty by effecting major changes in government and business.

IMPEDIMENTS TO CLERGY LEADERSHIP

The fact that clergy views of our society are often more informed by the transcendent truths of faith makes particularly important the clergy's task of interpreting the world to the laity, but certain trends in our society impede this task. Unlike the bishop's word picture, laity are not, for the most part, sitting there eager to hear tough talk about how the transcendent engages them in their homes, their jobs, and their daily lives. The receptivity to religious teaching on public issues has been adversely affected by the erosion of authority which was accelerated by the powerful movements of the 1960s and by the Watergate experience. This erosion is manifested in all areas of our society, as is exemplified by the increasing number of lawsuits against physicians, school boards, parents, *and* clergy.[1] Not only do laity in general trust religious leaders (or any leaders) less, materialism—especially its particularly virulent form in our society, consumerism—tends to deflect people away from the human and spiritual concerns and the ideas of service and sacrificial giving that clergy talk about in their preaching and teaching.

Other trends impeding the leadership role of clergy (or at least necessitating clergy role changes) include the increasing complexity of public issues and at the same time the increasing sophistication of the laity, who are achieving higher levels of education and gaining greater expertise. Consider, for example, the relevance of the explosion of knowledge about fetal development to the question of abortion, or the relevance of new discoveries in genetics to the question of homosexuality. If we are going to repaint the word picture of preaching, we might have the listeners saying under their breath, "Well that's your opinion, but how dare you say something about biology (or economics, or _____). I have a Ph.D. in that field."

In the contemporary picture, many of the brightest people, whose grandparents may have been in church or synagogue in that earlier day, will not be present to hear what clergy have to say. Possibly because of materialism, they are not focused on a spiritual dimension of life. Or perhaps they still hang on to some religion, but because of another trend in our society—privatism—they are focused on themselves and their families and believe they can practice their own religion in private. They do not believe in the need for religious institutions.

Transcendent truth in its application to current events is a tough sell in our society.

TWO AIDS TO VITAL CLERGY LEADERSHIP

Here are two ways clergy may use their teaching and preaching as a basis for vitalizing the faith of the laity.

First, clergy can raise consciousness about the sacred values of their religious tradition and use those values as leverage for changing the perspectives of the laity. Second, clergy can teach scriptural truths in the context of pastoral ministry. Though these activities have intrinsic importance apart from their implications for church growth, I believe that churches and synagogues will grow when clergy so vitalize the ministry *to* the affiliated laity and the ministry *of* the affiliated laity that the unaffiliated become curious about what they are missing. (Here I use "grow" with the broad, rich meaning that Loren Mead (Chapter 2) has given it—size is an important dimension of growth, but not the primary dimension).

Psychologist Milton Rokeach (1973) taught us that our value repertoire is configured as a hierarchy, that we normally have the more selfish values at the top, and that it is possible to reconfigure that hierarchy by consciousness-raising. An illustration of this process of raising members' consciousness of religious values as they consider controversial issues paraphrases a statement by a minister in a racially changing neighborhood who was dealing with his board's reluctance to face the issue of racial integration.

The question has arisen whether we foresee the time we will welcome people of other racial groups. This question cannot be answered today, but I do want to indicate additional questions raised by this one: (1) What does the New Testament say about Christian faith expressed in race relationships? (2) How would Jesus answer the matter of racial attitudes and race relationships? (3) Is the church in the first place "Christ's church," or, do we consider it as "our church primarily"? What are some of the conclusions to be drawn in each answer? As your pastor, I present these questions to which I hope you will give serious thought, study, and prayer. (Wood, 1981, pp. 87–88)

A more common use of consciousness-raising is for leveraging people into helping others in the community. In a 1986 study of Indiana residents I found that when respondents described organizations that recruited them into volunteer activities, churches were the organizations most often mentioned—more than twice as often as the next most mentioned type of organization, youth organizations. In a later study, I was able to link a person's perception of the pastor's role in motivating that volunteering. For example, in a sample of church members from forty Indiana and Illinois churches (Catholic and Protestant), more than 78% of those who volunteered in the community agreed that "I decided to volunteer because my pastor showed me how Jesus' teachings apply to today."

A second, and related, way clergy can vitalize the faith of the laity is by teaching and preaching in the context of ministry. When clergy ground their teaching and preaching in ministry, they are not only more likely to have a receptive audience, they are more likely to unlock the energy of their listeners and channel that energy in ministry to others—inside and outside the church or synagogue. By ministry I mean, first, in the light of God's transcendent truth, helping individuals to achieve their true personal needs, including self-esteem, self-security, and self-actualization, and second, shaping social structures that allow individuals the opportunity to meet those needs. For example, synagogues and churches that welcome gays and lesbians not only minister to the needs of these new members but also create a new interactional structure through which attitudes of other members may be changed. Moreover, they provide models of tolerance and acceptance for the surrounding communities.

To be effective teachers or preachers, especially when dealing with controversial issues, clergy have to carry on effective pastoral ministry *and* bring that pastoral ministry into their preaching and teaching. Here is an example from a sermon preached in an Alabama church I studied in the 1960s:

> Let not your hearts be troubled.... In my Father's house are many rooms...
> God loves us, there is room in God's house for each of us. There is room in God's plan, there is room in God's purpose, there is room in God's love for all. If we can believe this, we will no longer feel insecure. To our desire to be wanted, to be loved—God says I want you, I love you.
> Secure in God's love, we can also understand that at the same time God says yes to the deep longing of our hearts, God says no to all the fruitless ways in which we have sought security. And especially God says no to all those ways in which we have sought to build ourselves up at the expense of others, to make ourselves seem important by considering others unimportant.
> God invites to God's house persons whom we do not invite to our houses. There is room in God's love for persons for whom we have found no room in our love. (Sermon preached by the Reverend J.R. Wood at the Edgemont Methodist Church in Florence, Alabama on January 15, 1961)

This sermon reflects the pastor's genuine concern for those individuals who are unable to accept the dramatic changes occurring in the relationships between races with the desegregation of schools and public accommodations. The sermon affirms the worth of these individuals, grounded in God's love for them, yet suggests that God is at work in the reshaping of their social institutions.

LAITY'S EMERGING ROLE IN MINISTRY

The clergy's distinctive task is to connect transcendent truth with everyday life. Clergy will vitalize the laity by enlisting them as partners in this task. Once their consciousness of their religious values is raised, once they are secure in their faith, they can become a vital part of ministry to church and synagogue *and* to the community. Laity may help connect the transcendent message with everyday life.

Laity can increase the effectiveness of administration in churches and synagogues. Ruth Wallace in *They Call Her Pastor* (1992) studies twenty Catholic parishes that are administered by women because no priest was available. She concluded that these women are able to identify with their parishioners to a much greater extent than any previous pastor because they are not members of the clergy. Thus the constraints and limitations of their nonordained state are transformed into opportunities by their creation of a new leadership style that incorporates their parishioners as peers, and eventually leads to a greater spirit of community in these parishes (Wallace, 1992). This lesson that Catholics learned out of necessity is valuable for clergy seeking ways to enliven the participation of laity.

Laity can provide valuable resources for churches' and synagogues' ministry of counseling and social support for those facing crises in their lives. No person can know firsthand the wide experience of humanity, but clergy can create an atmosphere which encourages laity to share their experiences with those who need help in facing similar crises. A close friend in the church where I am a member lost twin boys at seven months of pregnancy. She confided to me that the pastor was helpful, but that she was best ministered to by several women who not only share her faith but who also had experienced similar losses.

Laity are indispensable in community outreach ministries. Glide Memorial United Methodist Church in San Francisco provides a dramatic example. That church grew by 844 members in 1992 and now has an average worship attendance of 2,500. Explaining this vitality, Pastor Cecil Williams said, "About four years ago, Glide began to deal with recovery in the area of substance abuse. We discovered that what was needed was spirituality, and I said, 'My God, that's what the church is about.' So we emphasize spirituality in every act we engage in." Last year, this church was featured in "Rainbow in the Clouds," a PBS special with Maya Angelou. The documentary showed dramatically how the church uses lay people who have been victims of incest, spousal or parental abuse, rape, AIDS, or unemployment in ministering to other victims (Peck, 1993).

Laity's potential role in teaching and preaching is the one most often neglected. Many clergy have gained valuable insights from coffee and discussion groups that follow the sermon. These occasions can be important opportunities for clergy to learn how well they are communicating with laity. I also like the idea of a group of laity meeting regularly with their minister or rabbi to study and discuss the scriptures for coming sermons. Though clergy are responsible for keeping the light of transcendent truth shining on issues, they may comprehend some issues only with lay help; and some issues may be addressed by a wide variety of specific actions for which laity are valuable resources. The laity are absolutely essential to the closer application of God's transcendent truth, both because they have certain knowledge and experience that clergy lack and because they are in the work places, board rooms, community organizations, and legislative bodies where the action is.

Perhaps the most valuable contribution of such groups is to keep the clergy aware of the many different strongly held opinions and the diverse perspectives they have to contend with in communicating the transcendent faith in particular circumstances. Samuel Blizzard, one of the first to study clergy roles, described the "social actionist" as one who "may conceive his role as somewhat akin to the Israelite prophets of the Old Testament times" and is often aggressive and directive (Blizzard, 1985, p. 72). Based on my study of fifty-eight Protestant ministers in Indianapolis, I have argued that clergy who ground their ministry in the transcendent truths of their faith and integrate their pastoral and preaching roles provoke less conflict *and* more effectively support social change than the social actionist described by Blizzard. Deep sharing with a group of laity in the process of preparing sermons is one way for clergy to discover how best to communicate their message.

Through such a group, one pastor was made concretely aware of the wide variety of strong reactions and the deep divisions in his church over the Persian Gulf war. This selection from a sermon preached soon after the beginning of the war shows how he acknowledged the genuineness of the reactions yet affirmed the truth that God cares about our enemies as well as our friends. This sermon was effective in part because it was given by one who trusted laity to help him make connections between the transcendent and what is happening day by day.

> In the Old Testament reading this morning, God called the boy Samuel who was an apprentice of the priest Eli. After God speaks to Samuel, Eli debriefs him. Eli demands that Samuel tell him *absolutely everything* that God has said—even the unpleasant judgments that God has made against Eli. *That's an important insight: if we want to hear God's voice we must take everything in.* In viewing this war, it is important, I think, to do our best to take it in from many perspectives. . . .
>
> What is it like to be a pilot's wife waiting with your children in an apartment near an air base in Virginia or Florida, with your heart sinking every time the telephone rings? What is it like to be a grieving parent in Israel whose infant suffocated to death because in the four minutes of panic before the first Scud missile attack, you didn't know that it was necessary to remove a piece of cardboard inside your child's gas mask? What is it like to be walking on a road as one of the two million Iraqi refugees that are soon expected to be fleeing Iraq, seeking another country? What will it be like to be a nineteen-year-old American marine in the first wave of a ground assault in Kuwait? . . .
>
> Simply watching a war doesn't seem like much, but at this early stage I don't know what else I can do. Of course, I will also pray, although at times like this I don't always know what to pray. I awoke about 3:00 A.M. on Saturday morning. I decided to pray, but what to say? When I don't know what to pray for others, I sometimes try to visualize them in my mind, and then I say several times: God have mercy, Christ have mercy. So I did that.
>
> I remembered our soldiers, sailors, and marines. I remembered those who are still safe and those who are missing in action, and I prayed: God have mercy, Christ

have mercy. I remembered our leaders, both civilian and military—President Bush and his circle of advisors and our generals. . . . I remembered those Americans who are waiting for loved ones to return. I remembered those of you who are waiting, and I prayed. I remembered the civilians in Iraq and Kuwait, unarmed yet at great physical risk, and I prayed. I remembered the Iraqi soldiers, not because I am pro-Iraq, but because they are huddling beneath the pounding bombs and because they are human, and I prayed. I remembered all whom I could remember; I remembered those who detest war and those who were itching for it; I remembered those who are protesting the war and those who are loyally supporting it; and then I prayed: God have mercy, Christ have mercy. ("Thoughts of War," sermon preached by the Reverend David Owen at St. Mark's United Methodist Church, Bloomington, Indana, January 20, 1991.)

INTEGRITY IN CHURCH AND SYNAGOGUE MINISTRY

Lay participation can enrich synagogues' and churches' administration, counseling, community outreach, and preaching and teaching. An important by-product will be the development of deeper faith and stronger commitment among those laity who are sharing ministry. Increased reliance on laity in ministry will provide those laity a powerful motive for participation in a church or synagogue, and their excitement about ministry will often attract unaffiliated persons.

In all of this give and take with the laity, however, there will be pressures to stray from the transcendent truth. That is why this chapter ends with a discussion of integrity—of moral soundness, especially as it is revealed in dealings that test steadfastness to truth. In discussing Blizzard's social actionist, I implied that clergy must not separate prophetic ministry from loving care and hard work. There are issues worth clergy losing their members or their jobs for, but clergy should have a broad program of ministry that will minimize the probability of those outcomes. Still, our faith often requires controversial social action. Such action sometimes actually stimulates church growth. Much of the discussion of Dean Kelley's (1972) thesis about growth fails to consider that prophetic social action can provide meaning and discipline which, in turn, can create commitment. Patrick McNamara's (1992) study of young American Catholics uncovered a "reservoir of social idealism," leading him to suggest that church leaders appealing to young Catholics combine doctrine with social work and outreach programs. Given their generation's role in a number of movements for social change, it is plausible that some of the baby boomers who did not come back to synagogue or church after college may yet be attracted by socially relevant ministries.

Sometimes taking a principled stand precipitates a crisis in ministry. Clergy must have their own support networks and nurture their own faith so that if ever, despite all their efforts to persuade with a pastor's heart, they are forced to choose between their jobs and their faith, they will make the right choice, trusting the future to God.

A recent book, *Terror in the Night: The Klan's Campaign Against the Jews* (Nelson, 1993), tells of the agony felt by many clergy in Mississippi in the 1960s. Nelson details the inner and outer struggles of two rabbis, Rabbi Perry Nussbaum, of Jackson, and Rabbi Milton Schlager, of Meridian, in the wake of terrorist actions by the Ku Klux Klan against anyone challenging the racial status quo in Mississippi. Despite enormous social pressures—and at the risk of their jobs and, as it turned out, their lives—these rabbis continued to work for the racial justice rooted in their faith.

One of my first sociological studies was of the effect of racial tensions on Methodist ministers in Alabama during the late 1950s and the early 1960s (Wood & Zald, 1966). Lay people, especially the Methodist Layman's Union, brought strong pressure on the bishop to silence those ministers who were outspoken advocates of interracial understanding. I was able to document the fact that the number of such ministers in the largest, most prestigious churches in Birmingham steadily decreased. For example, of the principal ministers of the thirteen top Methodist churches in Birmingham in 1955, five were conservative, two were moderate, and five were liberal in their views toward racial integration (my informants were unable to classify the thirteenth). By 1963, the count was eleven conservatives, one moderate, and no liberals.

During those years, I often interviewed John Rutland, an outspoken liberal who weathered the storm from 1955 through 1962 (in 1961 and 1962 he was the one remaining liberal in a top Birmingham Methodist church). I concluded that John Rutland was able to stay at his post partly because he was a good pastor who grounded his prophetic preaching in his pastoral ministry. In addition, he became a symbol for liberal ministers throughout the state who pressed the bishop to leave him in Birmingham. But despite the burning of a cross on his front lawn, verbal sniping of his parishioner Bull Connor, and pressure from his own bishop, he did not mute his voice for racial justice. Each year, the bishop insisted that he would move John Rutland out of Birmingham, but at the last moment would relent. I was in John Rutland's church the first Sunday of his last year in Birmingham. I will always remember that the chairman of the official board, John Jones (not his real name), a prominent industrialist, announced to the congregation with obvious glee: "The bishop has assured us that this will be Brother Rutland's last year as our pastor."

Recently I saw John Rutland and I reminded him of that Sunday. He said, "Let me tell you a story. I hadn't seen John Jones in twenty years. Then I was visiting a church in Birmingham after I retired. I looked across the parking lot and here came John Jones, running as fast as he could. He grabbed hold of me and swung me around, and he said, 'John Rutland, if I were half the man that you are, I would have called you fifteen years ago to tell you that you were right and I was wrong.' "

As clergy, we may not often have such dramatic affirmations of our integrity as witnesses to God's truth. But all of us, when we are discouraged by pressures from a secular society, can find strength in our faith that, though God's timetable may be different from our own timetables, God's truth will prevail.

NOTE

1. Of course, religious leaders should be held responsible for their actions. Reluctance of denominations and other religious organizations to discipline clergy who violate legal or moral standards contributes to the erosion of clergy authority. Perhaps a more prevalent problem is the existence of some clergy who, for lack of competence or motivation, simply fail to lead. In the fifty-eight churches included in the Indianapolis study discussed above, I found one minister who was far behind his people in willingness to extend the congregation's ministry to the surrounding community.

REFERENCES

Berger, P. (1967). *The Sacred Canopy*. Garden City, NY: Doubleday.

Blizzard, S. W. (1985). *The Protestant Parish Minister: A Behavioral Science Interpretation*. Storrs, CT: Society for the Scientific Study of Religion.

Feagin, J. R. (1975). *Subordinating the Poor: Welfare and American Beliefs*. Lexington, MA: Lexington Books.

Kelley, D. M. (1972). *Why Conservative Churches Are Growing*. New York: Harper & Row.

Martin, W. C. (1949). *To Fulfill This Ministry*. New York: Abingdon.

McNamara, P. H. (1992). *Conscience First, Tradition Second: A Study of Young American Catholics*. Albany: State University of New York Press.

Nelson, J. (1993). *Terror in the Night: The Klan's Campaign Against the Jews*. New York: Simon & Schuster.

Peck, J. R. (Ed.). (1993). *The United Methodist Newscope*, 21(20). Nashville: The United Methodist Publishing House.

Rokeach, M. (1973). *The Nature of Human Values*. New York: Free Press.

Shupe, A. D., Jr., & Wood, J. R. (1973). Sources of Leadership Ideology in Dissident Clergy. *Sociological Analysis, 34*, 185–201.

Wallace, R. A. (1992). *They Call Her Pastor*. Albany: State University of New York Press.

Wood, J. R. (1981). *Leadership in Voluntary Organizations: The Controversy over Social Action in Protestant Churches*. New Brunswick, NJ: Rutgers University Press.

Wood, J. R., & Zald, M. N. (1966). Aspects of Racial Integration in the Methodist Church: Sources of Resistance to Organizational Policy. *Social Forces, 45*, 255–265.

CHAPTER 12

The Role of National Religious Institutions in Congregational Affiliation and Growth

William McKinney

About a dozen years ago, the United Methodist Church, prompted by some of its Korean congregations, passed a resolution to grow from 9 million to 20 million by the year 2000. I wondered at the time how they decided 20 and not 15, or 25, or 30 million. It prompted me to ask how one would achieve such growth. What might a national strategy for growth look like? Can national denominations do anything to help local congregations grow?

To answer these questions, one needs a theory or set of assumptions about the way a local congregation or national denomination grows. I came up with a very simple formula. People come into religious organizations in three ways, and they leave in three ways. They are born into a religious tradition, transfer in from another tradition, or convert from the ranks of the unaffiliated. They leave because they die, transfer out into another tradition, or drop out into the ranks of the unaffiliated. For the Methodist Church to grow to 20 million, 11 million more persons must come into the church by birth, transfer, or conversion than leave because of death, transfer, or dropping out. A denomination's growth strategy needs to be sensitive to all six elements in the formula.

In *American Mainline Religion* (Roof & McKinney, 1987), we used this formula to look at future growth prospects for various religious groups: liberal Protestants, moderate Protestants, black Protestants, conservative Protestants, Catholics, Jews, and the unaffiliated. We relied on survey data from the General Social Survey, 1972–1984, a respected annual national poll of 1,500 Americans that includes data on religious affiliation (Davis & Smith, 1992). Our focus was on denominational switching (movement into and out of faith traditions) and its implications for growth. We found evidence that there are differences among groups that help explain rates of growth and decline. The birthrates of Jews, liberal Protestants, and moderate Protestants are relatively low, while those of black Protestants and conservative Protestants are higher; Catholic birth rates are close to the national average. Members of the groups with high birthrates tend to be older than those with low rates, which led us to speculate that over time they would not only gain fewer members through births but also lose more current members to deaths. Moreover, we found that low birthrate/high death rate religious groups also lose more members to the ranks of the religious unaffiliated, especially among the young.

For this chapter, I have taken data from the General Social Surveys of 1988–1991 to see if there have been changes in the patterns documented in our book. The survey data deal solely with religious identification, with what people say they are now and with what they say they were when age 16.[1] In *American Mainline Religion*, we found rather different patterns for those over and under age 45, so I have divided the sample into younger and older portions. I have also treated liberal and moderate Protestants as a single family with the label "old-line Protestant." I now avoid the term "mainline" to refer to this group of Protestant churches since it implies other groups are not. I will focus here on persons who give conservative Protestantism, old-line Protestantism, and Judaism as their religious affiliation.[2]

Survey data have obvious limitations for dealing with births and deaths, two factors important to our formula. Still, one can use survey data to explore intergroup differences and dynamics. For example, comparing the ratio of young to old affiliates in these three traditions tells us there are 103 younger old-line Protestants for every 100 older affiliates. For every 100 older conservative Protestants, however, there are 123 younger persons who cite a conservative Protestant preference. For Jews, this ratio drops to 94. This suggests quite clearly that old-line Protestant and Jewish death rates will be higher than those of other religious groups over the next half century. We see evidence of the change taking place in the demographic balance in American religious affiliation. Among the older generation, there are 193 old-line Protestants and 12 Jews for every 100 conservative Protestants. For the younger generation, there are 165 old-line Protestants and 9.7 Jews for every 100 conservative Protestants.

DENOMINATIONAL AFFILIATION

Figures 12.1, 12.2, and 12.3 look at persons who claim the three religious identifications that are our focus. To demonstrate how to read these figures, let me use older conservative Protestants as an example. The sample included 850 persons over age 45 who named a conservative Protestant denomination when asked for their current religious affiliation. These 850 persons (100%) include persons raised as conservative Protestants who have not left *plus* those raised in another religious tradition who switched to a conservative Protestant identification (transfers in, 23%), *minus* those who once thought of themselves as affiliated with a conservative Protestant denomination but who now consider themselves part of a different tradition (transfers out, 28%). For example, if I was a Presbyterian when growing up and transferred into the Catholic Church, I become a transfer out of old-line Protestantism and a transfer into Catholicism. Among those over age 45, conservative Protestantism has a net loss due to denominational switching by religious families.

Some persons over age 45 came into conservative Protestantism from outside the religious system; these formerly unaffiliated persons are converts (3%). Conservative Protestantism shows about the same percentage of persons over age 45 dropping out (2%). The other half of each figure looks at the same religious families and patterns for younger sample members.

What do these figures tell us about affiliation change? First, there is a lot of switching going on, and among old-line Protestants and Jews there is more of it among those under 45 than among those over 45. Generally speaking, among these three traditions those transferring in and transferring out tend to balance each other out. Intergroup switching does not benefit one tradition much more than any other. There is some movement from old-line Protestantism to other traditions among the young, but it does not fully account for the decline in this family of churches. None of the groups has been notably effective in attracting the unaffiliated.

The most important finding in these figures is the change in dropout rates, which is the increase in the number of persons who grew up in a tradition but now are unaffiliated. Among younger sample members 6% of those raised as conservative Protestants, 7% of those Jews raised, and 10% of those raised as old-line Protestants no longer identify with a religious tradition. The proportions are lower among older sample members.

ROLE OF THE NATIONAL DENOMINATIONS

Most national religious organizations have adopted a pattern of organization that divides domestic mission activities into three areas that conform very nicely to the three ways in which people come into religious organization (birth, transfer in, and conversion). The labels vary, but one customarily finds organized departments of education, extension, and evangelism, each corresponding to one of the sources of congregational growth. Education can be seen as focusing on the nurture of persons born into the religious tradition, extension on those who transfer into the tradition (often following a move to a new community), and evangelism on those essentially outside the religious system. I want to say a few things about denominational strategy and use of these three traditional categories of "home mission" activity.

Figure 12.1
Conservative Protestants—% Entering and Leaving

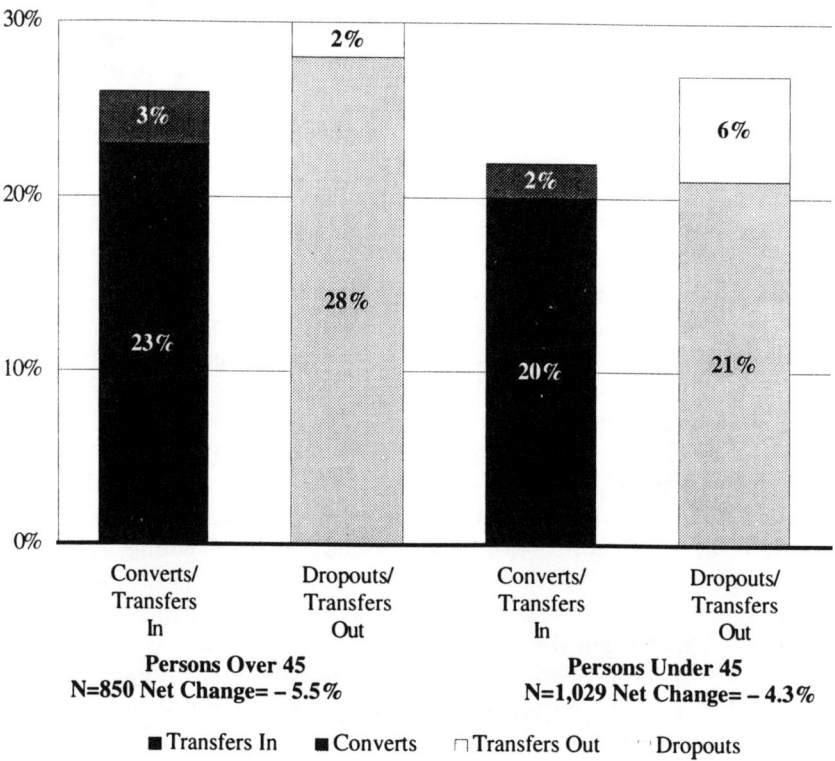

Education

The surest source of new adherents for religious organizations is the children of those already in the fold. Over 70% of conservative and old-line Protestants and over 90% of Jews started out in their current tradition. In other words, over 90% of those who are Jews today were Jews when they were growing up. Despite switching, despite trends toward increased choice in affiliation and identification, church and synagogue families are the largest single source of new affiliates. New research on baby boomers and religion (e.g., Roof, 1993) points to the importance of maintaining a connection to the religious community during the high school and college years. While it may not produce active congregational memberships in the short run, maintaining a relationship with persons in their teens and twenties increases the likelihood those persons will reaffiliate at some point in the future. Campus ministry and Hillel activities may be more important than national denominations have realized in the past.

Figure 12.2
Oldline Protestants—% Entering and Leaving

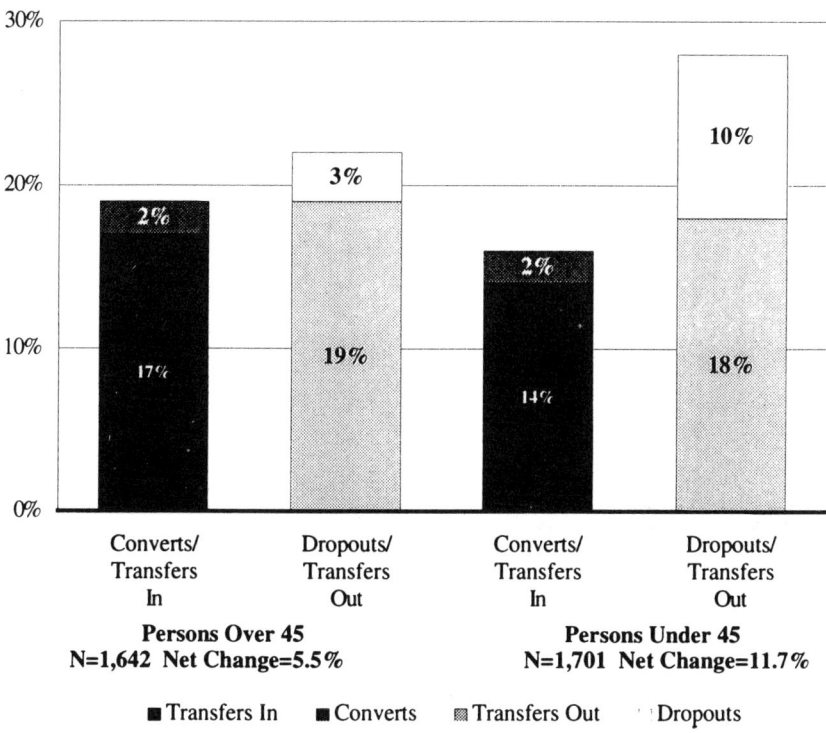

For Protestant Christians, and perhaps others as well, relying on educational strategies for growth results in the continuation of racial and ethnic homogeneity. Many denominations came into being to serve the religious needs of particular ethnic or racial groups. Immigrants in the eighteenth and nineteenth centuries often brought their churches with them, giving rise to the Dutch Reformed Church, the Augustana (Swedish) Lutheran Church, and so on. African Americans, tired of second-class treatment in white churches, formed independent denominations such as the African Methodist Episcopal Church or the National Baptist Convention. Even in denominations less tied to specific ethnic origins, congregations emerged to specialize in meeting the needs of people of a common national origin. Earlier in this century it was not unusual to find congregations of a single denomination serving Swedes, Germans, Italians, or others. Today, in most cities one discovers a plurality of congregations, each serving primarily one group, so that we now have Korean, Latino, Filipino, or Haitian congregations.

Many denominations have recognized that for theological and practical reasons depending on a single ethnic group for adherents is increasingly

Figure 12.3
Jews—% Entering and Leaving

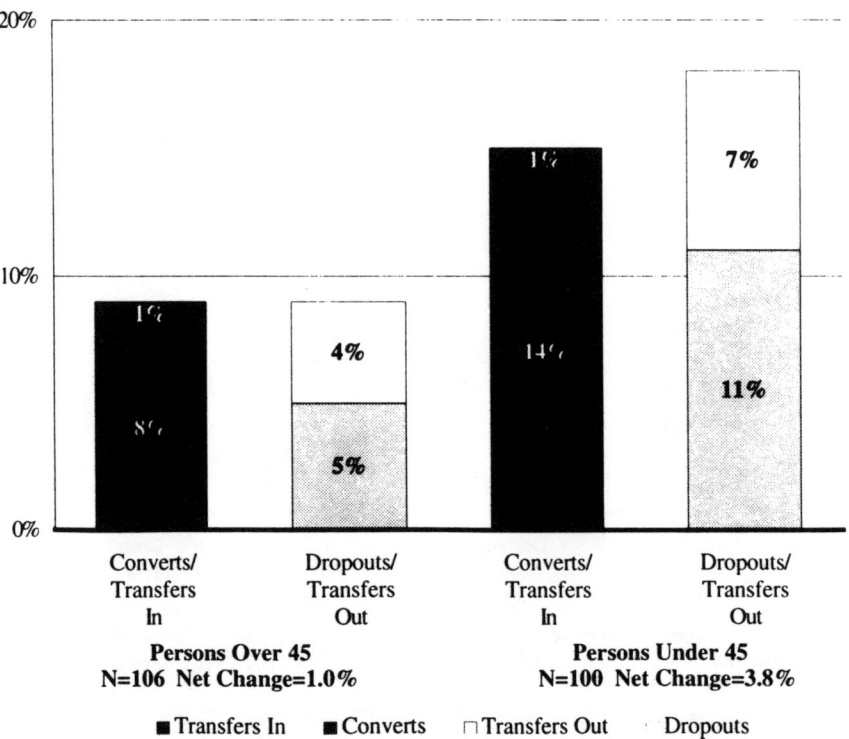

problematic. Theologically, within Christianity, there is an increasing realization of the multicultural character of the church; practically, changes in immigration laws have reduced the flow of persons from the nations that once supplied traditional adherents. As a result, given the changing composition of American society, depending solely on the children of current adherents for future generations of members presents an enormous challenge. A denomination or congregation that fails, for whatever reason, to broaden its ethnic and cultural base puts itself at a competitive disadvantage.

Extension

Congregational extension is in some ways the arena of interdenominational competition, especially within denominational family groups. In new or rapidly changing communities, incoming families are fair game for recruitment; Methodists, for example, seek a fair shot at former Presbyterians, and vice versa.

For development of denominational extension strategies, there are some helpful lessons to be learned from research on student recruitment in higher education. The classic approach to student recruitment is to think of moving people through an imaginary funnel. A college's strategy begins with the public, with identifying ways some of that public can be narrowed into prospective applicants. The following steps are to turn prospects into inquirers, inquirers into applicants, applicants into enrollers, enrollers into successful students, students into graduates, and graduates into alumni(ae) donors. At each stage of the funnel, a college's strategy must be different. It does not have one recruitment strategy but a package of strategies.

Extension work is a major program focus for most denominations, and substantial money has been spent helping congregations gain their share of transfer growth. Research done by Marjorie Royle (1994) on United Church of Christ church growth training programs and C. Kirk Hadaway (1990) on Christian Church (Disciples of Christ) efforts at transfer growth suggests that targeted programs do have an impact on congregational growth, but that the impact is mainly motivational. Training people to be effective evangelists or recruiters of new members is relatively low in payoff in terms of actual new members.

The phenomenology of denominational switching needs further study by national denominations. In my own denomination, the United Church of Christ, former Roman Catholics represent a third to a half of new adult members in New England. What does it mean to a person to change adherence? Similarly, little is known about church and synagogue shopping. Occasionally we study those who shop and stop in our congregations, that is, people we receive as a result of shopping for a congregation. But I know of no study of those who have shopped and then gone elsewhere.

New congregation development is another form of transfer growth since most members of new congregations are switchers from another congregation. There are some interesting recent studies of new church development (Bullock, 1991; Marler & Hadaway, 1994). These studies suggest that new congregation development does not cause growth in denominations, though the denominations would clearly grow less without it. Old-line Protestantism's losses would have been slightly worse without the limited new church development that has been undertaken.

Evangelism

The third way religious organizations gain new adherents is through evangelism. My personal view is that this is the arena in which the greatest national-level attention is needed. The question here is sharing faith as much as promoting church or synagogue participation. Most denominational membership and church growth resources developed by old-line Protestant churches have emphasized "selling" the church and "selling" a particular congregation to people already inclined to be part of a church. Relatively speaking, there has been little attention to sharing faith. Shifting the emphasis to more sharing of faith will take a major reorientation for the old-line religious community that has tended to view aggressive evangelistic activity as unseemly.

In conversion growth, an important challenge is to find entry or reentry points through which people can find their way into the life of a religious tradition and into some form of affiliation. High holy days in the Christian and Jewish traditions provide what an earlier section of this paper called inquirers. The high holy days are entry points that offer possibilities for turning inquirers into applicants. A national denomination can help identify and create similar points of entry/reentry.

NATIONAL STRATEGIES FOR GROWTH IN AFFILIATION

I close with four general comments about national strategies for growth in affiliation and membership.

First, it is a truism that denominations do not grow or decline—local churches and synagogues grow and decline. It therefore follows that a national denomination's role is to help local congregations as they reach out to new people.

This truism needs to be examined. It is possible that denominations may have a more active role to play. Historian Jean Miller Schmidt (1991), in her book *Souls or the Social Order*, reminds us that it is only in the twentith century that denominations have understood their principal role to serve local congregations. Mass evangelism was an important growth strategy and was sometimes quite separate from local churches. Evangelists were often supported denominationally; the evangelist was the actor, the congregation the recipient. Similarly, Milton J. Coalter (1991) documents a change in Presbyterian thinking about that denomination's role in evangelism. The Presbyterian denomination, he argues, once focused nationally on "unreached constituencies," in effect looking out at American society and determining what groups most needed to hear their message. In the 1940s, there began a shift from the needs of specific constituencies to the need for a visible evangelism program. As a result, says Coalter, Presbyterians now had an evangelism program but no longer had a growth strategy.

These studies lead me to ask whether denominations may still have a role in congregational growth beyond providing resources to congregations. At the very least, there is a need for clear thinking about denominational and congregational roles.

Second, I am convinced the most important contribution a national denomination can make to congregational growth is establishing an ethos that encourages growth. Establishing such an ethos involves more than recognizing fast-growing congregations at national meetings or increasing the amount of attention given to the strength of religious institutions. It means fostering a sense of social movement versus social institution. Denominational religion in its institutional manifestations is experiencing some tough times today, but religious traditions still have enormous appeal. How a denomination rethinks its ways of being and acting to convey a sense of movement is an important challenge.

Establishing a new ethos will require a new understanding of denominational religion in cultural terms. The character of a denomination's culture may have more to do with its growth than do its institutions or programs. In a recent essay, Donald Luidens (1990) looks at Presbyterian bodies, mostly conservative, which have left the major Presbyterian denominations. These schismatic groups are theologically conservative, so some would think they should be growing. Luidens looks at their growth rates over the past twenty years and finds that they are not; virtually all Presbyterian denominations are declining. He concludes there is something more involved than theological differences. I suspect what is involved are issues of class, race, and historical experience that lead some to be more (or less) willing to bear the label "Presbyterian."

Third, growth strategies need to address both growth and decline, new affiliates and disaffiliates. For many congregations, the problem is less the number of people who come in the front door than the number who leave through the back door.

For some national denominations, increased new congregation development is and will remain an important means for increasing affiliation. The strategy is incomplete, however, if it does not attend to the loss of old congregations. Even doubling the rate of new church development in the United Methodist, Presbyterian, Disciples of Christ, and United Church of Christ results in a net loss in the number of churches in these denominations at the end of each year because so many churches are being closed.

Finally, national denominations need to cultivate their ability to think about the future. The future strength of our religious traditions depends as much on the quality of our intellectual work as on the quantity or even the quality of our programs. I would suggest just a few research questions suitable for sustained ecumenical attention. There are many practical questions for which we lack answers: In emphasizing individual responsibility in matters of faith and morals, are liberal religious traditions in effect encouraging persons to practice their faith independent of organized faith communities? What is the impact of evangelism/membership development courses in theological seminaries? How does one warm up "frozen people" and help them to share their faith with friends and neighbors? What is the role of ministerial placement systems in congregational growth and decline?

National denominations have an important role to play in helping their congregations, clergy, and members pose and answer these questions.

Indeed, as national religious dollars become tighter this "research and development" function of denominations should grow in importance.

NOTES

1. The Think Tank on Congregational Affiliation (Brandeis University, October 1992) reinforced for me the importance of being clear and consistent in the use of concepts. I will use "affiliates" and "adherents" interchangeably to refer to persons who identify with a particular religious group, though they need not be "members" of any religious organization. Affiliation may mean nothing more than having a response to the question: "What is your religious preference? Is it Protestant, Catholic, Jewish, some other religion, or no religion?" (the question used by the National Opinion Research Center in the General Social Survey).

2. For definition of these groups, see Roof and McKinney (1987), *American Mainline Religion*, Appendix. While the focus in this paper is on only these three groups, the analysis included all groups in the General Social Surveys.

REFERENCES

Bullock, R. H., Jr. (1991). Twentieth-Century Presbyterian New Church Development: A Critical Period, 1940–1980. In M. J. Coalter, J. M. Mulder, & L. B. Weeks (Eds.), *The Diversity of Discipleship: The Presbyterians and Twentieth-Century Christian Witness* (pp. 55–82). Louisville: Westminster/John Knox.

Coalter, M. J. (1991). Presbyterian Evangelism: A Case of Parallel Allegiances Diverging. In M. J. Coalter, J. M. Mulder, & L. B. Weeks (Eds.), *The Diversity of Discipleship: The Presbyterians and Twentieth-Century Christian Witness* (pp. 33–54). Louisville: Westminster/John Knox.

Davis, J. A., & Smith, T. W. (1992). *General Social Surveys, 1972–1992* [Machine-readable data file]. Chicago: National Opinion Research Center.

Hadaway, C. K. (1990). Denominational Switching, Social Mobility and Membership Trends. In N. Williams (Ed.), *A Case Study of Mainstream Protestantism* (pp. 491–508). Grand Rapids, MI: Eerdman's.

Luidens, D. A. (1990). Numbering the Presbyterian Branches: Membership Trends Since Colonial Times. In M.J. Coalter, J. M. Mulder, & L. B. Weeks (Eds.), *The Mainstream Protestant "Decline": The Presbyterian Pattern* (pp. 29–65). Louisville: Westminster/John Knox.

Marler, P. L., & Hadaway, D. K. (1994). New Church Development and Denominational Growth (1950–1988): Symptom or Cause? In D. A. Roozen & C. K. Hadaway (Eds.), *Church and Denominational Growth* (pp. 47–86). Nashville: Abingdon.

Roof, W. C. (1993). *A Generation of Seekers*. San Francisco: Harper Collins.

Roof, W. C., & McKinney, W. (1987). *American Mainline Religion*. New Brunswick, NJ: Rutgers University Press.

Royle, M. H. (1994). The Effect of a Church Growth Strategy on United Church of Christ Congregations. In D. A. Roozen & C. K. Hadaway (Eds.), *Church and Denominational Growth* (pp. 155–168). Nashville: Abingdon.

Schmidt, J. M. (1991). *Souls or the Social Order: The Two-Party System in American Protestantism*. Brooklyn, NY: Carlson Publishing.

Afterword

James P. Wind

In *Lives of a Cell* (1974), the late Lewis Thomas, one of our nation's most preeminent physicians, wrote about—among other things—the behavior of ants, termites, and bees. Such topics might seem out of place in a book about congregational affiliation, just as they seemed out of place on the pages of the August *New England Journal of Medicine* (where they were first published) or in the circles Dr. Thomas moved in as dean of the Yale School of Medicine or president of the Memorial Sloan-Kettering Cancer Center. Thomas, who was a superb scientist as well as a gifted administrator, possessed a precious trait: he loved and was attentive to mystery. Hence he spent "moonlight" time as an essayist, trying to call his colleagues to the realm of wonder.

Which brings us to ants, bees, and termites. The solitary bug, say an ant, Thomas claimed, "can't be imagined to have a mind at all." A "ganglion on legs," this lone insect seems aimless and insignificant. Put four to ten of them together around a dead moth or a leaf and "they begin to look like an idea." Follow them home to the hill, where they mass in the thousands, becoming a black throbbing whole, and you "begin to see the whole beast, and now you observe it thinking, planning, calculating. It is an intelligence, a kind of live computer, with crawling bits for its wits" (Thomas, 1974, pp. 12–13). Thomas the scientist, fascinated by the difference between individual and collective behavior, speculated on the role of pheromones (unnoticed chemical substances members of a species give off that stimulate behaviors of other members of that species) in releasing the energy of the hill, or the buzz of the hive. Then Thomas the essayist wondered about the likenesses between humans and these so-called lowly creatures. Taking his own research community as exhibit A, he noted how through their journals, meetings, computer links, and the like, these humans built their own hill, their own marvelously intricate system of interactions. Like the bugs, they were caught up in processes larger than their consciousness, which shaped them and made them purposive.

The chapters in this book, while lacking in the sheer capacity for artful wonder that we find in Thomas's essays, nonetheless take us right up to the edge of an interface between individual and collective behavior that should leave us wondering. In this case, the collective is not the hill but congregations. From various points of view, the authors make moves like Thomas the scientist. They try to help us figure out why people are drawn to or repelled from these fascinating institutions. A variety of explanations are offered—none as intriguing as pheromones, but all with partial explanatory power. So we consider individual life stories, contextual factors such as demographic trends, denominational histories, or the qualities of clergy leadership that might help us with the riddle of affiliation. We ponder the breakdown of the American Protestant plausibility structure, the emergence of lay liberalism, the impact of interfaith marriage, the importance of certain kinds of programs and practices, the significance of life-cycle transitions, the role of passion and emotion, and the need for distinctive beliefs. Perhaps in this complex list of factors, or perhaps within their delicate interplay, we can find an answer.

But the mystery eludes us. Why do people join congregations? Why do they hang in there year after year? Why do they drop out? Why do they stay away? Why do they join and not participate? Why do they continue to identify themselves religiously, yet keep a safe distance from any congregation's door? Maybe the ants help us. They remain mysterious, but they continue the dance of life. They move this way and that for reasons that remain obscure.

In congregations we witness part of the dance of life: here the dance is complex, variegated, and wonderful. People approach congregations with all sorts of personal codings. They come with particular personal stories that are amalgams of family histories and personal experiences, mixes of tragedy and comedy, webs of social relations, and thickets of psychological dynamics. Entangled in each of these biographies is a personal religious negotiation, an encounter with and an avoidance of religious truth and reality. All of this can and often does go on outside of local congregations. What we have is roughly analogous to Thomas's individual ants or to the small groups of them that begin to look like an idea.

Then there is the congregation. Far more mysterious than the hill or the hive, this institution is a complex particular world. No two congregations are exactly alike, since each is made of particular sets of materials. A denominational tradition (itself a most complex reality), a regional character, a particular socioeconomic environment, an interplay of either a small or a large set of personal and family histories, and a collection of distinctive institutional practices and experiences come together within a congregation to form a distinct local culture. Encounters with the sacred, with symbols, with systems of organizational behavior, and with practices of formation, care, mission, and proclamation are put together in distinctive ways in each one of the more than 450,000 local churches and synagogues that color our landscape.

Part of the problem in our previous attempts to understand congregational and denominational affiliation patterns—and part of the problem that this book addresses—is that we have failed to fathom just how much is going on in the life of any individual who approaches a congregation, in any congregation itself, and in any interaction between the two. Since others are far more competent than I to probe individual worlds, and since so much has been written that seeks to open those worlds for us, let me go a bit deeper into the other side of the affiliation threshold, the congregation. To do so, I take a clue from H. Richard Niebuhr's classic, *The Responsible Self* (1963). Niebuhr, who was writing to a nation preoccupied with doing rather than being, wanted to help people learn to hesitate before asking "What shall I do?" (One thinks here especially of busy congregational and denominational leaders who feel tremendous pressure to do something about membership declines or plateaus.) The all-important prior question for Niebuhr was "What is going on?" For him, responsible selves need to work very hard to give full interpretations of the situations they are placed in. Such interpretations require discerning the social and historical dynamics at work in any situation. But they also require discerning what God is up to, setting situations in theological contexts.

In the past two decades, a remarkable probing of congregational life has gone on, some of it by contributors to this volume. The congregational portraits in these pages also testify to our growing awareness of congregational particularity. But there is much more to be learned. A stunning example of an attempt to answer Niebuhr's question (even if it does not invoke him) is Samuel G. Freedman's wonderful book, *Upon This Rock* (1993). *Upon This Rock*, the result of two years of painstaking study of St. Paul's Church, Brooklyn, New York, helps us see just how complex the congregational dance really is. Members, would-be members, dropouts, and church-shoppers dance along the affiliation threshold as they participate in a certain kind of African American neo-Pentecostal worship. As the preacher, the Reverend Johnny Ray Youngblood, lifts up key Biblical texts, focuses on the lived reality of his congregation members, and shares his own failures as father, spouse, and son, people are given specific occasions to step closer or draw further away from St. Paul's life. That same reality occurs as the congregation celebrates African roots, builds affordable housing in East Brooklyn, welcomes addicts into a small group, or makes the plight of black males a central concern. Very specific moves are being made—some of them as small as the smile as breakfast is served, some as large as the too familiar touch of a church elder or the show of solidarity as members rally in time of tragedy—all parts of a mostly subconscious choreography that appeals or repels individuals depending upon what they bring to the congregational dance. The reality is thick, ambiguous, and bewilderingly complex—at bottom, a dense mystery.

The dance between congregations and members is really a dance of dances as various histories, cultures, experiences, and interpretations jostle each other. The number of interactions and possible occasions for enticing someone to become more deeply involved or for forcing someone else further away is beyond our comprehension. Further, the dance is continually interrupted by the larger events and dynamics of nation and world. An event at an orphanage in Ghana, a major social movement in our own land, powerful dynamics like our national tendency to render religion a private affair lace through these individual and congregational histories in ways that constantly unsettle and reshuffle reality. Do we two-step, twist, line dance, or just improvise? The larger culture keeps making demands upon these local interactions, sometimes overtly, sometimes invisibly.

Professor Niebuhr, of course, was not satisfied with interpretation as an end in itself. After answering the question about what is going on, the responsible agent must decide what to do. But knowing what to do depends on the best possible answer to the prior interpretive question. For those of us interested in questions of membership and affiliation, it is time to ask ourselves where we are, what is going on in our collective enterprise, in our own hill. These essays are distinctive in that they have brought into one conversation leading interpreters, leading practitioners (read actors), and actual leaders and members of local congregations—from across a wide denominational spectrum. The conversation itself points us in new directions. As various presenters summarize what they have learned from years of researching or leading local churches and synagogues, a larger whole begins to come into view. That whole is the thick religious and cultural dance that goes on as individuals, congregations, denominations, social systems, cultures, traditions, and history interact.

The dance is a mystery, one that we have only begun to fathom. To be sure, the studies referred to in these pages shed light on portions of the dance, a step or two, or perhaps even major moments. But this volume shows us how much more we have to learn about the intricate web of interactions that lies beneath our affiliation statistics and analyses. If we can find ways to pool our various expertises and bring them sympathetically to bear upon the actual experiences of members, hangers-on, dropouts, shoppers, and turned off individuals, we may find that new explanations, perhaps even as interesting as Thomas's pheromones, await us. But even if the exotic or grand theory eludes us, we will have come a bit closer to the mystery that the very things that attract some repel others, that our natures seem to push and pull us in both directions, and that the dance goes on and on.

REFERENCES

Freedman, S. G. (1993). *Upon This Rock: The Miracles of a Black Church*. New York: HarperCollins.

Niebuhr, H. R. (1963). *The Responsible Self: An Essay in Christian Moral Philosophy*. New York: Harper and Row.

Thomas, L. (1974). *Lives of a Cell: Notes of a Biology Watcher*. New York: Viking.

For Further Reading

Carroll, J. W., Dudley, C. S., & McKinney, W. (1986). *Handbook for Congregational Studies*. Nashville: Abingdon.
Carroll, J. W., & Wade, C. R. (Eds.). (1993). *Beyond Establishment*. Louisville: Westminster/John Knox.
Dudley, C. S., & Johnson, S. A. (1993). *Energizing the Congregation: Images that Shape Your Church's Ministry*. Louisville: Westminster/John Knox.
Finke, R., & Stark, R. (1992). *The Churching of America 1976–1990*. New Brunswick: Rutgers University Press.
Goldstein, S. (1992). Profile of American Jewry: Insights from the 1990 National Jewish Population Survey. In D. Singer (Ed.), *American Jewish Year Book* (pp. 77–173). New York: American Jewish Committee and the Jewish Publication Society.
Hadaway, C. K. (1990). *What Can We Do about Church Dropouts?* Nashville: Abingdon.
Hoge, D. R., Johnson, B., & Luidens, D. A. (1994). *Vanishing Boundaries: The Religion of Mainline Protestant Baby Boomers*. Louisville: Westminster/John Knox.
Mead, L. B. (1993). *More than Numbers*. Washington, DC: The Alban Institute.
Roof, W. C. (Ed.). (1993a). *Religion in the Nineties. The Annals of the American Academy of Political and Social Science, Vol. 527*. Newbury Park: Sage.
Roof, W. C. (1993b). *A Generation of Seekers: The Spiritual Journey of the Baby Boomer Generation*. San Francisco, CA: HarperCollins.
Roof, W. C., & McKinney, W. (1987). *American Mainline Religion: Its Changing Shape and Future*. New Brunswick, NJ: Rutgers University Press.
Roozen, D. A., & Hadaway, C. K. (Eds.). (1994). *Church and Denominational Growth*. Nashville: Abingdon.
Wertheimer, J. (1993). *A People Divided: Judaism in Contemporary America*. New York: Basic Books.

Wertheimer, J. (Eds.) (1995). *The American Synagogue: A Sanctuary Transformed.* Hanover, NH: University Press of New England.

Wood, J. R. (1981). *Leadership in Voluntary Organizations: The Controversy over Social Action in Protestant Churches.* New Brunswick, NJ: Rutgers University Press.

Wuthnow, R. (1990). *The Struggle for America's Soul: Evangelicals, Liberals, and Secularism.* Grand Rapids, MI: Eerdmans.

Index

Active members, 42
Active young adults, 64–67
Activist orientation, 37
Albrecht, Stan, 42
American Mainline Religion, 167, 168
Apostolate of laity, 36

Bahr, Howard, 42
Baptists, Bethany Baptist Church, 135–42
Berger, Peter, 65, 156
Bethany Baptist Church, 135–42; and numerical growth planning, 136–38; and planning for church growth, 141–42; and social action as church mission, 138–41
Birth and death rates, 29
Blizzard, Samuel, 162
B'nai Jeshurun, 143–51; attracting target population, 144–45; and community building, 145–47; and eco-kashrut, 149; and education, 150; and homeless shelter, 148; and social action, 148–50; and women's role, 149–50
Buckle, Ted, 27–40

Carroll, J. W., 36

Catholics: congregational membership definitions of, 44; dropouts, 98–99
Christendom, 38
Christian Church, 173; outreach of, 16
Churched, 41–43; young adults, 63
Church involvement and life experiences, 70–71
Church members, 42, 62
Church of Latter Day Saints (LDS), 45
Civic orientation, 36–37
Clergy leadership, 155-57; aids to, 158–60; impediments to, 158
Coalter, Milton J., 174
Congregational affiliation: congregation response to challenges of, 8–12; declines in, 3–4; as emotional issue, 7–8; framework for, 15; global context of, 24; individual and congregation, 19–21; inreach and outreach, 11–12; institutional/contextual distinction, 18–19; local contextual factors, 22; mission, passion, and relevance, 8–10; national contextual factors, 23–24; national institutional factors, 22–23; national strategies for growth, 174–76; nature of, 4–5; per-

sonal and communal life contribution to, 2–3; and pluralism, relativism, individualism, 10–11; as relational concept, 20–21; and religious institutions as special organizations, 6–7; social context, 18–19
Congregation in congregational affiliation, 19–21
Congregations, components of, 20
Converts and dropouts, 30
Corporate culture of congregations, 20
Critics, marginal members as, 80, 84–86, 89

Decision making in organizational processes, 35
Denominational affiliation, 16, 45–46, 168–69
Denominational loyalists, 23
Denominations, 169–74; education in, 170–72; evangelism in, 173–74; and extension, 172–73
Disaffiliated, dropout case studies of, 95–111
Disaffiliation, 42
Disciples of Christ, 175
Disengagement, 42
Doctrinal beliefs of unchurched, 67–68
Dropouts, 95–111; Catholic, 98–99; current beliefs and practices, 100–102; future possibilities of, 108; Jewish, 96–97; Methodist, 99–100; next generation of, 102–5; and organized religion, 106–7; and personal religion, 107–8; Presbyterian, 97–98; and separation from affiliation, 107

Eco-kashrut, 149
Education: at B'nai Jeshurun, 150; in denominations, 170–72; ministry of, 31
Environmental factors in congregations, 29
Episcopalians, 3, 59; congregational membership definitions of, 44
Evangelism: in denominations, 173–74; outreach of, 47–49

Evangelistic orientation, 37
Extension in denominations, 172–73

Foster, Steven E., 109, 113–26
Freedman, Samuel G., 179

Gallup Poll Organization, 42
General Social Survey, 167–68
Geographical population shifts, 29
Glide Memorial United Methodist Church, 161
Growth: congregational, 49–50; definitions of, 15–16, 27–40; incarnational, 36–38; maturational, 31–33; numerical, 28–30; organic, 33–36; strategies for affiliation, 174–76

Hadaway, C. Kirk, 42, 56, 77–93, 173
Handbook for Congregational Studies, 20
Hoge, D. R., 18, 42, 55, 59–76
Homeless: and B'nai Jeshurun, 148; and Luther Place Memorial Church, 128–29

Identification, 51–52
Ideology, 50–51
Inactive members, 42
Inactives, 64–67, 78–79; religious identity of, 78
Incarnational growth in congregations, 16, 36–38; activist orientation of, 37; civic orientation of, 36–37; evangelistic orientation of, 37; and relation to community, 36–38; sanctuary orientation of, 37
Individualism in congregational affiliation, 10–11
Individuals in congregational affiliation, 19–21
Inreach, 11–12. *See also* Outreach
Institutional connection of denominational affiliation, 46
Institutional/contextual distinction, 18–19
Intermarriage and synagogue affiliation, 118–20

Jehovah's Witnesses, 78

Index

Jews, 3; and B'nai Jeshurun, 143–51; congregational membership definitions, 44; as dropouts, 96–97; in mixed-married families, 120–23; outreach of, 16, 48, 120–23; and "Stepping Stones—To a Jewish ME" program, 120–23; synagogue affiliation motivations for, 115–16; synagogue affiliation rates of, 113–14
Johnson, Benton, 42, 55, 59–76
Journey theology, 75

Kane, Charles, 28
Kashrut, 149
Kelley, Dean, 163

Laity in ministry, 31, 160–63
Lay liberalism, 71–73
Liberals as marginal members, 80, 82–84, 89
Life-crisis ministries in maturational growth of congregation, 32
Life experiences and church involvement, 70–71
Lifelong marginal members, 80, 86–88, 89–90
Lilly Endowment, 59, 78
Lives of a Cell, 177
Local church, 76
Local contextual factors, 22
Luidens, D. A., 23, 42, 55, 59–76, 175
Lutheran Church-Missouri Synod, 46
Lutherans, 3; congregational membership definitions of, 44; outreach, 47, 48, 49
Lutheran Volunteer Corps, 130
Luther Place Memorial Church, 127–33

McKinney, W., 36, 153
McNamara, Patrick, 163
Marginal members and marginality, 42, 77–93; as critics, 80, 84–86, 89; data and methods for identifying, 79–80; as liberals, 80, 82–84, 89; lifelong, 80, 86–88, 89–90; and religious identity of inactives, 78; as traditionalists, 80–82, 89
Marler, Penny Long, 42, 56, 77–93
Maturational growth of congregation, 16, 31–33, 49–50; through life-crisis ministries, 32; through ministry of education, 31; through worship, 32–33
Mead, Loren B., 15–16, 27–40
Membership, congregational, 43–45
Mennonite outreach, 49
Mental affiliates, 42; religious identity of inactives, 78
Methodist dropouts, 99–100
Methodist Layman's Union, 164
Meyer, Marshall T., 110, 143–51
Ministry: of education, 31; integrity in, 163–65
Minyan, 12
Mission in congregational affiliation, 8–10
Morality views of unchurched, 68–70
Mormons, 78; outreach of, 48

National contextual factors of congregation affiliation, 23–24
National institutional factors of congregation affiliation, 22–23
National Jewish Population Survey (NJPS), 113, 118, 150
Niebuhr, H. Richard, 179, 180
Nones, religious identity of inactives, 78
Norms in organizational culture, 34
Numerical growth of congregations, 28–30, 49–50; at Bethany Baptist Church, 136–38; environmental factors, 29; individual decisions, 29–30

Organic growth of congregations, 6, 16, 33–36; organizational culture of, 34–35; organizational processes of, 35–36
Organizational culture, 34–35; norms in, 34; roles in, 34; values in, 34–35
Organizational processes, 35
Organizational structure and processes of congregations, 20

Organized religion, dropouts of, 106–7
Outreach, 16, 36, 47–49; and congregational affiliation, 11–12; of evangelism, 47–48; to Jewish mixed-married families, 120–23; of Lutherans, 48, 49; of Mennonites, 48–49; of Mormons, 48–49

Participation, 52–53
Pastoral care, 32
Pluralism in congregational affiliation, 10–11
Population shifts, geographical, 29
Presbyterian Church, 3, 59, 175
Presbyterians, 60–76; congregational membership definitions of, 43; dropouts, 97–98
Program of congregation, 20
Protestants: marginal members, 79–90; unaffiliated, 59–76

Quayle, William, 156

Regional culture, 29
Relation to community in incarnational growth in congregations, 36–38
Relativism in congregational affiliation, 10–11
Religious boundaries, 73–75
Religious identity of inactives, 78
Religious institutions as special organizations, 6–7
Responsible Self, The, 179
Rokeach, Milton, 159
Roles in organizational culture, 34
Roof, Wade Clark, 42
Roozen, David A., 15, 17–26, 36, 42
Royle, Marjorie, 173
Rutland, John, 164

St. Paul's Church, Brooklyn, New York, 179
Sales, Amy L., 56, 95–111
Sample, Tex, 75
Sanctuary orientation, 37
Schmidt, Jean Miller, 174
Scott, James A., 110, 135–42

Self-proclaimed identity of denominational affiliation, 45
Social action: at Bethany Baptist Church, 138–41; at B'nai Jeshurun, 148–50
Social/community service, 49
Social context of congregation, 20
Socialization of new members in organizational processes, 35
Souls or the Social Order, 174
Southern Research Institute, 79
Steinbruck, John F., 110, 127–33
"Stepping Stones—To a Jewish ME" program, 109, 120–23
Synagogue affiliation: intermarriage and, 118–20; motivations for, 115–16; rates of, 113–14; reasons for dropping out, 116–18

Terror in the Night: The Klan's Campaign Against the Jews, 164
They Call Her Pastor, 160
Thomas, Lewis, 177
Traditional faith, 71–73
Traditionalists, marginal members as, 80–82, 89
Transfers of congregational members, 30
Turner, Gordon, 41

Unaffiliated, 46–47, 55–57; of Protestant adults, 59–76
Unchurched, 41–43; and criticism of church, 70; doctrinal beliefs of, 67–68; and views on morality, 68–70; young adults as, 64
United Church of Christ, 3, 59, 173, 175
United Methodist Church, 167, 175
United Methodists, congregational membership definition of, 43
Upon This Rock, 179

Values in organizational culture, 34–35

Wallace, Ruth, 160
Walrath, Doug, 19

Williams, Cecil, 161
Women's role at B'nai Jeshurun, 149–50

Wood, James R., 153–54, 155–65
Worship, maturational of faith through, 32–33

About the Editors and Contributors

RENNI S. ALTMAN is the associate rabbi of Temple Beth-El in Great Neck, New York. She was formerly the Director of Programs for the Unaffiliated at the Union of American Hebrew Congregations where she developed programs to help Reform congregations reach out to and involve more members. She was ordained from the Hebrew Union College-Jewish Institute of Religion in New York.

STEVEN E. FOSTER is senior rabbi of Congregation Emanuel in Denver, Colorado and the co-chairperson of the Union of American Hebrew Congregation's Task Force on the Unaffiliated. He received his M.A. in Hebrew letters, his rabbinical ordination from Hebrew Union College (Cincinnati), and his Doctor of Ministries from the Iliff School of Theology (Denver). He has served as board member and officer of a number of community and religious organizations including the Colorado State Civil Rights Commission and the Denver Area Interfaith Clergy Conference.

C. KIRK HADAWAY is secretary for research and evaluation at the United Church Board for Homeland Ministries (United Church of Christ). Previously, he held research positions with the Sunday School Board, the Center for Urban Church Studies, and the Home Mission Board of the Southern Baptist Convention. He received his Ph.D. in sociology from the University of Massachusetts (Amherst). He has published numerous articles and books on congregational affiliation and church growth.

DEAN R. HOGE is professor of sociology at the Catholic University of America. He received his B.D. degree from Harvard Divinity School and his Ph.D. in sociology from Harvard University. Hoge has published many articles and books on religious life in America.

BENTON JOHNSON is professor of sociology and head of the Department of Religious Studies at the University of Oregon. He received his B.A. degree from the University of North Carolina at Chapel Hill and his M.A. and Ph.D. from Harvard University. He has published widely on topics pertaining to religion in the United States including the holiness movement, church-sect distinction, new religious movements, and the relation between religion and politics.

DONALD A. LUIDENS is professor of sociology at Hope College in Holland, Michigan. He received his M.Div. from Princeton Theological Seminary and his M.A. and Ph.D. from Rutgers University. His research has focused on mainline Protestantism, with special attention to the Reformed Church in America, on which he has directed three nationwide surveys of clergy and laity since the mid-1970s. Luiden's articles have appeared in journals and in denominational and church-related periodicals.

WILLIAM MCKINNEY is dean and professor of religion and society at Hartford Seminary. Prior to joining the seminary faculty in 1985, he served for eleven years as research director for the United Church of Christ's Board for Homeland Ministries based in New York City. He holds a M.Div. from Hartford Seminary and a Ph.D. from Pennsylvania State University. He is an ordained minister in the United Church of Christ.

PENNY LONG MARLER is assistant professor of religion at Samford University. She holds an M.Div. and a Ph.D. from the Southern Baptist Theological Seminary and a Master of Social Work from the University of Louisville. Her recent research has focused on secularization and American religion, seminary cultures, religious mobility in America, and marginal church members.

LOREN B. MEAD, an Episcopal priest, is the president and founder of The Alban Institute, Inc. He is a graduate of Virginia Theological Seminary and has received honorary doctorates from the Protestant Episcopal Theological Seminary in Virginia, the University of the South, and Berkeley Divinity School. Mead has consulted with many churches, seminaries, agencies, and groups in the United States, and throughout the world. He is the author of numerous articles and books on congregations and the ministry.

MARSHALL T. MEYER (1930–1993) was a rabbi of Congregation B'nai Jeshurun in New York City. He received his M.A. in Hebrew literature and his Rabbinical Ordination from the Jewish Theological Seminary, and he completed postgraduate work at Hebrew University in Jerusalem, Columbia University, and Union Theological Seminary. He also received honorary degrees from the Jewish Theological Seminary, Kalamazoo College, Hebrew Union College, Dartmouth College, and the University of Buenos Aires. He served on the boards of numerous religious and human rights organizations in the United States and Latin America and received international awards for his religious scholarship and his human rights activities.

DAVID A. ROOZEN is director of Hartford Seminary's Center for Social and Religious Research, with which he has been affiliated since 1973. He holds a Ph.D. in the sociology of religion from Emory University. Roozen has published widely on American religious change, congregational life, mission, and theological education.

AMY L. SALES is a senior research associate at the Maurice and Marilyn Cohen Center for Modern Jewish Studies at Brandeis University. She received her Ph.D. in social psychology from Boston University. Sales has published research papers on diverse topics including organization culture, Jewish women in the "executive suite," the social adjustment of Soviet Jewish emigrés, and the values and attitudes of American Jewish teenagers.

JAMES A. SCOTT has been the minister of Bethany Baptist Church in Newark, New Jersey, for thirty years and, since 1971, has been associate professor in the Department of Education at Rutgers University. He holds a B.D. from Yale Divinity School and a Ph.D. in social planning and policy development from Rutgers University. He has been awarded honorary doctoral degrees by Bethune-Cookman College and Monrovia College in West Africa.

JOHN F. STEINBRUCK received his ordination in 1959. Since 1970, he has been the pastor of Luther Place Memorial Church in Washington, D.C. He holds a D.Min. degree from Lutheran Theological Seminary. Steinbruck has been awarded a number of honorary doctorates and citations for his contributions to interracial and interfaith understanding and cooperation. He has published articles in journals, religious publications, and books.

GARY A. TOBIN is director of the Maurice and Marilyn Cohen Center for Modern Jewish Studies at Brandeis University. He earned his Ph.D. in city and regional planning from the University of California, Berkeley, and served on the faculty of Washington University, St. Louis, for eleven years before coming to Brandeis in 1984. Tobin has written many books, articles, and planning reports about intermarriage, demography, anti-Semitism, Jewish community planning, and philanthropy in the Jewish community.

JAMES P. WIND is program director of the religion division of the Lilly Endowment, Inc. He received his M.Div. degree from the Lutheran School of Theology, Chicago, and his Ph.D. from the Divinity School at the University of Chicago. Before joining the Lilly Endowment, he served as director of research for the Park Ridge Center for the Study of Health, Faith and Ethics, for the Lutheran General Hospital (Park Ridge, Illinois) project on Health/Medicine and the Faith Traditions, and for the Evaluation of the Study of Congregation conducted by the Institute for the Advanced Study of Religion at the University of Chicago. Wind has published numerous books, articles, chapters, reviews and sermons on religion.

JAMES R. WOOD, professor of sociology at Indiana University, studies voluntary organizations and their role in American society. His current research examines the way the legislative bodies of church denominations arrive at consensus on controversial public issues. He holds an M.Div. from Yale University and a Ph.D. in sociology from Vanderbilt University.

BV 820 .C48 1995

Church and synagogue
 affiliation